ECONOMICS OF ENVIRONMENTAL DEVELOPMENT

ECONOMICS OF ENVIRONMENTAL DEVELOPMENT

H.K. Pathak

CYBER TECH PUBLICATIONS
4264/3, Ansari Road, Daryaganj, New Delhi-110002 (India)
Ph.: 011-23244078, 011-43559448 Fax: 011-23280028
E-Mail: cyberpublicationsdelhi@yahoo.com
Website: www.cybertechpublications.com

ECONOMICS OF ENVIRONMENTAL DEVELOPMENT

H.K. Pathak

First Edition 2010

Asian Offset Printers

Published by :

G.S. Rawat for **Cyber Tech Publications**
4264/3, Ansari Road, Daryaganj, New Delhi-110002 (India)
Ph.: 011-23244078, 011-43559448 Fax: 011-23280028
E-Mail: cyberpublicationsdelhi@yahoo.com
Website: www.cybertechpublications.com

Preface

The book "Economics of Environmental Development being a global issue is the basic approach in the global business. Hence, in this book the authors' presents a comprehensive and an analytical picture of the development in India in industrializing the country. The decade of the 1970s was marked by a growing climate consciousness, both popular and scientific. The new interest was sparked by a series of extreme climate events and related disruptions, and by scientific speculation as to increased climate variability and possible climate change. Two sets of events during this period attracted both scientific and public interest.

Nonetheless, it is widely agreed that one such change, a long-term global warming derived from the enrichment of the atmospheric content of the `greenhouse' gases, is underway. How to respond to such impacts adjusting to changing climate, coping with extremes, matching human needs to climate endowment are issues of considerable import. The scientific study of climate and society will inform societal response. Concepts of economically impact assessment are new, the methods are still under development.

This book will make a significant contribution to the existing environmental development sector in the changing business scenario.

—Author

Preface

CONTENTS

1

Introduction

In order to meet the challenges of environment and development, States have decided to establish a new global partnership. This partnership commits all States to engage in a continuous and constructive dialogue, inspired by the need to achieve a more efficient and equitable world economy, keeping in view the increasing interdependence of the community of nations and that sustainable development should become a priority item on the agenda of the international community. It is recognized that, for the success of this new partnership, it is important to overcome confrontation and to foster a climate of genuine cooperation and solidarity. It is equally important to strengthen national and international policies and multinational cooperation to adapt to the new realities.

Economic policies of individual countries and international economic relations both have great relevance to sustainable development. The reactivation and acceleration of development requires both a dynamic and a supportive international economic environment and determined policies at the national level. It will be frustrated in the absence of either of these requirements. A supportive external economic environment is crucial. The development process will not gather momentum if the global economy lacks dynamism and stability and is beset with uncertainties. Neither will it gather momentum if the developing countries are weighted down by external indebtedness, if development finance is inadequate, if barriers restrict access to markets and if commodity prices and the terms of trade of developing countries remain depressed. The record of the 1980s was essentially negative on each of these counts and needs to be reversed. The policies and measures needed to create an international environment that is strongly supportive of national development efforts are thus vital. International cooperation in this area should be designed to complement and support - not to diminish or subsume - sound domestic economic policies, in both developed and developing countries, if global progress towards sustainable development is to be achieved.

The international economy should provide a supportive international climate for achieving environment and development goals by:

PROGRAMME AREAS

Promoting Sustainable Development through Trade

Basis for Action

An open, equitable, secure, non-discriminatory and predictable multilateral trading system that is consistent with the goals of sustainable development and leads to the optimal distribution of global production in accordance with comparative advantage is of benefit to all trading partners. Moreover, improved market access for developing countries' exports in conjunction with sound macroeconomic and environmental policies would have a positive environmental impact and therefore make an important contribution towards sustainable development. Experience has shown that sustainable development requires a commitment to sound economic policies and management, an effective and predictable public administration, the integration of environmental concerns into decision-making and progress towards democratic government, in the light of country-specific conditions, which allows for full participation of all parties concerned. These attributes are essential for the fulfilment of the policy directions and objectives listed below.

The commodity sector dominates the economies of many developing countries in terms of production, employment and export earnings. An important feature of the world commodity economy in the 1980s was the prevalence of very low and declining real prices for most commodities in international markets and a resulting substantial contraction in commodity export earnings for many producing countries. The ability of those countries to mobilize, through international trade, the resources needed to finance investments required for sustainable development may be impaired by this development and by tariff and non-tariff impediments, including tariff escalation, limiting their access to export markets. The removal of existing distortions in international trade is essential. In particular, the achievement of this objective requires that there be substantial and progressive reduction in the support and protection of agriculture - covering internal regimes, market access and export subsidies - as well as of industry and other sectors, in order to avoid inflicting large losses on the more efficient producers, especially in developing countries. Thus, in agriculture, industry and other sectors, there is scope for initiatives aimed at trade liberalization and at policies to make production more responsive to environment and development needs. Trade liberalization should therefore be pursued on a global basis across economic sectors so as to contribute to sustainable development.

The international trading environment has been affected by a number of developments that have created new challenges and opportunities and have made multilateral economic cooperation of even greater importance. World trade has continued to grow faster than world output in recent years. However, the expansion of world trade has been unevenly spread, and only a limited number of developing countries have been capable of achieving appreciable growth in their exports. Protectionist pressures and unilateral policy actions continue to endanger the functioning of an open multilateral trading system, affecting particularly the export interests of developing countries. Economic integration processes have intensified in recent years and should impart dynamism to global trade and enhance the trade and development possibilities for developing countries. In recent years, a growing number of these countries have adopted courageous policy reforms involving ambitious autonomous trade liberalization, while far-reaching reforms and profound restructuring processes are taking place in Central and Eastern European countries, paving the way for their integration into the world economy and the international trading system. Increased attention is being devoted to enhancing the role of enterprises and promoting competitive markets through adoption of competitive policies. The GSP has proved to be a useful trade policy instrument, although its objectives will have to be fulfilled, and trade facilitation strategies relating to electronic data interchange (EDI) have been effective in improving the trading efficiency of the public and private sectors. The interactions between environment policies and trade issues are manifold and have not yet been fully assessed. An early, balanced, comprehensive and successful outcome of the Uruguay Round of multilateral trade negotiations would bring about further liberalization and expansion of world trade, enhance the trade and development possibilities of developing countries and provide greater security and predictability to the international trading system.

Objectives

In the years ahead, and taking into account the results of the Uruguay Round of multilateral trade negotiations, Governments should continue to strive to meet the following objectives:

(a) To promote an open, non-discriminatory and equitable multilateral trading system that will enable all countries - in particular, the developing countries - to improve their economic structures and improve the standard of living of their populations through sustained economic development;

(b) To improve access to markets for exports of developing countries;

(c) To improve the functioning of commodity markets and achieve sound, compatible and consistent commodity policies at national and international levels with a view to optimizing the contribution of the commodity sector to sustainable development, taking into account environmental considerations;

(d) To promote and support policies, domestic and international, that make economic growth and environmental protection mutually supportive.

Activities

(A) International and Regional Cooperation and Coordination

Promoting an international trading system that takes account of the needs of developing countries. Accordingly, the international community should:

(a) Halt and reverse protectionism in order to bring about further liberalization and expansion of world trade, to the benefit of all countries, in particular the developing countries;

(b) Provide for an equitable, secure, non-discriminatory and predictable international trading system;

(c) Facilitate, in a timely way, the integration of all countries into the world economy and the international trading system;

(d) Ensure that environment and trade policies are mutually supportive, with a view to achieving sustainable development;

(e) Strengthen the international trade policies system through an early, balanced, comprehensive and successful outcome of the Uruguay Round of multilateral trade negotiations.

The international community should aim at finding ways and means of achieving a better functioning and enhanced transparency of commodity markets, greater diversification of the commodity sector in developing economies within a macroeconomic framework that takes into consideration a country's economic structure, resource endowments and market opportunities, and better management of natural resources that takes into account the necessities of sustainable development. Therefore, all countries should implement previous commitments to halt and reverse protectionism and further expand market access, particularly in areas of interest to developing countries. This improvement of market access will be facilitated by appropriate structural adjustment in developed countries. Developing countries should continue the trade-policy reforms and structural adjustment they have undertaken. It is thus urgent to achieve an improvement in market access conditions for commodities, notably through the progressive removal of barriers that restrict imports, particularly from developing countries, of commodity products in primary and processed forms, as well as the substantial and progressive reduction of types of support that induce uncompetitive production, such as production and export subsidies.

(B) Management related activities Developing domestic policies that maximize the benefits of trade liberalization for sustainable development

For developing countries to benefit from the liberalization of trading systems, they should implement the following policies, as appropriate:

(a) Create a domestic environment supportive of an optimal balance between production for the domestic and export markets and remove biases against exports and discourage inefficient import-substitution;

(b) Promote the policy framework and the infrastructure required to improve the efficiency of export and import trade as well as the functioning of domestic markets.

The following policies should be adopted by developing countries with respect to commodities consistent with market efficiency:

(a) Expand processing, distribution and improve marketing practices and the competitiveness of the commodity sector;

(b) Diversify in order to reduce dependence on commodity exports;

(c) Reflect efficient and sustainable use of factors of production in the formation of commodity prices, including the reflection of environmental, social and resources costs.

(C) Data and information

Encouraging data collection and research

GATT, UNCTAD and other relevant institutions should continue to collect appropriate trade data and information. The

Secretary-General of the United Nations is requested to strengthen the Trade Control Measures Information System managed by UNCTAD.

Improving international cooperation in commodity trade and the diversification of the sector.

With regard to commodity trade, Governments should, directly or through appropriate international organizations, where appropriate:

(a) Seek optimal functioning of commodity markets, inter alia, through improved market transparency involving exchanges of views and information on investment plans, prospects and markets for individual commodities. Substantive negotiations between producers and consumers should be pursued with a view to achieving viable and more efficient international agreements that take into account market trends, or arrangements, as well as study groups. In this regard, particular attention should be paid to the agreements on cocoa, coffee, sugar and tropical timber. The importance of international commodity agreements and arrangements is underlined. Occupational health and safety matters, technology transfer and services associated with the production, marketing and promotion of commodities, as well as environmental considerations, should be taken into account;

(b) Continue to apply compensation mechanisms for shortfalls in commodity export earnings of developing countries in order to encourage diversification efforts;

(c) Provide assistance to developing countries upon request in the design and implementation of commodity policies and the gathering and utilization of information on commodity markets;

(d) Support the efforts of developing countries to promote the policy framework and infrastructure required to improve the efficiency of export and import trade;

(e) Support the diversification initiatives of the developing countries at the national, regional and international levels.

Means of implementation

A) Financing and Cost Evaluation

The Conference secretariat has estimated the average total annual cost (1993-2000) of implementing the activities in this programme area to be about $8.8 billion from the international community on grant or concessional terms. These are indicative and order-of-magnitude estimates only and have not been reviewed by Governments. Actual costs and financial terms, including any that are non-concessional, will depend upon, inter alia, the specific strategies and programmes Governments decide upon for implementation.

B) Capacity-building

The above-mentioned technical cooperation activities aim at strengthening national capabilities for design and implementation of commodity policy, use and management of national resources and the gathering and utilization of information on commodity markets.

Making Trade and Environment Mutually Supportive

Basis for Action

Environment and trade policies should be mutually supportive. An open, multilateral trading system makes possible a more efficient allocation and use of resources and thereby contributes to an increase in production and incomes and to lessening demands on the environment. It thus provides additional resources needed for economic growth and development and improved environmental protection. A sound environment, on the other hand, provides the ecological and other resources needed to sustain growth and underpin a continuing expansion of trade. An open, multilateral trading system, supported by the adoption of sound environmental policies, would have a positive impact on the environment and contribute to sustainable development.

International cooperation in the environmental field is growing, and in a number of cases trade provisions in multilateral environment agreements have played a role in tackling global environmental challenges. Trade measures have thus been used in certain specific instances, where considered necessary, to enhance the effectiveness of environmental regulations for the protection of the environment. Such regulations should address the root causes of environmental degradation so as not to result in unjustified restrictions on trade. The challenge is to ensure that trade and environment policies are consistent and reinforce the process of sustainable development. However, account should be taken of the fact that environmental standards valid for developed countries may have unwarranted social and economic costs in developing countries.

Objectives

Governments should strive to meet the following objectives, through relevant multilateral forums, including GATT, UNCTAD and other international organizations:

(a) To make international trade and environment policies mutually supportive in favour of sustainable development;

(b) To clarify the role of GATT, UNCTAD and other international organizations in dealing with trade and environment-related issues, including, where relevant, conciliation procedure and dispute settlement;

(c) To encourage international productivity and competitiveness and encourage a constructive role on the part of industry in dealing with environment and development issues.

Activities

Developing an Environment/trade and Development Agenda

Governments should encourage GATT, UNCTAD and other relevant international and regional economic institutions to examine, in accordance with their respective mandates and competences, the following propositions and principles:

(a) Elaborate adequate studies for the better understanding of the relationship between trade and environment for the promotion of sustainable development;

(b) Promote a dialogue between trade, development and environment communities;

(c) In those cases when trade measures related to environment are used, ensure transparency and compatibility with international obligations;

(d) Deal with the root causes of environment and development problems in a manner that avoids the adoption of environmental measures resulting in unjustified restrictions on trade;

(e) Seek to avoid the use of trade restrictions or distortions as a means to offset differences in cost arising from differences in environmental standards and regulations, since their application could lead to trade distortions and increase protectionist tendencies;

(f) Ensure that environment-related regulations or standards, including those related to health and safety standards, do not constitute a means of arbitrary or unjustifiable discrimination or a disguised restriction on trade;

(g) Ensure that special factors affecting environment and trade policies in the developing countries are borne in mind in the application of environmental standards, as well as in the use of any trade measures. It is worth noting that standards that are valid in the most advanced countries may be inappropriate and of unwarranted social cost for the developing countries;

(h) Encourage participation of developing countries in multilateral agreements through such mechanisms as special transitional rules;

(i) Avoid unilateral actions to deal with environmental challenges outside the jurisdiction of the importing country. Environmental measures addressing transborder or global environmental problems should, as far as possible, be based on an international consensus. Domestic measures targeted to achieve certain environmental objectives may need trade measures to render them effective. Should trade policy measures be found necessary for the enforcement of environmental policies, certain principles and rules should apply. These could include, inter alia, the principle of non-discrimination; the principle that the trade measure chosen should be the least trade-restrictive necessary to achieve the objectives; an obligation to ensure transparency in the use of trade measures related to the environment and to provide adequate notification of national regulations; and the need to give consideration to the special conditions and developmental requirements of developing countries as they move towards internationally agreed environmental objectives;

(j) Develop more precision, where necessary, and clarify the relationship between GATT provisions and some of the multilateral measures adopted in the environment area;

(k) Ensure public input in the formation, negotiation and implementation of trade policies as a means of fostering increased transparency in the light of country-specific conditions;

(l) Ensure that environmental policies provide the appropriate legal and institutional framework to respond to new needs for the protection of the environment that may result from changes in production and trade specialization.

Providing Adequate Financial Resources to Developing Countries

Basis for Action

Investment is critical to the ability of developing countries to achieve needed economic growth to improve the welfare of their populations and to meet their basic needs in a sustainable manner, all without deteriorating or depleting the resource base that underpins development. Sustainable development requires increased investment, for which domestic and external financial resources are needed. Foreign private investment and the return of flight capital, which depend on a healthy investment climate, are an important source of financial resources. Many developing countries have experienced a decade-long situation of negative net transfer of financial resources, during which their financial receipts were exceeded by payments they had to make, in particular for debt-servicing. As a result, domestically mobilized resources had to be transferred abroad instead of being invested locally in order to promote sustainable economic development.

For many developing countries, the reactivation of development will not take place without an early and durable solution to the problems of external indebtedness, taking into account the fact that, for many developing countries, external debt burdens are a significant problem. The burden of debt-service payments on those countries has imposed severe constraints on their ability to accelerate growth and eradicate poverty and has led to a contraction in imports, investment and consumption. External indebtedness has emerged as a main factor in the economic stalemate in the developing countries. Continued vigorous implementation of the evolving international debt strategy is aimed at restoring debtor countries' external financial viability, and the resumption of their growth and development would assist in achieving sustainable growth and development. In this context, additional financial resources in favour of developing countries and the efficient utilization of such resources are essential.

Objectives

The specific requirements for the implementation of the sectoral and cross-sectoral programmes included in Agenda 21 are dealt with in the relevant programme areas and in chapter 33 (Financial resources and mechanisms).

Activities

A) Meeting International Targets of Official Development Assistance Funding

As discussed in chapter 33, new and additional resources should be provided to support Agenda 21 programmes.

(B) Addressing the Debt Issue

In regard to the external debt incurred with commercial banks, the progress being made under the strengthened debt strategy is recognized and a more rapid implementation of this strategy is encouraged. Some countries have already benefited from the combination of sound adjustment policies and commercial bank debt reduction or equivalent measures. The international community encourages:

(a) Other countries with heavy debts to banks to negotiate similar commercial bank debt reduction with their creditors;

(b) The parties to such a negotiation to take due account of both the medium-term debt reduction and new money requirements of the debtor country;

(c) Multilateral institutions actively engaged in the strengthened international debt strategy to continue to support debt-reduction packages related to commercial bank debt with a view to ensuring that the magnitude of such financing is consonant with the evolving debt strategy;

(d) Creditor banks to participate in debt and debt-service reduction;

(e) Strengthened policies to attract direct investment, avoid unsustainable levels of debt and foster the return of flight capital.

With regard to debt owed to official bilateral creditors, the recent measures taken by the Paris Club with regard to more generous terms of relief to the poorest most indebted countries are welcomed. Ongoing efforts to implement these "Trinidad terms" measures in a manner commensurate with the payments capacity of those countries and in a way that gives additional support to their economic reform efforts are welcomed. The substantial bilateral debt reduction undertaken by some creditor countries is also welcomed, and others which are in a position to do so are encouraged to take similar action.

The actions of low-income countries with substantial debt burdens which continue, at great cost, to service their debt and safeguard their creditworthiness are commended. Particular attention should be paid to their resource needs. Other debt-distressed developing countries which are making great efforts to continue to service their debt and meet their external financial obligations also deserve due attention.

In connection with multilateral debt, it is urged that serious attention be given to continuing to work towards growth-oriented solutions to the problem of developing countries with serious debt-servicing problems, including those whose debt is mainly to official creditors or to multilateral financial institutions. Particularly in the case of low-income countries in the process of economic reform, the support of the multilateral financial institutions in the form of new disbursements and the use of their concessional funds is welcomed. The use of support groups should be continued in providing resources to clear arrears of countries embarking upon vigorous economic reform programmes supported by IMF and the World Bank. Measures by the multilateral financial institutions such as the refinancing of interest on non-concessional loans with IDA reflows - "fifth dimension" - are noted with appreciation.

MEANS OF IMPLEMENTATION

Financing and Cost Evaluation

Encouraging Economic Policies Conducive to Sustainable Development

Basis for Action: The unfavourable external environment facing developing countries makes domestic resource mobilization and efficient allocation and utilization of domestically mobilized resources all the more important for the promotion of sustainable development. In a number of countries, policies are necessary to correct misdirected public spending, large budget deficits and other macroeconomic imbalances, restrictive policies and distortions in the areas of exchange rates, investment and finance, and obstacles to entrepreneurship. In developed countries, continuing policy reform and adjustment, including appropriate savings rates, would help generate resources to support the transition to sustainable development both domestically and in developing countries.

Good management that fosters the association of effective, efficient, honest, equitable and accountable public administration with individual rights and opportunities is an essential element for sustainable, broadly based development and sound economic performance at all development levels. All countries should increase their efforts to eradicate mismanagement of public and private affairs, including corruption, taking into account the factors responsible for, and agents involved in, this phenomenon.

Many indebted developing countries are undergoing structural adjustment programmes relating to debt rescheduling or new loans. While such programmes are necessary for improving the balance in fiscal budgets and balance-of-payments accounts, in some cases they have resulted in adverse social and environmental effects, such as cuts in allocations for health care, education and environmental protection. It is important to ensure that structural adjustment programmes do not have negative impacts on the environment and social development so that such programmes can be more in line with the objectives of sustainable development.

Objectives

It is necessary to establish, in the light of the country-specific conditions, economic policy reforms that promote the efficient planning and utilization of resources for sustainable development through sound economic and social policies, foster entrepreneurship and the incorporation of social and environmental costs in resource pricing, and remove sources of distortion in the area of trade and investment.

ACTIVITIES

A) Management-related Activities

Promoting Sound Economic Policies

The industrialized countries and other countries in a position to do so should strengthen their efforts:

(a) To encourage a stable and predictable international economic environment, particularly with regard to monetary stability, real rates of interest and fluctuations in key exchange rates;

(b) To stimulate savings and reduce fiscal deficits;

(c) To ensure that the processes of policy coordination take into account the interests and concerns of the developing countries, including the need to promote positive action to support the efforts of the least developed countries to halt their marginalization in the world economy;

(d) To undertake appropriate national macroeconomic and structural policies aimed at promoting non-inflationary growth, narrowing their major external imbalances and increasing the adjustment capacity of their economies.

Developing countries should consider strengthening their efforts to implement sound economic policies:

(a) That maintain the monetary and fiscal discipline required to promote price stability and external balance;

(b) That result in realistic exchange rates;

(c) That raise domestic savings and investment, as well as improve returns to investment.

More specifically, all countries should develop policies that improve efficiency in the allocation of resources and take full advantage of the opportunities offered by the changing global economic environment. In particular, wherever appropriate, and taking into account national strategies and objectives, countries should:

(a) Remove the barriers to progress caused by bureaucratic inefficiencies, administrative strains, unnecessary controls and the neglect of market conditions;

(b) Promote transparency in administration and decision-making;

(c) Encourage the private sector and foster entrepreneurship by improving institutional facilities for enterprise creation and market entry. The essential objective would be to simplify or remove the restrictions, regulations and formalities that make it more complicated, costly and time-consuming to set up and operate enterprises in many developing countries;

(d) Promote and support the investment and infrastructure required for sustainable economic growth and diversification on an environmentally sound and sustainable basis;

(e) Provide scope for appropriate economic instruments, including market mechanisms, in harmony with the objectives of sustainable development and fulfilment of basic needs;

(f) Promote the operation of effective tax systems and financial sectors;

(g) Provide opportunities for small-scale enterprises, both farm and non-farm, and for the indigenous population and local communities to contribute fully to the attainment of sustainable development;

(h) Remove biases against exports and in favour of inefficient import substitution and establish policies that allow them to benefit fully from the flows of foreign investment, within the framework of national, social, economic and developmental goals;

(i) Promote the creation of a domestic economic environment supportive of an optimal balance between production for the domestic and export markets.

B) International and Regional Cooperation and Coordination

Governments of developed countries and those of other countries in a position to do so should, directly or through appropriate international and regional organizations and international lending institutions, enhance their efforts to provide developing countries with increased technical assistance for the following:

(a) Capacity-building in the nation's design and implementation of economic policies, upon request;

(b) Design and operation of efficient tax systems, accounting systems and financial sectors;

(c) Promotion of entrepreneurship.

International financial and development institutions should further review their policies and programmes in the light of the objective of sustainable development.

Stronger economic cooperation among developing countries has long been accepted as an important component of efforts to promote economic growth and technological capabilities and to accelerate development in the developing world. Therefore, the efforts of the developing countries to promote economic cooperation among themselves should be enhanced and continue to be supported by the international community.

MEANS OF IMPLEMENTATION

(A) Financing and Cost Evaluation

The Conference secretariat has estimated the average total annual cost (1993-2000) of implementing the activities in this programme area to be about $50 million from the international community on grant or concessional terms. These are indicative and order-of-magnitude estimates only and have not been reviewed by Governments. Actual costs and financial terms, including any that are non-concessional, will depend upon, inter alia, the specific strategies and programmes Governments decide upon for implementation.

(B) Capacity-building

The above-mentioned policy changes in developing countries involve substantial national efforts for capacity-building in the areas of public administration, central banking, tax administration, savings institutions and financial markets.

Particular efforts in the implementation of the four programme areas identified in this chapter are warranted in view of the especially acute environmental and developmental problems of the least developed countries.

2

Combating Poverty

PROGRAMME AREA

Enabling the Poor to Achieve Sustainable Livelihoods

Basis for action: Poverty is a complex multidimensional problem with origins in both the national and international domains. No uniform solution can be found for global application. Rather, country-specific programmes to tackle poverty and international efforts supporting national efforts, as well as the parallel process of creating a supportive international environment, are crucial for a solution to this problem. The eradication of poverty and hunger, greater equity in income distribution and human resource development remain major challenges everywhere. The struggle against poverty is the shared responsibility of all countries.

While managing resources sustainably, an environmental policy that focuses mainly on the conservation and protection of resources must take due account of those who depend on the resources for their livelihoods. Otherwise it could have an adverse impact both on poverty and on chances for long-term success in resource and environmental conservation. Equally, a development policy that focuses mainly on increasing the production of goods without addressing the sustainability of the resources on which production is based will sooner or later run into declining productivity, which could also have an adverse impact on poverty. A specific anti-poverty strategy is therefore one of the basic conditions for ensuring sustainable development. An effective strategy for tackling the problems of poverty, development and environment simultaneously should begin by focusing on resources, production and people and should cover demographic issues, enhanced health care and education, the rights of women, the role of youth and of indigenous people and local communities and a democratic participation process in association with improved governance. Integral to such action is, together with international support, the promotion of economic growth in developing countries that is both sustained and sustainable and direct action in eradicating poverty by strengthening employment and income-generating programmes.

Objectives

The long-term objective of enabling all people to achieve sustainable livelihoods should provide an integrating factor that allows policies to address issues of development, sustainable resource management and poverty eradication simultaneously. The objectives of this programme area are:

(a) To provide all persons urgently with the opportunity to earn a sustainable livelihood;

(b) To implement policies and strategies that promote adequate levels of funding and focus on integrated human development policies, including income generation, increased local control of resources, local institution-strengthening and capacity-building and greater involvement of non-governmental organizations and local levels of government as delivery mechanisms;

(c) To develop for all poverty-stricken areas integrated strategies and programmes of sound and sustainable management of the environment, resource mobilization, poverty eradication and alleviation, employment and income generation;

(d) To create a focus in national development plans and budgets on investment in human capital, with special policies and programmes directed at rural areas, the urban poor, women and children.

Activities

Activities that will contribute to the integrated promotion of sustainable livelihoods and environmental protection cover a variety of sectoral interventions involving a range of actors, from local to global, and are essential at every level, especially the community and local levels. Enabling actions will be necessary at the national and international levels, taking full account of regional and subregional conditions to support a locally driven and country-specific approach. In general design, the programmes should:

(a) Focus on the empowerment of local and community groups through the principle of delegating authority, accountability and resources to the most appropriate level to ensure that the programme will be geographically and ecologically specific;

(b) Contain immediate measures to enable those groups to alleviate poverty and to develop sustainability;

(c) Contain a long-term strategy aimed at establishing the best possible conditions for sustainable local, regional and national development that would eliminate poverty and reduce the inequalities between various population groups. It should assist the most disadvantaged groups - in particular, women, children and youth within those groups - and refugees. The groups will include poor smallholders, pastoralists, artisans, fishing communities, landless people, indigenous communities, migrants and the urban informal sector.

The focus here is on specific cross-cutting measures - in particular, in the areas of basic education, primary/maternal health care, and the advancement of women.

A) Empowering Communities

Sustainable development must be achieved at every level of society. Peoples' organizations, women's groups and non-governmental organizations are important sources of innovation and action at the local level and have a strong interest and proven ability to promote sustainable livelihoods. Governments, in cooperation with appropriate international and non-governmental organizations, should support a community-driven approach to sustainability, which would include, inter alia:

(a) Empowering women through full participation in decision-making;

(b) Respecting the cultural integrity and the rights of indigenous people and their communities;

(c) Promoting or establishing grass-roots mechanisms to allow for the sharing of experience and knowledge between communities;

(d) Giving communities a large measure of participation in the sustainable management and protection of the local natural resources in order to enhance their productive capacity;

(e) Establishing a network of community-based learning centres for capacity-building and sustainable development.

B) Management-related Activities

Governments, with the assistance of and in cooperation with appropriate international, non-governmental and local community organizations, should establish measures that will directly or indirectly:

(a) Generate remunerative employment and productive occupational opportunities compatible with country-specific factor endowments, on a scale sufficient to take care of prospective increases in the labour force and to cover backlogs;

(b) With international support, where necessary, develop adequate infrastructure, marketing systems, technology systems, credit systems and the like and the human resources needed to support the above actions and to achieve a widening of options for resource-poor people. High priority should be given to basic education and professional training;

(c) Provide substantial increases in economically efficient resource productivity and measures to ensure that the local population benefits in adequate measure from resource use;

(d) Empower community organizations and people to enable them to achieve sustainable livelihoods;

(e) Set up an effective primary health care and maternal health care system accessible to all;

(f) Consider strengthening/developing legal frameworks for land management, access to land resources and land ownership - in particular, for women - and for the protection of tenants;

(g) Rehabilitate degraded resources, to the extent practicable, and introduce policy measures to promote sustainable use of resources for basic human needs;

(h) Establish new community-based mechanisms and strengthen existing mechanisms to enable communities to gain sustained access to resources needed by the poor to overcome their poverty;

(i) Implement mechanisms for popular participation - particularly by poor people, especially women - in local community groups, to promote sustainable development;

(j) Implement, as a matter of urgency, in accordance with country-specific conditions and legal systems, measures to ensure that women and men have the same right to decide freely and responsibly on the number and spacing of their children and have access to the information, education and means, as appropriate, to enable them to exercise this right in keeping with their freedom, dignity and personally held values, taking into account ethical and cultural considerations. Governments should take active steps to implement programmes to establish and strengthen preventive and curative health facilities, which include women-centred, women-managed, safe and effective reproductive health care and affordable, accessible services, as appropriate, for the responsible planning of family size, in keeping with freedom, dignity and personally held values, taking into account ethical and cultural considerations. Programmes should focus on providing comprehensive health care, including pre-natal care, education and information on health and responsible parenthood and should provide the opportunity for all women to breast-feed fully, at least during the first four months post-partum. Programmes should fully support women's productive and reproductive roles and well-being, with special attention to the need for providing equal and improved health care for all children and the need to reduce the risk of maternal and child mortality and sickness;

(k) Adopt integrated policies aiming at sustainability in the management of urban centres;

(l) Undertake activities aimed at the promotion of food security and, where appropriate, food self-sufficiency within the context of sustainable agriculture;

(m) Support research on and integration of traditional methods of production that have been shown to be environmentally sustainable;

(n) Actively seek to recognize and integrate informal-sector activities into the economy by removing regulations and hindrances that discriminate against activities in those sectors;

(o) Consider making available lines of credit and other facilities for the informal sector and improved access to land for the landless poor so that they can acquire the means of production and reliable access to natural resources. In many instances special considerations for women are required. Strict feasibility appraisals are needed for borrowers to avoid debt crises;

(p) Provide the poor with access to fresh water and sanitation;

(q) Provide the poor with access to primary education.

C) Data, Information and Evaluation

Governments should improve the collection of information on target groups and target areas in order to facilitate the design of focused programmes and activities, consistent with the target-group needs and aspirations. Evaluation of such programmes should be gender-specific, since women are a particularly disadvantaged group.

D) International and Regional Cooperation and Coordination

The United Nations system, through its relevant organs, organizations and bodies, in cooperation with Member States and with appropriate international and non-governmental organizations, should make poverty alleviation a major priority and should:

(a) Assist Governments, when requested, in the formulation and implementation of national action programmes on poverty alleviation and sustainable development. Action-oriented activities of relevance to the above objectives, such as poverty eradication, projects and programmes supplemented where relevant by food aid, and support and special emphasis on employment and income generation, should be given particular attention in this regard;

(b) Promote technical cooperation among developing countries for poverty eradication activities;

(c) Strengthen existing structures in the United Nations system for coordination of action relating to poverty eradication, including the establishment of a focal point for information exchange and the formulation and implementation of replicable pilot projects to combat poverty;

(d) In the follow-up of the implementation of Agenda 21, give high priority to the review of the progress made in eradicating poverty;

(e) Examine the international economic framework, including resource flows and structural adjustment programmes, to ensure that social and environmental concerns are addressed, and in this connection, conduct a review of the policies of international organizations, bodies and agencies, including financial institutions, to ensure the continued provision of basic services to the poor and needy;

(f) Promote international cooperation to address the root causes of poverty. The development process will not gather momentum if developing countries are weighted down by external indebtedness, if development finance is inadequate, if barriers restrict access to markets and if commodity prices and the terms of trade in developing countries remain depressed.

MEANS OF IMPLEMENTATION

A) Financing and Cost Evaluation

The secretariat of the Conference has estimated the average total annual cost (1993-2000) of implementing the activities of this programme to be about $30 billion, including about $15 billion from the international community on grant or concessional terms. These are indicative and order-of-magnitude estimates only and have not been reviewed by Governments. This estimate overlaps estimates in other parts of Agenda 21. Actual costs and financial terms, including any that are non-concessional, will depend upon, inter alia, the specific strategies and programmes Governments decide upon for implementation.

C) Capacity-building

National capacity-building for implementation of the above activities is crucial and should be given high priority. It is particularly important to focus capacity-building at the local community level in order to support a community-driven approach to sustainability and to establish and strengthen mechanisms to allow sharing of experience and knowledge between community groups at national and international levels. Requirements for such activities are considerable and are related to the various relevant sectors of Agenda 21 calling for requisite international, financial and technological support.

CHANGING CONSUMPTION PATTERNS

It contains the following programme areas:

(a) Focusing on unsustainable patterns of production and consumption;

(b) Developing national policies and strategies to encourage changes in unsustainable consumption patterns.

Since the issue of changing consumption patterns is very broad, it is addressed in several parts of Agenda 21, notably those dealing with energy, transportation and wastes, and in the chapters on economic instruments and the transfer of technology. The present chapter should also be read in conjunction with chapter 5 (Demographic dynamics and sustainability).

PROGRAMME AREAS

A) Focusing on Unsustainable Patterns of Production and Consumption

Basis for Action

Poverty and environmental degradation are closely interrelated. While poverty results in certain kinds of environmental stress, the major cause of the continued deterioration of the global environment is the unsustainable pattern of consumption and production, particularly in industrialized countries, which is a matter of grave concern, aggravating poverty and imbalances. Measures to be undertaken at the international level for the protection and enhancement of the environment must take fully into account the current imbalances in the global patterns of consumption and production.

Special attention should be paid to the demand for natural resources generated by unsustainable consumption and to the efficient use of those resources consistent with the goal of minimizing depletion and reducing pollution. Although consumption patterns are very high in certain parts of the world, the basic consumer needs of a large section of humanity are not being met. This results in excessive demands and unsustainable lifestyles among the richer segments, which place immense stress on the environment. The poorer segments, meanwhile, are unable to meet food, health care, shelter and educational needs. Changing consumption patterns will require a multipronged strategy focusing on demand, meeting the basic needs of the poor, and reducing wastage and the use of finite resources in the production process.

Growing recognition of the importance of addressing consumption has also not yet been matched by an understanding of its implications. Some economists are questioning traditional concepts of economic growth and underlining the importance of pursuing economic objectives that take account of the full value of natural resource capital. More needs to be known about the role of consumption in relation to economic growth and population dynamics in order to formulate coherent international and national policies.

Objectives

Action is needed to meet the following broad objectives:

(a) To promote patterns of consumption and production that reduce environmental stress and will meet the basic needs of humanity;

(b) To develop a better understanding of the role of consumption and how to bring about more sustainable consumption patterns.

ACTIVITIES

(A) Management-related Activities

Adopting an international approach to achieving sustainable consumption patterns: In principle, countries should be guided by the following basic objectives in their efforts to address consumption and lifestyles in the context of environment and development:

(a) All countries should strive to promote sustainable consumption patterns;

(b) Developed countries should take the lead in achieving sustainable consumption patterns;

Developing countries should seek to achieve sustainable consumption patterns in their development process, guaranteeing the provision of basic needs for the poor, while avoiding those unsustainable patterns, particularly in industrialized countries, generally recognized as unduly hazardous to the environment, inefficient and wasteful, in their development processes. This requires enhanced technological and other assistance from industrialized countries. In the follow-up of the implementation of Agenda 21 the review of progress made in achieving sustainable consumption patterns should be given high priority.

B) DATA AND INFORMATION

Undertaking Research on Consumption

In order to support this broad strategy, Governments, and/ or private research and policy institutes, with the assistance of regional and international economic and environmental organizations, should make a concerted effort to:

(a) Expand or promote databases on production and consumption and develop methodologies for analysing them;

(b) Assess the relationship between production and consumption, environment, technological adaptation and innovation, economic growth and development, and demographic factors;

(c) Examine the impact of ongoing changes in the structure of modern industrial economies away from material-intensive economic growth;

(d) Consider how economies can grow and prosper while reducing the use of energy and materials and the production of harmful materials;

(e) Identify balanced patterns of consumption worldwide which the Earth can support in the long term.

Developing new Concepts of Sustainable Economic Growth and Prosperity

Consideration should also be given to the present concepts of economic growth and the need for new concepts of wealth and prosperity which allow higher standards of living through changed lifestyles and are less dependent on the Earth's finite resources and more in harmony with the Earth's carrying capacity. This should be reflected in the evolution of new systems of national accounts and other indicators of sustainable development.

C) International Cooperation and Coordination

While international review processes exist for examining economic, development and demographic factors, more attention needs to be paid to issues related to consumption and production patterns and sustainable lifestyles and environment. In the follow-up of the implementation of Agenda 21, reviewing the role and impact of unsustainable production and consumption patterns and lifestyles and their relation to sustainable development should be given high priority.

Financing and Cost Evaluation

The Conference secretariat has estimated that

implementation of this programme is not likely to require significant new financial resources.

B. Developing National Policies and Strategies to Encourage Changes in Unsustainable Consumption Patterns

Basis for Action

Achieving the goals of environmental quality and sustainable development will require efficiency in production and changes in consumption patterns in order to emphasize optimization of resource use and minimization of waste. In many instances, this will require reorientation of existing production and consumption patterns that have developed in industrial societies and are in turn emulated in much of the world. Progress can be made by strengthening positive trends and directions that are emerging, as part of a process aimed at achieving significant changes in the consumption patterns of industries, Governments, households and individuals.

Objectives

In the years ahead, Governments, working with appropriate organizations, should strive to meet the following broad objectives:

(a) To promote efficiency in production processes and reduce wasteful consumption in the process of economic growth, taking into account the development needs of developing countries;

(b) To develop a domestic policy framework that will encourage a shift to more sustainable patterns of production and consumption;

(c) To reinforce both values that encourage sustainable production and consumption patterns and policies that encourage the transfer of environmentally sound technologies to developing countries.

ACTIVITIES

A) Encouraging Greater Efficiency in the use of Energy and Resources

Reducing the amount of energy and materials used per

unit in the production of goods and services can contribute both to the alleviation of environmental stress and to greater economic and industrial productivity and competitiveness. Governments, in cooperation with industry, should therefore intensify efforts to use energy and resources in an economically efficient and environmentally sound manner by:

(a) Encouraging the dissemination of existing environmentally sound technologies;

(b) Promoting research and development in environmentally sound technologies;

(c) Assisting developing countries to use these technologies efficiently and to develop technologies suited to their particular circumstances;

(d) Encouraging the environmentally sound use of new and renewable sources of energy;

(e) Encouraging the environmentally sound and sustainable use of renewable natural resources.

B) Minimizing the Generation of Wastes

At the same time, society needs to develop effective ways of dealing with the problem of disposing of mounting levels of waste products and materials. Governments, together with industry, households and the public, should make a concerted effort to reduce the generation of wastes and waste products by:

(a) Encouraging recycling in industrial processes and at the consumed level;

(b) Reducing wasteful packaging of products;

(c) Encouraging the introduction of more environmentally sound products.

C) Assisting Individuals and Households to Make Environmentally Sound Purchasing Decisions

The recent emergence in many countries of a more environmentally conscious consumer public, combined with increased interest on the part of some industries in providing environmentally sound consumer products, is a significant development that should be encouraged. Governments and international organizations, together with the private sector, should develop criteria and methodologies for the assessment of environmental impacts and resource requirements throughout the full life cycle of products and processes. Results of those assessments should be transformed into clear indicators in order to inform consumers and decision makers.

Governments, in cooperation with industry and other relevant groups, should encourage expansion of environmental labelling and other environmentally related product information programmes designed to assist consumers to make informed choices.

They should also encourage the emergence of an informed consumer public and assist individuals and households to make environmentally informed choices by:

(a) Providing information on the consequences of consumption choices and behaviour so as to encourage demand for environmentally sound products and use of products;
(b) Making consumers aware of the health and environmental impact of products, through such means as consumer legislation and environmental labelling;
(c) Encouraging specific consumer-oriented programmes, such as recycling and deposit/refund systems.

D) Exercising Leadership through Government Purchasing

Governments themselves also play a role in consumption, particularly in countries where the public sector plays a large role in the economy and can have a considerable influence on both corporate decisions and public perceptions. They should therefore review the purchasing policies of their agencies and departments so that they may improve, where possible, the environmental content of government procurement policies, without prejudice to international trade principles.

E) Moving Towards Environmentally Sound Pricing

Without the stimulus of prices and market signals that make clear to producers and consumers the environmental costs of the consumption of energy, materials and natural resources and the generation of wastes, significant changes in consumption and production patterns seem unlikely to occur in the near future. Some progress has begun in the use of appropriate economic instruments to influence consumer behaviour. These instruments include environmental charges and taxes, deposit/refund systems, etc. This process should be encouraged in the light of country-specific conditions.

F) Reinforcing Values that Support Sustainable Consumption

Governments and private-sector organizations should promote more positive attitudes towards sustainable consumption through education, public awareness programmes and other means, such as positive advertising of products and services that utilize environmentally sound technologies or encourage sustainable production and consumption patterns. In the review of the implementation of Agenda 21, an assessment of the progress achieved in developing these national policies and strategies should be given due consideration.

Means of Implementation

This programme is concerned primarily with changes in unsustainable patterns of consumption and production and values that encourage sustainable consumption patterns and lifestyles. It requires the combined efforts of Governments, consumers and producers. Particular attention should be paid to the significant role played by women and households as consumers and the potential impacts of their combined purchasing power on the economy.

DEMOGRAPHIC DYNAMICS AND SUSTAINABILITY

It contains the following programme areas:

(a) Developing and disseminating knowledge concerning the links between demographic trends and factors and sustainable development;

(b) Formulating integrated national policies for environment and development, taking into account demographic trends and factors;

(c) Implementing integrated, environment and development programmes at the local level, taking into account demographic trends and factors.

PROGRAMME AREAS

Developing and Disseminating Knowledge Concerning the Links between Demographic Trends and Factors and Sustainable Development

Basis for Action

Demographic trends and factors and sustainable development have a synergistic relationship.

The growth of world population and production combined with unsustainable consumption patterns places increasingly severe stress on the life-supporting capacities of our planet. These interactive processes affect the use of land, water, air, energy and other resources. Rapidly growing cities, unless well-managed, face major environmental problems. The increase in both the number and size of cities calls for greater attention to issues of local government and municipal management. The human dimensions are key elements to consider in this intricate set of relationships and they should be adequately taken into consideration in comprehensive policies for sustainable development. Such policies should address the linkages of demographic trends and factors, resource use, appropriate technology dissemination, and development. Population policy should also recognize the role played by human beings in environmental and development concerns. There is a need to increase awareness of this issue among decision makers at all levels and to provide both better information on which to base national and international policies and a framework against which to interpret this information. There is a need to develop strategies to mitigate both the adverse impact on the environment of human activities and the adverse impact of environmental change on human populations. The world's population is expected to exceed 8 billion by the year 2020. Sixty per cent of the world's population already live in coastal areas, while 65 per cent of cities with populations above 2.5 million are located along the world coasts; several of them are already at or below the present sea level.

Objectives

The following objectives should be achieved as soon as practicable:

(a) To incorporate demographic trends and factors in the global analysis of environment and development issues;

(b) To develop a better understanding of the relationships among demographic dynamics, technology, cultural behaviour, natural resources and life support systems;

(c) To assess human vulnerability in ecologically sensitive areas and centres of population to determine the priorities for action at all levels, taking full account of community defined needs.

Activities: Research on the interaction between demographic trends and factors and sustainable development

Relevant international, regional and national institutions should consider undertaking the following activities:

(a) Identifying the interactions between demographic processes, natural resources and life support systems, bearing in mind regional and subregional variations deriving from, inter alia, different levels of development;

(b) Integrating demographic trends and factors into the ongoing study of environmental change, using the expertise of international, regional and national research networks and of local communities, first, to study the human dimensions of environmental change and, second, to identify vulnerable areas;

(c) Identifying priority areas for action and developing strategies and programmes to mitigate the adverse impact of environmental change on human populations, and vice versa.

MEANS OF IMPLEMENTATION

A) Financing and Cost Evaluation

The Conference secretariat has estimated the average total annual cost (1993-2000) of implementing the activities of this programme to be about $10 million from the international community on grant or concessional terms. These are indicative and order-of-magnitude estimates only and have not been reviewed by Governments. Actual costs and financial terms, including any that are non-concessional, will depend upon, inter alia, the specific strategies and programmes Governments decide upon for implementation.

B) Strengthening Research Programmes that Integrate Population, Environment and Development

In order to integrate demographic analysis into a broader social science perspective on environment and development, interdisciplinary research should be increased. International institutions and networks of experts should enhance their scientific capacity, taking full account of community experience and knowledge, and should disseminate the experience gained in multidisciplinary approaches and in linking theory to action.

Better modelling capabilities should be developed, identifying the range of possible outcomes of current human activities, especially the interrelated impact of demographic trends and factors, per capita resource use and wealth distribution, as well as the major migration flows that may be expected with increasing climatic events and cumulative environmental change that may destroy people's local livelihoods.

C) Developing Information and Public Awareness

Socio-demographic information should be developed in a suitable format for interfacing with physical, biological and socio-economic data. Compatible spatial and temporal scales, cross-country and time-series information, as well as global behavioural indicators should be developed, learning from local communities' perceptions and attitudes.

Awareness should be increased at all levels concerning the need to optimize the sustainable use of resources through efficient resource management, taking into account the development needs of the populations of developing countries.

Awareness should be increased of the fundamental linkages between improving the status of women and demographic dynamics, particularly through women's access to education, primary and reproductive health care programmes, economic independence and their effective, equitable participation in all levels of decision-making.

Results of research concerned with sustainable development issues should be disseminated through technical reports, scientific journals, the media, workshops, forums or other means so that the information can be used by decision makers at all levels and increase public awareness.

D) Developing and/or Enhancing Institutional Capacity and Collaboration

Collaboration and exchange of information should be increased between research institutions and international; regional and national agencies and all other sectors (including the private sector, local communities, non-governmental organizations and scientific institutions) from both the industrialized and developing countries, as appropriate.

Efforts should be intensified to enhance the capacities of national and local governments, the private sector and non-governmental organizations in developing countries to meet the growing needs for improved management of rapidly growing urban areas.

FORMULATING INTEGRATED NATIONAL POLICIES FOR ENVIRONMENT AND DEVELOPMENT

Basis for Action

Existing plans for sustainable development have generally recognized demographic trends and factors as elements that have a critical influence on consumption patterns, production, lifestyles and long-term sustainability. But in future, more attention will have to be given to these issues in general policy formulation and the design of development plans. To do this, all countries will have to improve their own capacities to assess the environment and development implications of their demographic trends and factors. They will also need to formulate and implement policies and action programmes where appropriate. Policies should be designed to address the consequences of population growth built into population momentum, while at the same time incorporating measures to bring about demographic transition. They should combine environmental concerns and population issues within a holistic view of development whose primary goals include the alleviation of poverty; secure livelihoods; good health; quality of life; improvement of the status and income of women and their access to schooling and professional training, as well as fulfilment of their personal aspirations; and empowerment of individuals and communities. Recognizing that large increases in the size and number of cities will occur in developing countries under any likely population scenario, greater attention should be given to preparing for the needs, in particular of women and children, for improved municipal management and local government.

Objective

Full integration of population concerns into national planning, policy and decision-making processes should continue. Population policies and programmes should be considered, with full recognition of women's rights.

Activities

Governments and other relevant actors could, inter alia, undertake the following activities, with appropriate assistance from aid agencies, and report on their status of implementation to the International Conference on Population and Development to be held in 1994, especially to its committee on population and environment.

A) Assessing the Implications of National Demographic Trends and Factors

The relationships between demographic trends and factors and environmental change and between environmental degradation and the components of demographic change should be analysed.

Research should be conducted on how environmental factors interact with socio-economic factors as a cause of migration.

Vulnerable population groups (such as rural landless workers, ethnic minorities, refugees, migrants, displaced people, women heads of household) whose changes in demographic structure may have specific impacts on sustainable development should be identified. An assessment should be made of the implications of the age structure of the population on resource demand and dependency burdens, ranging from educational expenses for the young to health care and support for the elderly, and on household income generation.

An assessment should also be made of national population carrying capacity in the context of satisfaction of human needs and sustainable development, and special attention should be given to critical resources, such as water and land, and environmental factors, such as ecosystem health and biodiversity.

The impact of national demographic trends and factors on the traditional livelihoods of indigenous groups and local communities, including changes in traditional land use because of internal population pressures, should be studied.

B) Building and Strengthening a National Information Base

National databases on demographic trends and factors and environment should be built and/or strengthened, disaggregating data by ecological region (ecosystem approach), and population/environment profiles should be established by region.

Methodologies and instruments should be developed to identify areas where sustainability is, or may be, threatened by the environmental effects of demographic trends and factors, incorporating both current and projected demographic data linked to natural environmental processes.

Case-studies of local level responses by different groups to demographic dynamics should be developed, particularly in areas subject to environmental stress and in deteriorating urban centres.

Population data should be disaggregated by, inter alia, sex and age in order to take into account the implications of the gender division of labour for the use and management of natural resources.

C) Incorporating Demographic Features into Policies and Plans

In formulating human settlements policies, account should be taken of resource needs, waste production and ecosystem health.

The direct and induced effects of demographic changes on environment and development programmes should, where appropriate, be integrated, and the impact on demographic features assessed.

National population policy goals and programmes that are consistent with national environment and development plans for sustainability and in keeping with the freedom, dignity and personally held values of individuals should be established and implemented.

Appropriate socio-economic policies for the young and the elderly, both in terms of family and state support systems, should be developed.

Policies and programmes should be developed for handling the various types of migrations that result from or induce environmental disruptions, with special attention to women and vulnerable groups.

Demographic concerns, including concerns for environmental migrants and displaced people, should be incorporated in the programmes for sustainable development of relevant international and regional institutions.

National reviews should be conducted and the integration of population policies in national development and environment strategies should be monitored nationally.

MEANS OF IMPLEMENTATION

A) Financing and Cost Evaluation

The Conference secretariat has estimated the average total annual cost (1993-2000) of implementing the activities of this programme to be about $90 million from the international community on grant or concessional terms. These are indicative and order-of-magnitude estimates only and have not been reviewed by Governments. Actual costs and financial terms, including any that are non-concessional, will depend upon, inter alia, the specific strategies and programmes Governments decide upon for implementation.

B) Raising Awareness of Demographic and Sustainable Development Interactions

Understanding of the interactions between demographic trends and factors and sustainable development should be increased in all sectors of society. Stress should be placed on local and national action. Demographic and sustainable development education should be coordinated and integrated in both the formal and non-formal education sectors. Particular attention should be given to population literacy programmes, notably for women. Special emphasis should be placed on the linkage between these programmes, primary environmental care and the provision of primary health care and services.

C) Strengthening Institutions

The capacity of national, regional and local structures to deal with issues relating to demographic trends and factors and sustainable development should be enhanced.

This would involve strengthening the relevant bodies responsible for population issucs to enable them to elaborate policies consistent with the national prospects for sustainable development. Cooperation among government, national research institutions, non-governmental organizations and local communities in assessing problems and evaluating policies should also be enhanced.

The capacity of the relevant United Nations organs, organizations and bodies, international and regional intergovernmental bodies, non-governmental organizations and local communities should, as appropriate, be enhanced to help countries develop sustainable development policies on request and, as appropriate, provide assistance to environmental migrants and displaced people.

Inter-agency support for national sustainable development policies and programmes should be improved through better coordination of population and environment activities.

D) Promoting Human Resource Development

The international and regional scientific institutions should assist Governments, upon request, to include concerns regarding the population/environment interactions at the global, ecosystem and micro-levels in the training of demographers and population and environment specialists. Training should include research on linkages and ways to design integrated strategies.

C. Implementing Integrated Environment and Development Programmes at the Local Level, Taking into Account Demographic Trends and Factors

Basis for Action

Population programmes are more effective when implemented together with appropriate cross-sectoral policies. To attain sustainability at the local level, a new framework is needed that integrates demographic trends and factors with such factors as ecosystem health, technology and human settlements, and with socio-economic structures and access to resources. Population programmes should be consistent with socio-economic and environmental planning. Integrated sustainable development programmes should closely correlate action on demographic trends and factors with resource management activities and development goals that meet the needs of the people concerned.

Objective

Population programmes should be implemented along with natural resource management and development programmes at the local level that will ensure sustainable use of natural resources, improve the quality of life of the people and enhance environmental quality.

Activities

Governments and local communities, including community-based women's organizations and national non-governmental organizations, consistent with national plans, objectives, strategies and priorities, could, inter alia, undertake the activities set out below with the assistance and cooperation of international organizations, as appropriate. Governments could share their experience in the implementation of Agenda 21 at the International Conference on Population and Development, to be held in 1994, especially its committee on population and environment.

A) Developing a Framework for Action

An effective consultative process should be established and implemented with concerned groups of society where the formulation and decision-making of all components of the programmes are based on a nationwide consultative process drawing on community meetings, regional workshops and national seminars, as appropriate. This process should ensure that views of women and men on needs, perspective and constraints are equally well reflected in the design of programmes, and that solutions are rooted in specific experience. The poor and underprivileged should be priority groups in this process.

Nationally determined policies for integrated and multifaceted programmes, with special attention to women, to the poorest people living in critical areas and to other vulnerable groups should be implemented, ensuring the involvement of groups with a special potential to act as agents for change and sustainable development. Special emphasis should be placed on those programmes that achieve multiple objectives, encouraging sustainable economic development, and mitigating adverse impacts of demographic trends and factors, and avoiding long-term environmental damage. Food security, access to secure tenure, basic shelter, and essential infrastructure, education, family welfare, women's reproductive health, family credit schemes, reforestation programmes, primary environmental care, women's employment should, as appropriate, be included among other factors.

An analytical framework should be developed to identify complementary elements of sustainable development policies as well as the national mechanisms to monitor and evaluate their effects on population dynamics.

Special attention should be given to the critical role of women in population/environment programmes and in achieving sustainable development. Projects should take advantage of opportunities to link social, economic and environmental gains for women and their families. Empowerment of women is essential and should be assured through education, training and policies to accord and improve women's right and access to assets, human and civil rights, labour-saving measures, job opportunities and participation in decision-making. Population/ environment programmes must enable women to mobilize themselves to alleviate their burden and improve their capacity to participate in and benefit from socio-economic development. Specific measures should be undertaken to close the gap between female and male illiteracy rates.

B) Supporting Programmes that Promote Changes in Demographic Trends and Factors Towards Sustainability

Reproductive health programmes and services, should, as appropriate, be developed and enhanced to reduce maternal and infant mortality from all causes and enable women and men to fulfil their personal aspirations in terms of family size, in a way in keeping with their freedom and dignity and personally held values.

Governments should take active steps to implement, as a matter of urgency, in accordance with country-specific conditions and legal systems, measures to ensure that women and men have the same right to decide freely and responsibly on the number and spacing of their children, to have access to the information, education and means, as appropriate, to enable them to exercise this right in keeping with their freedom, dignity and personally held values taking into account ethical and cultural considerations.

Governments should take active steps to implement programmes to establish and strengthen preventive and curative health facilities that include women-centred, women-managed, safe and effective reproductive health care and affordable, accessible services, as appropriate, for the responsible planning of family size, in keeping with freedom, dignity and personally held values and taking into account ethical and cultural considerations. Programmes should focus on providing comprehensive health care, including pre-natal care, education and information on health and responsible parenthood and should provide the opportunity for all women to breast-feed fully, at least during the first four months post-partum. Programmes should fully support women's productive and reproductive roles and well being, with special attention to the need for providing equal and improved health care for all children and the need to reduce the risk of maternal and child mortality and sickness.

Consistent with national priorities, culturally based information and education programmes that transmit reproductive health messages to men and women that are easily understood should be developed.

C) Creating Appropriate Institutional Conditions

Constituencies and institutional conditions to facilitate the implementation of demographic activities should, as appropriate, be fostered. This requires support and commitment from political, indigenous, religious and traditional authorities, the private sector and the national scientific community. In developing these appropriate institutional conditions, countries should closely involve established national machinery for women.

Population assistance should be coordinated with bilateral and multilateral donors to ensure that population needs and requirements of all developing countries are addressed, fully respecting the overall coordinating responsibility and the choice and strategies of the recipient countries.

Coordination should be improved at local and international levels. Working practices should be enhanced in order to make optimum use of resources, draw on collective experience and improve the implementation of programmes. UNFPA and other relevant agencies should strengthen the coordination of international cooperation activities with recipient and donor countries in order to ensure that adequate funding is available to respond to growing needs.

Proposals should be developed for local, national and international population/environment programmes in line with specific needs for achieving sustainability. Where appropriate, institutional changes must be implemented so that old-age security does not entirely depend on input from family members.

MEANS OF IMPLEMENTATION

A) Financing and Cost Evaluation

The Conference secretariat has estimated the average total annual cost (1993-2000) of implementing the activities of this programme to be about $7 billion, including about $3.5 billion from the international community on grant or concessional terms.

These are indicative and order-of-magnitude estimates only and have not been reviewed by Governments. Actual costs and financial terms, including any that are non-concessional, will depend upon, inter alia, the specific strategies and programmes Governments decide upon for implementation.

B) Research

Research should be undertaken with a view to developing specific action programmes; it will be necessary to establish priorities between proposed areas of research.

Socio-demographic research should be conducted on how populations respond to a changing environment.

Understanding of socio-cultural and political factors that can positively influence acceptance of appropriate population policy instruments should be improved.

Surveys of changes in needs for appropriate services relating to responsible planning of family size, reflecting variations among different socio-economic groups and variations in different geographical regions should be undertaken.

C) Human Resource Development and Capacity-building

The areas of human resource development and capacity-building, with particular attention to the education and training of women, are areas of critical importance and are a very high priority in the implementation of population programmes.

Workshops to help programme and projects managers to link population programmes to other development and environmental goals should be conducted.

Educational materials, including guides/workbooks for planners and decision makers and other actors of population/ environment/development programmes, should be developed.

Cooperation should be developed between Governments, scientific institutions and non-governmental organizations within the region, and similar institutions outside the region. Cooperation with local organizations should be fostered in ordered to raise awareness, engage in demonstration projects and report on the experience gained.

3

Protecting and Promoting Human Health

Health and development are intimately interconnected. Both insufficient development leading to poverty and inappropriate development resulting in overconsumption, coupled with an expanding world population, can result in severe environmental health problems in both developing and developed nations. Action items under Agenda 21 must address the primary health needs of the world's population, since they are integral to the achievement of the goals of sustainable development and primary environmental care. The linkage of health, environmental and socio-economic improvements requires intersectoral efforts. Such efforts, involving education, housing, public works and community groups, including businesses, schools and universities and religious, civic and cultural organizations, are aimed at enabling people in their communities to ensure sustainable development. Particularly relevant is the inclusion of prevention programmes rather than relying solely on remediation and treatment. Countries ought to develop plans for priority actions, drawing on the programme areas in this chapter, which are based on cooperative planning by the various levels of government, non-governmental organizations and local communities. An appropriate international organization, such as WHO, should coordinate these activities.

The following programme areas are contained in this chapter:

(a) Meeting primary health care needs, particularly in rural areas;

(b) Control of communicable diseases;
(c) Protecting vulnerable groups;
(d) Meeting the urban health challenge;
(e) Reducing health risks from environmental pollution and hazards.

PROGRAMME AREAS

A. Meeting Primary Health Care needs, Particularly in Rural Areas Basis for Action

Health ultimately depends on the ability to manage successfully the interaction between the physical, spiritual, biological and economic/social environment. Sound development is not possible without a healthy population; yet most developmental activities affect the environment to some degree, which in turn causes or exacerbates many health problems. Conversely, it is the very lack of development that adversely affects the health condition of many people, which can be alleviated only through development. The health sector cannot meet basic needs and objectives on its own; it is dependent on social, economic and spiritual development, while directly contributing to such development. It is also dependent on a healthy environment, including the provision of a safe water supply and sanitation and the promotion of a safe food supply and proper nutrition. Particular attention should be directed towards food safety, with priority placed on the elimination of food contamination; comprehensive and sustainable water policies to ensure safe drinking water and sanitation to preclude both microbial and chemical contamination; and promotion of health education, immunization and provision of essential drugs. Education and appropriate services regarding responsible planning of family size, with respect for cultural, religious and social aspects, in keeping with freedom, dignity and personally held values and taking into account ethical and cultural considerations, also contribute to these intersectoral activities.

Objectives

Within the overall strategy to achieve health for all by the year 2000, the objectives are to meet the basic health needs of rural peri-urban and urban populations; to provide the necessary specialized environmental health services; and to coordinate the involvement of citizens, the health sector, the health-related sectors and relevant non-health sectors (business, social, educational and religious institutions) in solutions to health problems. As a matter of priority, health service coverage should be achieved for population groups in greatest need, particularly those living in rural areas.

Activities

National Governments and local authorities, with the support of relevant non-governmental organizations and international organizations, in the light of countries' specific conditions and needs, should strengthen their health sector programmes, with special attention to rural needs, to:

(a) Build basic health infrastructures, monitoring and planning systems:

i. Develop and strengthen primary health care systems that are practical, community-based, scientifically sound, socially acceptable and appropriate to their needs and that meet basic health needs for clean water, safe food and sanitation;

ii. Support the use and strengthening of mechanisms that improve coordination between health and related sectors at all appropriate levels of government, and in communities and relevant organizations;

iii. Develop and implement rational and affordable approaches to the establishment and maintenance of health facilities;

iv. Ensure and, where appropriate, increase provision of social services support;

v. Develop strategies, including reliable health indicators, to monitor the progress and evaluate the effectiveness of health programmes;

vi. Explore ways to finance the health system based on the assessment of the resources needed and identify the various financing alternatives;

vii. Promote health education in schools, information exchange, technical support and training;

viii. Support initiatives for self-management of services by vulnerable groups;

ix. Integrate traditional knowledge and experience into national health systems, as appropriate;

x. Promote the provisions for necessary logistics for outreach activities, particularly in rural areas;

xi. Promote and strengthen community-based rehabilitation activities for the rural handicapped.

(b) Support research and methodology development:

i. Establish mechanisms for sustained community involvement in environmental health activities, including optimization of the appropriate use of community financial and human resources;

ii. Conduct environmental health research, including behaviour research and research on ways to increase coverage and ensure greater utilization of services by peripheral, underserved and vulnerable populations, as appropriate to good prevention services and health care;

iii. Conduct research into traditional knowledge of prevention and curative health practices.

MEANS OF IMPLEMENTATION

A) Financing and Cost Evaluation

The Conference secretariat has estimated the average total annual cost (1993-2000) of implementing the activities of this programme to be about $40 billion, including about $5 billion from the international community on grant or concessional terms. These are indicative and order-of-magnitude estimates only and have not been reviewed by Governments. Actual costs and financial terms, including any that are non-concessional, will depend upon, inter alia, the specific strategies and programmes Governments decide upon for implementation.

B) Scientific and Technological Means

New approaches to planning and managing health care

systems and facilities should be tested, and research on ways of integrating appropriate technologies into health infrastructures supported. The development of scientifically sound health technology should enhance adaptability to local needs and maintainability by community resources, including the maintenance and repair of equipment used in health care. Programmes to facilitate the transfer and sharing of information and expertise should be developed, including communication methods and educational materials.

C) Human Resource Development

Intersectoral approaches to the reform of health personnel development should be strengthened to ensure its relevance to the "Health for All" strategies. Efforts to enhance managerial skills at the district level should be supported, with the aim of ensuring the systematic development and efficient operation of the basic health system.

Intensive, short, practical training programmes with emphasis on skills in effective communication, community organization and facilitation of behaviour change should be developed in order to prepare the local personnel of all sectors involved in social development for carrying out their respective roles. In cooperation with the education sector, special health education programmes should be developed focusing on the role of women in the health-care system.

D) Capacity-building

Governments should consider adopting enabling and facilitating strategies to promote the participation of communities in meeting their own needs, in addition to providing direct support to the provision of health-care services. A major focus should be the preparation of community-based health and health-related workers to assume an active role in community health education, with emphasis on team work, social mobilization and the support of other development workers. National programmes should cover district health systems in urban, peri-urban and rural areas, the delivery of health programmes at the district level, and the development and support of referral services.

CONTROL OF COMMUNICABLE DISEASES

Basis for Action

Advances in the development of vaccines and chemotherapeutic agents have brought many communicable diseases under control. However, there remain many important communicable diseases for which environmental control measures are indispensable, especially in the field of water supply and sanitation. Such diseases include cholera, diarrhoeal diseases, leishmaniasis, malaria and schistosomiasis. In all such instances, the environmental measures, either as an integral part of primary health care or undertaken outside the health sector, form an indispensable component of overall disease control strategies, together with health and hygiene education, and in some cases, are the only component.

With HIV infection levels estimated to increase to 30-40 million by the year 2000, the socio-economic impact of the pandemic is expected to be devastating for all countries, and increasingly for women and children. While direct health costs will be substantial, they will be dwarfed by the indirect costs of the pandemic - mainly costs associated with the loss of income and decreased productivity of the workforce. The pandemic will inhibit growth of the service and industrial sectors and significantly increase the costs of human capacity-building and retraining. The agricultural sector is particularly affected where production is labour-intensive.

Objectives

A number of goals have been formulated through extensive consultations in various international forums attended by virtually all Governments, relevant United Nations organizations (including WHO, UNICEF, UNFPA, UNESCO, UNDP and the World Bank) and a number of non-governmental organizations. Goals (including but not limited to those listed below) are recommended for implementation by all countries where they are applicable, with appropriate adaptation to the specific situation of each country in terms of phasing, standards, priorities and availability of resources, with respect for cultural, religious and social aspects, in keeping with freedom, dignity and personally held values and taking into account ethical considerations. Additional goals that are particularly relevant to a country's specific situation should be added in the country's national plan of action (Plan of Action for Implementing the World Declaration on the Survival, Protection and Development of Children in the 1990s). 1/ Such national level action plans should be coordinated and monitored from within the public health sector. Some major goals are:

(a) By the year 2000, to eliminate guinea worm disease (dracunculiasis);

(b) By the year 2000, eradicate polio;

(c) By the year 2000, to effectively control onchocerciasis (river blindness) and leprosy;

(d) By 1995, to reduce measles deaths by 95 per cent and reduce measles cases by 90 per cent compared with pre-immunization levels;

(e) By continued efforts, to provide health and hygiene education and to ensure universal access to safe drinking water and universal access to sanitary measures of excreta disposal, thereby markedly reducing waterborne diseases such as cholera and schistosomiasis and reducing:

   i. By the year 2000, the number of deaths from childhood diarrhoea in developing countries by 50 to 70 per cent;

   ii. By the year 2000, the incidence of childhood diarrhoea in developing countries by at least 25 to 50 per cent;

(f) By the year 2000, to initiate comprehensive programmes to reduce mortality from acute respiratory infections in children under five years by at least one third, particularly in countries with high infant mortality;

(g) By the year 2000, to provide 95 per cent of the world's child population with access to appropriate care for acute respiratory infections within the community and at first referral level;

(h) By the year 2000, to institute anti-malaria programmes in all countries where malaria presents a significant health problem and maintain the transmission-free status of areas freed from endemic malaria;

(i) By the year 2000, to implement control programmes in countries where major human parasitic infections are endemic and achieve an overall reduction in the prevalence of schistosomiasis and of other trematode infections by 40 per cent and 25 per cent, respectively, from a 1984 baseline, as well as a marked reduction in incidence, prevalence and intensity of filarial infections;

(j) To mobilize and unify national and international efforts against AIDS to prevent infection and to reduce the personal and social impact of HIV infection;

(k) To contain the resurgence of tuberculosis, with particular emphasis on multiple antibiotic resistant forms;

(l) To accelerate research on improved vaccines and implement to the fullest extent possible the use of vaccines in the prevention of disease.

Activities

Each national Government, in accordance with national plans for public health, priorities and objectives, should consider developing a national health action plan with appropriate international assistance and support, including, at a minimum, the following components:

(a) National public health systems:

i. Programmes to identify environmental hazards in the causation of communicable diseases;

ii. Monitoring systems of epidemiological data to ensure adequate forecasting of the introduction, spread or aggravation of communicable diseases;

iii. Intervention programmes, including measures consistent with the principles of the global AIDS strategy;

iv. Vaccines for the prevention of communicable diseases;

(b) Public information and health education: Provide education and disseminate information on the risks of endemic communicable diseases and build awareness on environmental methods for control of communicable diseases to enable communities to play a role in the control of communicable diseases;

(c) Intersectoral cooperation and coordination:

  i. Second experienced health professionals to relevant sectors, such as planning, housing and agriculture;

  ii. Develop guidelines for effective coordination in the areas of professional training, assessment of risks and development of control technology;

(d) Control of environmental factors that influence the spread of communicable diseases: Apply methods for the prevention and control of communicable diseases, including water supply and sanitation control, water pollution control, food quality control, integrated vector control, garbage collection and disposal and environmentally sound irrigation practices;

(e) Primary health care system:

  i. Strengthen prevention programmes, with particular emphasis on adequate and balanced nutrition;

  ii. Strengthen early diagnostic programmes and improve capacities for early preventative/treatment action;

  iii. Reduce the vulnerability to HIV infection of women and their offspring;

(f) Support for research and methodology development:

  i. Intensify and expand multidisciplinary research, including focused efforts on the mitigation and environmental control of tropical diseases;

  ii. Carry out intervention studies to provide a solid epidemiological basis for control policies and to evaluate the efficiency of alternative approaches;

  iii. Undertake studies in the population and among health workers to determine the influence of cultural, behavioural and social factors on control policies;

(g) Development and dissemination of technology:
   i. Develop new technologies for the effective control of communicable diseases;
   ii. Promote studies to determine how to optimally disseminate results from research;
   iii. Ensure technical assistance, including the sharing of knowledge and know-how.

MEANS OF IMPLEMENTATION

Financing and Cost Evaluation

The Conference secretariat has estimated the average total annual cost (1993-2000) of implementing the activities of this programme to be about $4 billion, including about $900 million from the international community on grant or concessional terms. These are indicative and order-of-magnitude estimates only and have not been reviewed by Governments. Actual costs and financial terms, including any that are non-concessional, will depend upon, inter alia, the specific strategies and programmes Governments decide upon for implementation.

Scientific and Technological Means

Efforts to prevent and control diseases should include investigations of the epidemiological, social and economic bases for the development of more effective national strategies for the integrated control of communicable diseases. Cost-effective methods of environmental control should be adapted to local developmental conditions.

Human Resource Development

National and regional training institutions should promote broad intersectoral approaches to prevention and control of communicable diseases, including training in epidemiology and community prevention and control, immunology, molecular biology and the application of new vaccines. Health education materials should be developed for use by community workers and for the education of mothers for the prevention and treatment of diarrhoeal diseases in the home.

Capacity-building

The health sector should develop adequate data on the distribution of communicable diseases, as well as the institutional capacity to respond and collaborate with other sectors for prevention, mitigation and correction of communicable disease hazards through environmental protection. The advocacy at policy- and decision-making levels should be gained, professional and societal support mobilized, and communities organized in developing self-reliance.

Protecting Vulnerable Groups

Basis for Action

In addition to meeting basic health needs, specific emphasis has to be given to protecting and educating vulnerable groups, particularly infants, youth, women, indigenous people and the very poor as a prerequisite for sustainable development. Special attention should also be paid to the health needs of the elderly and disabled population. Infants and children. Approximately one third of the world's population are children under 15 years old. At least 15 million of these children die annually from such preventable causes as birth trauma, birth asphyxia, acute respiratory infections, malnutrition, communicable diseases and diarrhoea. The health of children is affected more severely than other population groups by malnutrition and adverse environmental factors, and many children risk exploitation as cheap labour or in prostitution.

Youth. As has been the historical experience of all countries, youth are particularly vulnerable to the problems associated with economic development, which often weakens traditional forms of social support essential for the healthy development, of young people. Urbanization and changes in social mores have increased substance abuse, unwanted pregnancy and sexually transmitted diseases, including AIDS. Currently more than half of all people alive are under the age of 25, and four of every five live in developing countries. Therefore it is important to ensure that historical experience is not replicated.

Women. In developing countries, the health status of women remains relatively low, and during the 1980s poverty, malnutrition and general ill-health in women were even rising. Most women in developing countries still do not have adequate basic educational opportunities and they lack the means of promoting their health, responsibly controlling their reproductive life and improving their socio-economic status. Particular attention should be given to the provision of pre-natal care to ensure healthy babies.

Indigenous people and their communities. Indigenous people had their communities make up a significant percentage of global population. The outcomes of their experience have tended to be very similar in that the basis of their relationship with traditional lands has been fundamentally changed. They tend to feature disproportionately in unemployment, lack of housing, poverty and poor health. In many countries the number of indigenous people is growing faster than the general population. Therefore it is important to target health initiatives for indigenous people.

Objectives

The general objectives of protecting vulnerable groups are to ensure that all such individuals should be allowed to develop to their full potential (including healthy physical, mental and spiritual development); to ensure that young people can develop, establish and maintain healthy lives; to allow women to perform their key role in society; and to support indigenous people through educational, economic and technical opportunities.

Specific major goals for child survival, development and protection were agreed upon at the World Summit for Children and remain valid also for Agenda 21. Supporting and sectoral goals cover women's health and education, nutrition, child health, water and sanitation, basic education and children in difficult circumstances.

Governments should take active steps to implement, as a matter of urgency, in accordance with country specific conditions and legal systems, measures to ensure that women and men have the same right to decide freely and responsibly on the number and spacing of their children, to have access to the information, education and means, as appropriate, to enable them to exercise this right in keeping with their freedom, dignity and personally held values, taking into account ethical and cultural considerations.

Governments should take active steps to implement programmes to establish and strengthen preventive and curative health facilities which include women-centred, women-managed, safe and effective reproductive health care and affordable, accessible services, as appropriate, for the responsible planning of family size, in keeping with freedom, dignity and personally held values and taking into account ethical and cultural considerations.

Programmes should focus on providing comprehensive health care, including pre-natal care, education and information on health and responsible parenthood and should provide the opportunity for all women to breast-feed fully, at least during the first four months post-partum. Programmes should fully support women's productive and reproductive roles and well being, with special attention to the need for providing equal and improved health care for all children and the need to reduce the risk of maternal and child mortality and sickness.

Activities

National Governments, in cooperation with local and non-governmental organizations, should initiate or enhance programmes in the following areas:

(a) Infants and children:

i. Strengthen basic health-care services for children in the context of primary health-care delivery, including prenatal care, breast-feeding, immunization and nutrition programmes;

ii. Undertake widespread adult education on the use of oral rehydration therapy for diarrhoea, treatment of respiratory infections and prevention of communicable diseases;

iii. Promote the creation, amendment and enforcement of a legal framework protecting children from sexual and workplace exploitation;

iv. Protect children from the effects of environmental and occupational toxic compounds;

(b) Youth: Strengthen services for youth in health, education and social sectors in order to provide better information, education, counselling and treatment for specific health problems, including drug abuse;

(c) Women:

i. Involve women's groups in decision-making at the national and community levels to identify health risks and incorporate health issues in national action programmes on women and development;

ii. Provide concrete incentives to encourage and maintain attendance of women of all ages at school and adult education courses, including health education and training in primary, home and maternal health care;

iii. Carry out baseline surveys and knowledge, attitude and practice studies on the health and nutrition of women throughout their life cycle, especially as related to the impact of environmental degradation and adequate resources;

(d) Indigenous people and their communities:

i. Strengthen, through resources and self-management, preventative and curative health services;

ii. Integrate traditional knowledge and experience into health systems.

MEANS OF IMPLEMENTATION

Financing and Cost Evaluation

The Conference secretariat has estimated the average total annual cost (1993-2000) of implementing the activities of this programme to be about $3.7 billion, including about $400 billion from the international community on grant or concessional terms. These are indicative and order-of-magnitude estimates only and have not been reviewed by Governments. Actual costs and financial terms, including any that are non-concessional, will depend upon, inter alia, the specific strategies and programmes Governments decide upon for implementation.

Scientific and Technological Means

Educational, health and research institutions should be strengthened to provide support to improve the health of vulnerable groups. Social research on the specific problems of these groups should be expanded and methods for implementing flexible pragmatic solutions explored, with emphasis on preventive measures. Technical support should be provided to Governments, institutions and non-governmental organizations for youth, women and indigenous people in the health sector.

Human Resources Development

The development of human resources for the health of children, youth and women should include reinforcement of educational institutions, promotion of interactive methods of education for health and increased use of mass media in disseminating information to the target groups.

This requires the training of more community health workers, nurses, midwives, physicians, social scientists and educators, the education of mothers, families and communities and the strengthening of ministries of education, health, population etc.

Capacity-building

Governments should promote, where necessary: (i) the organization of national, intercountry and interregional symposia and other meetings for the exchange of information among agencies and groups concerned with the health of children, youth, women and indigenous people, and (ii) women's organizations, youth groups and indigenous people's organizations to facilitate health and consult them on the creation, amendment and enforcement of legal frameworks to ensure a healthy environment for children, youth, women and indigenous peoples.

Meeting the Urban Health Challenge

Basis for Action

For hundreds of millions of people, the poor living conditions in urban and peri-urban areas are destroying lives, health, and social and moral values. Urban growth has outstripped society's capacity to meet human needs, leaving hundreds of millions of people with inadequate incomes, diets, housing and services. Urban growth exposes populations to serious environmental hazards and has outstripped the capacity of municipal and local governments to provide the environmental health services that the people need.

All too often, urban development is associated with destructive effects on the physical environment and the resource base needed for sustainable development. Environmental pollution in urban areas is associated with excess morbidity and mortality. Overcrowding and inadequate housing contribute to respiratory diseases, tuberculosis, meningitis and other diseases. In urban environments, many factors that affect human health are outside the health sector. Improvements in urban health therefore will depend on coordinated action by all levels of government, health care providers, businesses, religious groups, social and educational institutions and citizens.

Objectives

The health and well-being of all urban dwellers must be improved so that they can contribute to economic and social development. The global objective is to achieve a 10 to 40 per cent improvement in health indicators by the year 2000. The same rate of improvement should be achieved for environmental, housing and health service indicators. These include the development of quantitative objectives for infant mortality, maternal mortality, percentage of low birth weight newborns and specific indicators (e.g. tuberculosis as an indicator of crowded housing, diarrhoeal diseases as indicators of inadequate water and sanitation, rates of industrial and transportation accidents that indicate possible opportunities for prevention of injury, and social problems such as drug abuse, violence and crime that indicate underlying social disorders).

Activities

Local authorities, with the appropriate support of national Governments and international organizations should be encouraged to take effective measures to initiate or strengthen the following activities:

(a) Develop and implement municipal and local health plans:

i. Establish or strengthen intersectoral committees at both the political and technical level, including active collaboration on linkages with scientific, cultural, religious, medical, business, social and other city institutions, using networking arrangements;

ii. Adopt or strengthen municipal or local "enabling strategies" that emphasize "doing with" rather than "doing for" and create supportive environments for health;

iii. Ensure that public health education in schools, workplace, mass media etc. is provided or strengthened;

iv. Encourage communities to develop personal skills and awareness of primary health care;

v. Promote and strengthen community-based rehabilitation activities for the urban and peri-urban disabled and the elderly;

(b) Survey, where necessary, the existing health, social and environmental conditions in cities, including documentation of intra-urban differences;

(c) Strengthen environmental health services:

i. Adopt health impact and environmental impact assessment procedures;

ii. Provide basic and in-service training for new and existing personnel;

(d) Establish and maintain city networks for collaboration and exchange of models of good practice.

MEANS OF IMPLEMENTATION

Financing and Cost Evaluation

The Conference secretariat has estimated the average total

annual cost (1993-2000) of implementing the activities of this programme to be about $222 million, including about $22 million from the international community on grant or concessional terms. These are indicative and order-of-magnitude estimates only and have not been reviewed by Governments. Actual costs and financial terms, including any that are non-concessional, will depend upon, inter alia, the specific strategies and programmes Governments decide upon for implementation.

Scientific and Technological Means

Decision-making models should be further developed and more widely used to assess the costs and the health and environment impacts of alternative technologies and strategies. Improvement in urban development and management requires better national and municipal statistics based on practical, standardized indicators. Development of methods is a priority for the measurement of intra-urban and intra-district variations in health status and environmental conditions, and for the application of this information in planning and management.

Human Resources Development

Programmes must supply the orientation and basic training of municipal staff required for the healthy city processes. Basic and in-service training of environmental health personnel will also be needed.

Capacity-building

The programme is aimed towards improved planning and management capabilities in the municipal and local government and its partners in central Government, the private sector and universities. Capacity development should be focused on obtaining sufficient information, improving coordination mechanisms linking all the key actors, and making better use of available instruments and resources for implementation.

Reducing Health Risks from Environmental Pollution and Hazards

Basis for Action

In many locations around the world the general environment (air, water and land), workplaces and even individual dwellings are so badly polluted that the health of hundreds of millions of people is adversely affected. This is, inter alia, due to past and present developments in consumption and production patterns and lifestyles, in energy production and use, in industry, in transportation etc., with little or no regard for environmental protection. There have been notable improvements in some countries, but deterioration of the environment continues.

The ability of countries to tackle pollution and health problems is greatly restrained because of lack of resources. Pollution control and health protection measures have often not kept pace with economic development. Considerable development-related environmental health hazards exist in the newly industrializing countries. Furthermore, the recent analysis of WHO has clearly established the interdependence among the factors of health, environment and development and has revealed that most countries are lacking such integration as would lead to an effective pollution control mechanism. Without prejudice to such criteria as may be agreed upon by the international community, or to standards which will have to be determined nationally, it will be essential in all cases to consider the systems of values prevailing in each country and the extent of the applicability of standards that are valid for the most advanced countries but may be inappropriate and of unwarranted social cost for the developing countries.

Objectives

The overall objective is to minimize hazards and maintain the environment to a degree that human health and safety is not impaired or endangered and yet encourage development to proceed. Specific programme objectives are:

(a) By the year 2000, to incorporate appropriate environmental and health safeguards as part of national development programmes in all countries;

(b) By the year 2000, to establish, as appropriate, adequate national infrastructure and programmes for providing environmental injury, hazard surveillance and the basis for abatement in all countries;

(c) By the year 2000, to establish, as appropriate, integrated programmes for tackling pollution at the source and at the disposal site, with a focus on abatement actions in all countries;

(d) To identify and compile, as appropriate, the necessary statistical information on health effects to support cost/benefit analysis, including environmental health impact assessment for pollution control, prevention and abatement measures.

Activities

Nationally determined action programmes, with international assistance, support and coordination, where necessary, in this area should include:

(a) Urban air pollution:

i. Develop appropriate pollution control technology on the basis of risk assessment and epidemiological research for the introduction of environmentally sound production processes and suitable safe mass transport;

ii. Develop air pollution control capacities in large cities, emphasizing enforcement programmes and using monitoring networks, as appropriate;

(b) Indoor air pollution:

i. Support research and develop programmes for applying prevention and control methods to reducing indoor air pollution, including the provision of economic incentives for the installation of appropriate technology;

ii. Develop and implement health education campaigns, particularly in developing countries, to reduce the health impact of domestic use of biomass and coal;

(c) Water pollution:

i. Develop appropriate water pollution control technologies on the basis of health risk assessment;

ii. Develop water pollution control capacities in large cities;

(d) Pesticides: Develop mechanisms to control the distribution and use of pesticides in order to minimize the risks to human health by transportation, storage, application and residual effects of pesticides used in agriculture and preservation of wood;

(e) Solid waste:

i. Develop appropriate solid waste disposal technologies on the basis of health risk assessment;

ii. Develop appropriate solid waste disposal capacities in large cities;

(f) Human settlements: Develop programmes for improving health conditions in human settlements, in particular within slums and non-tenured settlements, on the basis of health risk assessment;

(g) Noise: Develop criteria for maximum permitted safe noise exposure levels and promote noise assessment and control as part of environmental health programmes;

(h) Ionizing and non-ionizing radiation: Develop and implement appropriate national legislation, standards and enforcement procedures on the basis of existing international guidelines;

(i) Effects of ultraviolet radiation:

i. Effects of ultraviolet radiation: Undertake, as a matter of urgency, research on the effects on human health of the increasing ultraviolet radiation reaching the earth's surface as a consequence of depletion of the stratospheric ozone layer;

ii. On the basis of the outcome of this research, consider taking appropriate remedial measures to mitigate the above-mentioned effects on human beings;

(j) Industry and energy production:

i. Establish environmental health impact assessment procedures for the planning and development of new industries and energy facilities;

ii. Incorporate appropriate health risk analysis in all national programmes for pollution control and management, with particular emphasis on toxic compounds such as lead;

iii. Establish industrial hygiene programmes in all major industries for the surveillance of workers' exposure to health hazards;

iv. Promote the introduction of environmentally sound technologies within the industry and energy sectors;

(k) Monitoring and assessment: Establish, as appropriate, adequate environmental monitoring capacities for the surveillance of environmental quality and the health status of populations;

(l) Injury monitoring and reduction:

i. Support, as appropriate, the development of systems to monitor the incidence and cause of injury to allow well-targeted intervention/prevention strategies;

ii. Develop, in accordance with national plans, strategies in all sectors (industry, traffic and others) consistent with the WHO safe cities and safe communities programmes, to reduce the frequency and severity of injury;

iii. Emphasize preventive strategies to reduce occupationally derived diseases and diseases caused by environmental and occupational toxins to enhance worker safety;

(m) Research promotion and methodology development:

i. Support the development of new methods for the quantitative assessment of health benefits and cost associated with different pollution control strategies;

ii. Develop and carry out interdisciplinary research on the combined health effects of exposure to multiple environmental hazards, including epidemiological investigations of long-term exposures to low levels of pollutants and the use of biological markers capable of estimating human exposures, adverse effects and susceptibility to environmental agents.

MEANS OF IMPLEMENTATION

Financing and Cost Evaluation

The Conference secretariat has estimated the average total annual cost (1993-2000) of implementing the activities of this programme to be about $3 billion, including about $115 million from the international community on grant or concessional terms.

These are indicative and order-of-magnitude estimates only and have not been reviewed by Governments. Actual costs and financial terms, including any that are non-concessional, will depend upon, inter alia, the specific strategies and programmes Governments decide upon for implementation.

Scientific and Technological Means

Although technology to prevent or abate pollution is readily available for a large number of problems, for programme and policy development countries should undertake research within an intersectoral framework.

Such efforts should include collaboration with the business sector. Cost/effect analysis and environmental impact assessment methods should be developed through cooperative international programmes and applied to the setting of priorities and strategies in relation to health and development.

In the activities listed in paragraph 6.41 (a) to (m) above, developing country efforts should be facilitated by access to and transfer of technology, know-how and information, from the repositories of such knowledge and technologies, in conformity with chapter 34.

Human Resource Development

Comprehensive national strategies should be designed to overcome the lack of qualified human resources, which is a major impediment to progress in dealing with environmental health hazards.

Training should include environmental and health officials at all levels from managers to inspectors. More emphasis needs to be placed on including the subject of environmental health in the curricula of secondary schools and universities and on educating the public.

Capacity-building

Each country should develop the knowledge and practical skills to foresee and identify environmental health hazards, and the capacity to reduce the risks. Basic capacity requirements must include knowledge about environmental health problems and awareness on the part of leaders, citizens and specialists; operational mechanisms for intersectoral and intergovernmental cooperation in development planning and management and in combating pollution; arrangements for involving private and community interests in dealing with social issues; delegation of authority and distribution of resources to intermediate and local levels of government to provide front-line capabilities to meet environmental health needs.

4

Promoting Sustainable Human Settlement Development

In industrialized countries, the consumption patterns of cities are severely stressing the global ecosystem, while settlements in the developing world need more raw material, energy, and economic development simply to overcome basic economic and social problems. Human settlement conditions in many parts of the world, particularly the developing countries, are deteriorating mainly as a result of the low levels of investment in the sector attributable to the overall resource constraints in these countries. In the low-income countries for which recent data are available, an average of only 5.6 per cent of central government expenditure went to housing, amenities, social security and welfare. Expenditure by international support and finance organizations is equally low. For example, only 1 per cent of the United Nations system's total grant-financed expenditures in 1988 went to human settlements, while in 1991, loans from the World Bank and the International Development Association (IDA) for urban development and water supply and sewerage amounted to 5.5 and 5.4 per cent, respectively, of their total lending.

On the other hand, available information indicates that technical cooperation activities in the human settlement sector generate considerable public and private sector investment. For example, every dollar of UNDP technical cooperation expenditure on human settlements in 1988 generated a follow-up investment of $122, the highest of all UNDP sectors of assistance.

This is the foundation of the "enabling approach" advocated for the human settlement sector. External assistance will help to generate the internal resources needed to improve the living and working environments of all people by the year 2000 and beyond, including the growing number of unemployed - the no-income group. At the same time the environmental implications of urban development should be recognized and addressed in an integrated fashion by all countries, with high priority being given to the needs of the urban and rural poor, the unemployed and the growing number of people without any source of income.

Human Settlement Objective

The overall human settlement objective is to improve the social, economic and environmental quality of human settlements and the living and working environments of all people, in particular the urban and rural poor. Such improvement should be based on technical cooperation activities, partnerships among the public, private and community sectors and participation in the decision-making process by community groups and special interest groups such as women, indigenous people, the elderly and the disabled.

These approaches should form the core principles of national settlement strategies. In developing these strategies, countries will need to set priorities among the eight programme areas in this chapter in accordance with their national plans and objectives, taking fully into account their social and cultural capabilities. Furthermore, countries should make appropriate provision to monitor the impact of their strategies on marginalized and disenfranchised groups, with particular reference to the needs of women.

The programme areas included in this chapter are:

(a) Providing adequate shelter for all;

(b) Improving human settlement management;

(c) Promoting sustainable land-use planning and management;

(d) Promoting the integrated provision of environmental infrastructure: water, sanitation, drainage and solid-waste management;

(e) Promoting sustainable energy and transport systems in human settlements;

(f) Promoting human settlement planning and management in disaster-prone areas;

(g) Promoting sustainable construction industry activities;

(h) Promoting human resource development and capacity-building for human settlement development.

PROGRAMME AREAS

Providing Adequate Shelter for All

Basis for Action

Access to safe and healthy shelter is essential to a person's physical, psychological, social and economic well-being and should be a fundamental part of national and international action. The right to adequate housing as a basic human right is enshrined in the Universal Declaration of Human Rights and the International Covenant on Economic, Social and Cultural Rights. Despite this, it is estimated that at the present time, at least 1 billion people do not have access to safe and healthy shelter and that if appropriate action is not taken, this number will increase dramatically by the end of the century and beyond.

A major global programme to address this problem is the Global Strategy for Shelter to the Year 2000, adopted by the General Assembly in December 1988 (resolution 43/181, annex). Despite its widespread endorsement, the Strategy needs a much greater level of political and financial support to enable it to reach its goal of facilitating adequate shelter for all by the end of the century and beyond.

Objective

The objective is to achieve adequate shelter for rapidly growing populations and for the currently deprived urban and rural poor through an enabling approach to shelter development and improvement that is environmentally sound.

Activities

The following activities should be undertaken:

(a) As a first step towards the goal of providing adequate shelter for all, all countries should take immediate measures to provide shelter to their homeless poor, while the international community and financial institutions should undertake actions to support the efforts of the developing countries to provide shelter to the poor;

(b) All countries should adopt and/or strengthen national shelter strategies, with targets based, as appropriate, on the principles and recommendations contained in the Global Strategy for Shelter to the Year 2000. People should be protected by law against unfair eviction from their homes or land;

(c) All countries should, as appropriate, support the shelter efforts of the urban and rural poor, the unemployed and the no-income group by adopting and/or adapting existing codes and regulations, to facilitate their access to land, finance and low-cost building materials and by actively promoting the regularization and upgrading of informal settlements and urban slums as an expedient measure and pragmatic solution to the urban shelter deficit;

(d) All countries should, as appropriate, facilitate access of urban and rural poor to shelter by adopting and utilizing housing and finance schemes and new innovative mechanisms adapted to their circumstances;

(e) All countries should support and develop environmentally compatible shelter strategies at national, state/provincial and municipal levels through partnerships among the private, public and community sectors and with the support of community-based organizations;

(f) All countries, especially developing ones, should, as appropriate, formulate and implement programmes to reduce the impact of the phenomenon of rural to urban drift by improving rural living conditions;

(g) All countries, where appropriate, should develop and implement resettlement programmes that address the specific problems of displaced populations in their respective countries;

(h) All countries should, as appropriate, document and monitor the implementation of their national shelter strategies by using, inter alia, the monitoring guidelines adopted by the Commission on Human Settlements and the shelter performance indicators being produced jointly by the United Nations Centre for Human Settlements (Habitat) and the World Bank;

(i) Bilateral and multilateral cooperation should be strengthened in order to support the implementation of the national shelter strategies of developing countries;

(j) Global progress reports covering national action and the support activities of international organizations and bilateral donors should be produced and disseminated on a biennial basis, as requested in the Global Strategy for Shelter to the Year 2000.

MEANS OF IMPLEMENTATION

Financing and Cost Evaluation

The Conference secretariat has estimated the average total annual cost (1993-2000) of implementing the activities of this programme to be about $75 billion, including about $10 billion from the international community on grant or concessional terms. These are indicative and order-of-magnitude estimates only and have not been reviewed by Governments. Actual costs and financial terms, including any that are non-concessional, will depend upon, inter alia, the specific strategies and programmes Governments decide upon for implementation.

Scientific and Technological Means

The requirements under this heading are addressed in each of the other programme areas included in the present chapter.

Human Resource Development and Capacity-building

Developed countries and funding agencies should provide specific assistance to developing countries in adopting an enabling approach to the provision of shelter for all, including the no-income group, and covering research institutions and training activities for government officials, professionals, communities and non-governmental organizations and by strengthening local capacity for the development of appropriate technologies.

Improving Human Settlement Management

Basis for Action

By the turn of the century, the majority of the world's population will be living in cities. While urban settlements, particularly in developing countries, are showing many of the symptoms of the global environment and development crisis, they nevertheless generate 60 per cent of gross national product and, if properly managed, can develop the capacity to sustain their productivity, improve the living conditions of their residents and manage natural resources in a sustainable way.

Some metropolitan areas extend over the boundaries of several political and/or administrative entities (counties and municipalities) even though they conform to a continuous urban system. In many cases this political heterogeneity hinders the implementation of comprehensive environmental management programmes.

Objective

The objective is to ensure sustainable management of all urban settlements, particularly in developing countries, in order to enhance their ability to improve the living conditions of residents, especially the marginalized and disenfranchised, thereby contributing to the achievement of national economic development goals.

ACTIVITIES

Improving Urban Management

One existing framework for strengthening management is in the United Nations Development Programme/World Bank/ United Nations Centre for Human Settlements (Habitat) Urban Management Programme (UMP), a concerted global effort to assist developing countries in addressing urban management issues. Its coverage should be extended to all interested countries during the period 1993-2000. All countries should, as appropriate and in accordance with national plans, objectives and priorities and with the assistance of non-governmental organizations and representatives of local authorities, undertake the following activities at the national, state/provincial and local levels, with the assistance of relevant programmes and support agencies:

(a) Adopting and applying urban management guidelines in the areas of land management, urban environmental management, infrastructure management and municipal finance and administration;

(b) Accelerating efforts to reduce urban poverty through a number of actions, including:

  i. Generating employment for the urban poor, particularly women, through the provision, improvement and maintenance of urban infrastructure and services and the support of economic activities in the informal sector, such as repairs, recycling, services and small commerce;

  ii. Providing specific assistance to the poorest of the urban poor through, inter alia, the creation of social infrastructure in order to reduce hunger and homelessness, and the provision of adequate community services;

  iii. Encouraging the establishment of indigenous community-based organizations, private voluntary organizations and other forms of non-governmental entities that can contribute to the efforts to reduce poverty and improve the quality of life for low-income families;

(c) Adopting innovative city planning strategies to address environmental and social issues by:

  i. Reducing subsidies on, and recovering the full costs of, environmental and other services of high standard (e.g. water supply, sanitation, waste collection, roads, telecommunications) provided to higher income neighbourhoods;

ii. Improving the level of infrastructure and service provision in poorer urban areas;

(d) Developing local strategies for improving the quality of life and the environment, integrating decisions on land use and land management, investing in the public and private sectors and mobilizing human and material resources, thereby promoting employment generation that is environmentally sound and protective of human health.

Strengthening Urban Data Systems

During the period 1993-2000 all countries should undertake, with the active participation of the business sector as appropriate, pilot projects in selected cities for the collection, analysis and subsequent dissemination of urban data, including environmental impact analysis, at the local, state/provincial, national and international levels and the establishment of city data management capabilities. United Nations organizations, such as Habitat, UNEP and UNDP, could provide technical advice and model data management systems.

Encouraging Intermediate City Development

In order to relieve pressure on large urban agglomerations of developing countries, policies and strategies should be implemented towards the development of intermediate cities that create employment opportunities for unemployed labour in the rural areas and support rural-based economic activities, although sound urban management is essential to ensure that urban sprawl does not expand resource degradation over an ever wider land area and increase pressures to convert open space and agricultural/buffer lands for development.

Therefore all countries should, as appropriate, conduct reviews of urbanization processes and policies in order to assess the environmental impacts of growth and apply urban planning and management approaches specifically suited to the needs, resource capabilities and characteristics of their growing intermediate-sized cities. As appropriate, they should also concentrate on activities aimed at facilitating the transition from rural to urban lifestyles and settlement patterns and at promoting the development of small-scale economic activities, particularly the production of food, to support local income generation and the production of intermediate goods and services for rural hinterlands.

All cities, particularly those characterized by severe sustainable development problems, should, in accordance with national laws, rules and regulations, develop and strengthen programmes aimed at addressing such problems and guiding their development along a sustainable path. Some international initiatives in support of such efforts, as in the Sustainable Cities Programme of Habitat and the Healthy Cities Programme of WHO, should be intensified. Additional initiatives involving the World Bank, the regional development banks and bilateral agencies, as well as other interested stakeholders, particularly international and national representatives of local authorities, should be strengthened and coordinated. Individual cities should, as appropriate:

(a) Institutionalize a participatory approach to sustainable urban development, based on a continuous dialogue between the actors involved in urban development (the public sector, private sector and communities), especially women and indigenous people;

(b) Improve the urban environment by promoting social organization and environmental awareness through the participation of local communities in the identification of public services needs, the provision of urban infrastructure, the enhancement of public amenities and the protection and/or rehabilitation of older buildings, historic precincts and other cultural artifacts. In addition, "green works" programmes should be activated to create self-sustaining human development activities and both formal and informal employment opportunities for low-income urban residents;

(c) Strengthen the capacities of their local governing bodies to deal more effectively with the broad range of developmental and environmental challenges associated with rapid and sound urban growth through comprehensive approaches to planning that recognize the individual needs of cities and are based on ecologically sound urban design practices;

(d) Participate in international "sustainable city networks" to exchange experiences and mobilize national and international technical and financial support;

(e) Promote the formulation of environmentally sound and culturally sensitive tourism programmes as a strategy for sustainable development of urban and rural settlements and as a way of decentralizing urban development and reducing discrepancies among regions;

(f) Establish mechanisms, with the assistance of relevant international agencies, to mobilize resources for local initiatives to improve environmental quality;

(g) Empower community groups, non-governmental organizations and individuals to assume the authority and responsibility for managing and enhancing their immediate environment through participatory tools, techniques and approaches embodied in the concept of environmental care.

Cities of all countries should reinforce cooperation among themselves and cities of the developed countries, under the aegis of non-governmental organizations active in this field, such as the International Union of Local Authorities (IULA), the International Council for Local Environmental Initiatives (ICLEI) and the World Federation of Twin Cities.

MEANS OF IMPLEMENTATION

Financing and Cost Evaluation

The Conference secretariat has estimated the average total annual cost (1993-2000) of implementing the activities of this programme to be about $100 billion, including about $15 billion from the international community on grant or concessional terms. These are indicative and order-of-magnitude estimates only and have not been reviewed by Governments. Actual costs and financial terms, including any that are non-concessional, will depend upon, inter alia, the specific strategies and programmes Governments decide upon for implementation.

Human Resource Development and Capacity-building

Developing countries should, with appropriate international assistance, consider focusing on training and developing a cadre of urban managers, technicians, administrators and other relevant stakeholders who can successfully manage environmentally sound urban development and growth and are equipped with the skills necessary to analyse and adapt the innovative experiences of other cities. For this purpose, the full range of training methods - from formal education to the use of the mass media - should be utilized, as well as the "learning by doing" option.

Developing countries should also encourage technological training and research through joint efforts by donors, non-governmental organizations and private business in such areas as the reduction of waste, water quality, saving of energy, safe production of chemicals and less polluting transportation.

Capacity-building activities carried out by all countries, assisted as suggested above, should go beyond the training of individuals and functional groups to include institutional arrangements, administrative routines, inter-agency linkages, information flows and consultative processes.

In addition, international efforts, such as the Urban Management Programme, in cooperation with multilateral and bilateral agencies, should continue to assist the developing countries in their efforts to develop a participatory structure by mobilizing the human resources of the private sector, non-governmental organizations and the poor, particularly women and the disadvantaged.

Promoting Sustainable Land-use Planning and Management

Basis for Action

Access to land resources is an essential component of sustainable low-impact lifestyles. Land resources are the basis for (human) living systems and provide soil, energy, water and the opportunity for all human activity. In rapidly growing urban areas, access to land is rendered increasingly difficult by the conflicting demands of industry, housing, commerce, agriculture, land tenure structures and the need for open spaces. Furthermore, the rising costs of urban land prevent the poor from gaining access to suitable land. In rural areas, unsustainable practices, such as the exploitation of marginal lands and the encroachment on forests and ecologically fragile areas by commercial interests and landless rural populations, result in environmental degradation, as well as in diminishing returns for impoverished rural settlers.

Objective

The objective is to provide for the land requirements of human settlement development through environmentally sound physical planning and land use so as to ensure access to land to all households and, where appropriate, the encouragement of communally and collectively owned and managed land. Particular attention should be paid to the needs of women and indigenous people for economic and cultural reasons.

Activities

All countries should consider, as appropriate, undertaking a comprehensive national inventory of their land resources in order to establish a land information system in which land resources will be classified according to their most appropriate uses and environmentally fragile or disaster-prone areas will be identified for special protection measures.

Subsequently, all countries should consider developing national land-resource management plans to guide land-resource development and utilization and, to that end, should:

(a) Establish, as appropriate, national legislation to guide the implementation of public policies for environmentally sound urban development, land utilization, housing and for the improved management of urban expansion;

(b) Create, where appropriate, efficient and accessible land markets that meet community development needs by, inter alia, improving land registry systems and streamlining procedures in land transactions;

(c) Develop fiscal incentives and land-use control measures, including land-use planning solutions for a more rational and environmentally sound use of limited land resources;

(d) Encourage partnerships among the public, private and community sectors in managing land resources for human settlements development;

(e) Strengthen community-based land-resource protection practices in existing urban and rural settlements;

(f) Establish appropriate forms of land tenure that provide security of tenure for all land-users, especially indigenous people, women, local communities, the low-income urban dwellers and the rural poor;

(g) Accelerate efforts to promote access to land by the urban and rural poor, including credit schemes for the purchase of land and for building/acquiring or improving safe and healthy shelter and infrastructure services;

(h) Develop and support the implementation of improved land-management practices that deal comprehensively with potentially competing land requirements for agriculture, industry, transport, urban development, green spaces, preserves and other vital needs;

(i) Promote understanding among policy makers of the adverse consequences of unplanned settlements in environmentally vulnerable areas and of the appropriate national and local land-use and settlements policies required for this purpose.

At the international level, global coordination of land-resource management activities should be strengthened by the various bilateral and multilateral agencies and programmes, such as UNDP, FAO, the World Bank, the regional development banks, other interested organizations and the UNDP/World Bank/Habitat Urban Management Programme, and action should be taken to promote the transfer of applicable experience on sustainable land-management practices to and among developing countries.

MEANS OF IMPLEMENTATION

Financing and Cost Evaluation

The Conference secretariat has estimated the average total annual cost (1993-2000) of implementing the activities of this programme to be about $3 billion, including about $300 million from the international community on grant or concessional terms. These are indicative and order-of-magnitude estimates only and have not been reviewed by Governments. Actual costs and financial terms, including any that are non-concessional, will depend upon, inter alia, the specific strategies and programmes Governments decide upon for implementation.

Scientific and Technological Means

All countries, particularly developing countries, alone or in regional or subregional groupings, should be given access to modern techniques of land-resource management, such as geographical information systems, satellite photography/imagery and other remote-sensing technologies.

Human Resource Development and Capacity-building

Environmentally focused training activities in sustainable land-resources planning and management should be undertaken in all countries, with developing countries being given assistance through international support and funding agencies in order to:

(a) Strengthen the capacity of national, state/provincial and local educational research and training institutions to provide formal training of land-management technicians and professionals;

(b) Facilitate the organizational review of government ministries and agencies responsible for land questions, in order to devise more efficient mechanisms of land-resource management, and carry out periodic in-service refresher courses for the managers and staff of such ministries and agencies in order to familiarize them with up-to-date land-resource-management technologies;

(c) Where appropriate, provide such agencies with modern equipment, such as computer hardware and software and survey equipment;

(d) Strengthen existing programmes and promote an international and interregional exchange of information and experience in land management through the establishment of professional associations in land-management sciences and related activities, such as workshops and seminars.

Promoting the Integrated Provision of Environmental Infrastructure: Water, Sanitation, Drainage and Solid-waste Management

Basis for Action

The sustainability of urban development is defined by many parameters relating to the availability of water supplies, air quality and the provision of environmental infrastructure for sanitation and waste management. As a result of the density of users, urbanization, if properly managed, offers unique opportunities for the supply of sustainable environmental infrastructure through adequate pricing policies, educational programmes and equitable access mechanisms that are economically and environmentally sound. In most developing countries, however, the inadequacy and lack of environmental infrastructure is responsible for widespread ill-health and a large number of preventable deaths each year. In those countries conditions are set to worsen due to growing needs that exceed the capacity of Governments to respond adequately.

An integrated approach to the provision of environmentally sound infrastructure in human settlements, in particular for the urban and rural poor, is an investment in sustainable development that can improve the quality of life, increase productivity, improve health and reduce the burden of investments in curative medicine and poverty alleviation.

Most of the activities whose management would be improved by an integrated approach, are covered in Agenda 21 as follows: chapter 6 (Protecting and promoting human health conditions), chapters 9 (Protecting the atmosphere), 18 (Protecting the quality and supply of freshwater resources) and 21 (Environmentally sound management of solid wastes and sewage-related issues).

Objective

The objective is to ensure the provision of adequate environmental infrastructure facilities in all settlements by the year 2025. The achievement of this objective would require that all developing countries incorporate in their national strategies programmes to build the necessary technical, financial and human resource capacity aimed at ensuring better integration of infrastructure and environmental planning by the year 2000.

Activities

All countries should assess the environmental suitability of infrastructure in human settlements, develop national goals for sustainable management of waste, and implement environmentally sound technology to ensure that the environment, human health and quality of life are protected. Settlement infrastructure and environmental programmes designed to promote an integrated human settlements approach to the planning, development, maintenance and management of environmental infrastructure (water supply, sanitation, drainage, solid-waste management) should be strengthened with the assistance of bilateral and multilateral agencies. Coordination among these agencies and with collaboration from international and national representatives of local authorities, the private sector and community groups should also be strengthened. The activities of all agencies engaged in providing environmental infrastructure should, where possible, reflect an ecosystem or metropolitan area approach to settlements and should include monitoring, applied research, capacity-building, transfer of appropriate technology and technical cooperation among the range of programme activities.

Developing countries should be assisted at the national and local levels in adopting an integrated approach to the provision of water supply, energy, sanitation, drainage and solid-waste management, and external funding agencies should ensure that this approach is applied in particular to environmental infrastructure improvement in informal settlements based on regulations and standards that take into account the living conditions and resources of the communities to be served.

All countries should, as appropriate, adopt the following principles for the provision of environmental infrastructure:

(a) Adopt policies that minimize if not altogether avoid environmental damage, whenever possible;

(b) Ensure that relevant decisions are preceded by environmental impact assessments and also take into account the costs of any ecological consequences;

(c) Promote development in accordance with indigenous practices and adopt technologies appropriate to local conditions;

(d) Promote policies aimed at recovering the actual cost of infrastructure services, while at the same time recognizing the need to find suitable approaches (including subsidies) to extend basic services to all households;

(e) Seek joint solutions to environmental problems that affect several localities.

The dissemination of information from existing programmes should be facilitated and encouraged among interested countries and local institutions.

MEANS OF IMPLEMENTATION

Financing and Cost Evaluation

The Conference secretariat has estimated most of the costs of implementing the activities of this programme in other chapters. The secretariat estimates the average total annual cost (1993-2000) of technical assistance from the international community grant or concessional terms to be about $50 million. These are indicative and order-of-magnitude estimates only and have not been reviewed by Governments. Actual costs and financial terms, including any that are non-concessional, will depend upon, inter alia, the specific strategies and programmes Governments decide upon for implementation.

Scientific and Technological Means

Scientific and technological means within the existing programmes should be coordinated wherever possible and should:

(a) Accelerate research in the area of integrated policies of environmental infrastructure programmes and projects based on cost/benefit analysis and overall environmental impact;

(b) Promote methods of assessing "effective demand", utilizing environment and development data as criteria for selecting technology.

Human Resource Development and Capacity-building

With the assistance and support of funding agencies, all countries should, as appropriate, undertake training and popular participation programmes aimed at:

(a) Raising awareness of the means, approaches and benefits of the provision of environmental infrastructure facilities, especially among indigenous people, women, low-income groups and the poor;

(b) Developing a cadre of professionals with adequate skills in integrated infrastructural service planning and maintenance of resource-efficient, environmentally sound and socially acceptable systems;

(c) Strengthening the institutional capacity of local authorities and administrators in the integrated provision of adequate infrastructure services in partnership with local communities and the private sector;

(d) Adopting appropriate legal and regulatory instruments, including cross-subsidy arrangements, to extend the benefits of adequate and affordable environmental infrastructure to unserved population groups, especially the poor.

Promoting Sustainable Energy and Transport Systems in Human Settlements

Basis for Action

Most of the commercial and non-commercial energy produced today is used in and for human settlements, and a substantial percentage of it is used by the household sector. Developing countries are at present faced with the need to increase their energy production to accelerate development and raise the living standards of their populations, while at the same time reducing energy production costs and energy-related pollution. Increasing the efficiency of energy use to reduce its polluting effects and to promote the use of renewable energies must be a priority in any action taken to protect the urban environment.

Developed countries, as the largest consumers of energy, are faced with the need for energy planning and management, promoting renewable and alternate sources of energy, and evaluating the life-cycle costs of current systems and practices as a result of which many metropolitan areas are suffering from pervasive air quality problems related to ozone, particulate matters and carbon monoxide. The causes have much to do with technological inadequacies and with an increasing fuel consumption generated by inefficiencies, high demographic and industrial concentrations and a rapid expansion in the number of motor vehicles.

Transport accounts for about 30 per cent of commercial energy consumption and for about 60 per cent of total global consumption of liquid petroleum. In developing countries, rapid motorization and insufficient investments in urban-transport planning, traffic management and infrastructure, are creating increasing problems in terms of accidents and injury, health, noise, congestion and loss of productivity similar to those occurring in many developed countries. All of these problems have a severe impact on urban populations, particularly the low-income and no-income groups.

Objectives

The objectives are to extend the provision of more energy-efficient technology and alternative/renewable energy for human settlements and to reduce negative impacts of energy production and use on human health and on the environment.

Activities

The principal activities relevant to this programme area are included in chapter 9 (Protection of the atmosphere), programme area B, subprogramme 1 (Energy development, efficiency and consumption) and subprogramme 2 (Transportation).

A comprehensive approach to human settlements development should include the promotion of sustainable energy development in all countries, as follows:

(a) Developing countries, in particular, should:

i. Formulate national action programmes to promote and support reafforestation and national forest regeneration with a view to achieving sustained provision of the biomass energy needs of the low-income groups in urban areas and the rural poor, in particular women and children;

ii. Formulate national action programmes to promote integrated development of energy-saving and renewable energy technologies, particularly for the use of solar, hydro, wind and biomass sources;

iii. Promote wide dissemination and commercialization of renewable energy technologies through suitable measures, inter alia, fiscal and technology transfer mechanisms;

iv. Carry out information and training programmes directed at manufacturers and users in order to promote energy-saving techniques and energy-efficient appliances;

(b) International organizations and bilateral donors should:

i. Support developing countries in implementing national energy programmes in order to achieve widespread use of energy-saving and renewable energy technologies, particularly the use of solar, wind, biomass and hydro sources;

ii. Provide access to research and development results to increase energy-use efficiency levels in human settlements.

Promoting efficient and environmentally sound urban transport systems in all countries should be a comprehensive approach to urban-transport planning and management. To this end, all countries should:

(a) Integrate land-use and transportation planning to encourage development patterns that reduce transport demand;

(b) Adopt urban-transport programmes favouring high-occupancy public transport in countries, as appropriate;

(c) Encourage non-motorized modes of transport by providing safe cycleways and footways in urban and suburban centres in countries, as appropriate;

(d) Devote particular attention to effective traffic management, efficient operation of public transport and maintenance of transport infrastructure;

(e) Promote the exchange of information among countries and representatives of local and metropolitan areas;

(f) Re-evaluate the present consumption and production patterns in order to reduce the use of energy and national resources.

MEANS OF IMPLEMENTATION

Financing and Cost Evaluation

The Conference secretariat has estimated the costs of implementing the activities of this programme in chapter 9 (Protection of the atmosphere).

Human Resource Development and Capacity-building

In order to enhance the skills of energy service and transport professionals and institutions, all countries should, as appropriate:

(a) Provide on-the-job and other training of government officials, planners, traffic engineers and managers involved in the energy-service and transport section;

(b) Raise public awareness of the environmental impacts of transport and travel behaviour through mass media campaigns and support for non-governmental and community initiatives promoting the use of non-motorized transport, shared driving and improved traffic safety measures;

(c) Strengthen regional, national, state/provincial, and private sector institutions that provide education and training on energy service and urban transport planning and management.

Promoting Human Settlement Planning and Management in Disaster-prone Areas

Basis for action

Natural disasters cause loss of life, disruption of economic activities and urban productivity, particularly for highly susceptible low-income groups, and environmental damage, such as loss of fertile agricultural land and contamination of water resources, and can lead to major resettlement of populations. Over the past two decades, they are estimated to have caused some 3 million deaths and affected 800 million people. Global economic losses have been estimated by the Office of the United Nations Disaster Relief Coordinator to be in the range of $30-50 billion per year. The General Assembly, in resolution 44/236, proclaimed the 1990s as the International Decade for Natural Disaster Reduction. The goals of the Decade bear relevance to the objectives of the present programme area.

In addition, there is an urgent need to address the prevention and reduction of man-made disasters and/or disasters caused by, inter alia, industries, unsafe nuclear power generation and toxic wastes.

Objective

The objective is to enable all countries, in particular those that are disaster-prone, to mitigate the negative impact of natural and man-made disasters on human settlements, national economies and the environment.

ACTIVITIES

Three distinct areas of activity are foreseen under this programme area, namely, the development of a "culture of safety", pre-disaster planning and post-disaster reconstruction.

Developing a Culture of Safety

To promote a "culture of safety" in all countries, especially those that are disaster-prone, the following activities should be carried out:

(a) Completing national and local studies on the nature and occurrence of natural disasters, their impact on people and economic activities, the effects of inadequate construction and land use in hazard-prone areas, and the social and economic advantages of adequate pre-disaster planning;

(b) Implementing nationwide and local awareness campaigns through all available media, translating the above knowledge into information easily comprehensible to the general public and to the populations directly exposed to hazards;

(c) Strengthening, and/or developing global, regional, national and local early warning systems to alert populations to impending disasters;

(d) Identifying industrially based environmental disaster areas at the national and international levels and implementing strategies aimed at the rehabilitation of these areas through, inter alia:

   i. Restructuring of the economic activities and promoting new job opportunities in environmentally sound sectors;
   ii. Promoting close collaboration between governmental and local authorities, local communities and non-governmental organizations and private business;
   iii. Developing and enforcing strict environmental control standards.

Developing Pre-disaster Planning

Pre-disaster planning should form an integral part of human settlement planning in all countries. The following should be included:

(a) Undertaking complete multi-hazard research into risk and vulnerability of human settlements and settlement infrastructure, including water and sewerage, communication and transportation networks, as one type of risk reduction may increase vulnerability to another (e.g., an earthquake-resistant house made of wood will be more vulnerable to wind storms);

(b) Developing methodologies for determining risk and vulnerability within specific human settlements and incorporating risk and vulnerability reduction into the human settlement planning and management process;

(c) Redirecting inappropriate new development and human settlements to areas not prone to hazards;

(d) Preparing guidelines on location, design and operation of potentially hazardous industries and activities;

(e) Developing tools (legal, economic etc.) to encourage disaster-sensitive development, including means of ensuring that limitations on development options are not punitive to owners, or incorporate alternative means of compensation;

(f) Further developing and disseminating information on disaster-resistant building materials and construction technologies for buildings and public works in general;

(g) Developing training programmes for contractors and builders on disaster-resistant construction methods. Some programmes should be directed particularly to small enterprises, which build the great majority of housing and other small buildings in the developing countries, as well as to the rural populations, which build their own houses;

(h) Developing training programmes for emergency site managers, non-governmental organizations and community groups which cover all aspects of disaster mitigation, including urban search and rescue, emergency communications, early warning techniques, and pre-disaster planning;

(i) Developing procedures and practices to enable local communities to receive information about hazardous installations or situations in these areas, and facilitate their participation in early warning and disaster abatement and response procedures and plans;

(j) Preparing action plans for the reconstruction of settlements, especially the reconstruction of community life-lines.

Initiating Post-disaster Reconstruction and Rehabilitation Planning

The international community, as a major partner in post-reconstruction and rehabilitation, should ensure that the countries involved derive the greatest benefits from the funds allocated by undertaking the following activities:

(a) Carrying out research on past experiences on the social and economic aspects of post-disaster reconstruction and adopting effective strategies and guidelines for post-disaster reconstruction, with particular focus on development-focused strategies in the allocation of scarce reconstruction resources, and on the opportunities that post-disaster reconstruction provides to introduce sustainable settlement patterns;

(b) Preparing and disseminating international guidelines for adaptation to national and local needs;

(c) Supporting efforts of national Governments to initiate contingency planning, with participation of affected communities, for post-disaster reconstruction and rehabilitation.

MEANS OF IMPLEMENTATION

Financing and Cost Evaluation

The Conference secretariat has estimated the average total annual cost (1993-2000) of implementing the activities of this programme to be about $50 million from the international community on grant or concessional terms. These are indicative and order-of-magnitude estimates only and have not been reviewed by Governments. Actual costs and financial terms, including any that are non-concessional, will depend upon, inter alia, the specific strategies and programmes Governments decide upon for implementation.

Scientific and Technological Means

Scientists and engineers specializing in this field in both developing and developed countries should collaborate with urban and regional planners in order to provide the basic knowledge and means to mitigate losses owing to disasters as well as environmentally inappropriate development.

Human Resource Development and Capacity-building

Developing countries should conduct training programmes on disaster-resistant construction methods for contractors and builders, who build the majority of housing in the developing countries. This should focus on the small business enterprises, which build the majority of housing in the developing countries.

Training programmes should be extended to government officials and planners and community and non-governmental organizations to cover all aspects of disaster mitigation, such as early warning techniques, pre-disaster planning and construction, post-disaster construction and rehabilitation.

Promoting Sustainable Construction Industry Activities

Basis for action

The activities of the construction sector are vital to the achievement of the national socio-economic development goals of providing shelter, infrastructure and employment. However, they can be a major source of environmental damage through depletion of the natural resource base, degradation of fragile eco-zones, chemical pollution and the use of building materials harmful to human health.

Objectives

The objectives are, first, to adopt policies and technologies and to exchange information on them in order to enable the construction sector to meet human settlement development goals, while avoiding harmful side-effects on human health and on the biosphere, and, second, to enhance the employment-generation capacity of the construction sector. Governments should work in close collaboration with the private sector in achieving these objectives.

Activities

All countries should, as appropriate and in accordance with national plans, objectives and priorities:

(a) Establish and strengthen indigenous building materials industry, based, as much as possible, on inputs of locally available natural resources;

(b) Formulate programmes to enhance the utilization of local materials by the construction sector by expanding technical support and incentive schemes for increasing the capabilities and economic viability of small-scale and informal operatives which make use of these materials and traditional construction techniques;

(c) Adopt standards and other regulatory measures which promote the increased use of energy-efficient designs and technologies and sustainable utilization of natural resources in an economically and environmentally appropriate way;

(d) Formulate appropriate land-use policies and introduce planning regulations specially aimed at the protection of eco-sensitive zones against physical disruption by construction and construction-related activities;

(e) Promote the use of labour-intensive construction and maintenance technologies which generate employment in the construction sector for the underemployed labour force found in most large cities, while at the same time promoting the development of skills in the construction sector;

(f) Develop policies and practices to reach the informal sector and self-help housing builders by adopting measures to increase the affordability of building materials on the part of the urban and rural poor, through, inter alia, credit schemes and bulk procurement of building materials for sale to small-scale builders and communities.

All countries should:

a. Promote the free exchange of information on the entire range of environmental and health aspects of construction, including the development and dissemination of databases on the adverse environmental effects of building materials through the collaborative efforts of the private and public sectors;

b. Promote the development and dissemination of databases on the adverse environmental and health effects of building materials and introduce legislation and financial incentives to promote recycling of energy-intensive materials in the construction industry and conservation of waste energy in building-materials production methods;

c. Promote the use of economic instruments, such as product charges, to discourage the use of construction materials and products that create pollution during their life cycle;

d. Promote information exchange and appropriate technology transfer among all countries, with particular attention to developing countries, for resource management in construction, particularly for non-renewable resources;

e. Promote research in construction industries and related activities, and establish and strengthen institutions in this sector.

MEANS OF IMPLEMENTATION

Financing and Cost Evaluation

The Conference secretariat has estimated the average total annual cost (1993-2000) of implementing the activities of this programme to be about $40 billion, including about $4 billion from the international community on grant or concessional terms. These are indicative and order-of-magnitude estimates only and have not been reviewed by Governments. Actual costs and financial terms, including any that are non-concessional, will depend upon, inter alia, the specific strategies and programmes Governments decide upon for implementation.

Human Resource Development and Capacity-building

Developing countries should be assisted by international support and funding agencies in upgrading the technical and managerial capacities of the small entrepreneur and the vocational skills of operatives and supervisors in the building materials industry, using a variety of training methods. These countries should also be assisted in developing programmes to encourage the use of non-waste and clean technologies through appropriate transfer of technology.

General education programmes should be developed in all countries, as appropriate, to increase builder awareness of available sustainable technologies.

Local authorities are called upon to play a pioneering role in promoting the increased use of environmentally sound building materials and construction technologies, e.g., by pursuing an innovative procurement policy.

Promoting Human Resource Development and Capacity-building for Human Settlements Development

Basis for action

Most countries, in addition to shortcomings in the availability of specialized expertise in the areas of housing, settlement management, land management, infrastructure, construction, energy, transport, and pre-disaster planning and reconstruction, face three cross-sectoral human resource development and capacity-building shortfalls. First is the absence of an enabling policy environment capable of integrating the resources and activities of the public sector, the private sector and the community, or social sector; second is the weakness of specialized training and research institutions; and third is the insufficient capacity for technical training and assistance for low-income communities, both urban and rural.

Objective

The objective is to improve human resource development and capacity-building in all countries by enhancing the personal and institutional capacity of all actors, particularly indigenous people and women, involved in human settlement development. In this regard, account should be taken of traditional cultural practices of indigenous people and their relationship to the environment.

Activities

Specific human resource development and capacity-building activities have been built into each of the programme areas of this chapter. More generally, however, additional steps should be taken to reinforce those activities. In order to do so, all countries, as appropriate, should take the following action:

(a) Strengthening the development of human resources and of capacities of public sector institutions through technical assistance and international cooperation so as to achieve by the year 2000 substantial improvement in the efficiency of governmental activities;

(b) Creating an enabling policy environment supportive of the partnership between the public, private and community sectors;

(c) Providing enhanced training and technical assistance to institutions providing training for technicians, professionals and administrators, and appointed, elected and professional members of local governments and strengthening their capacity to address priority training needs, particularly in regard to social, economic and environmental aspects of human settlements development;

(d) Providing direct assistance for human settlement development at the community level, inter alia, by:

   i. Strengthening and promoting programmes for social mobilization and raising awareness of the potential of women and youth in human settlements activities;

   ii. Facilitating coordination of the activities of women, youth, community groups and non-governmental organizations in human settlements development;

   iii. Promoting research on women's programmes and other groups, and evaluating progress made with a view to identifying bottlenecks and needed assistance;

(e) Promoting the inclusion of integrated environmental management into general local government activities.

Both international organizations and non-governmental organizations should support the above activities by, inter alia, strengthening subregional training institutions, providing updated training materials and disseminating the results of successful human resource and capacity-building activities, programmes and projects.

MEANS OF IMPLEMENTATION

Financing and Cost Evaluation

The Conference secretariat has estimated the average total annual cost (1993-2000) of implementing the activities of this programme to be about $65 million from the international community on grant or concessional terms. These are indicative and order-of-magnitude estimates only and have not been reviewed by Governments. Actual costs and financial terms, including any that are non-concessional, will depend upon, inter alia, the specific strategies and programmes Governments decide upon for implementation.

Scientific and technological means

Both formal training and non-formal types of human resource development and capacity-building programmes should be combined, and use should be made of user-oriented training methods, up-to-date training materials and modern audio-visual communication systems.

5

Integrating Environment and Development in Decision-making

This chapter contains the following programme areas:

(a) Integrating environment and development at the policy, planning and management levels;

(b) Providing an effective legal and regulatory framework;

(c) Making effective use of economic instruments and market and other incentives;

(d) Establishing systems for integrated environmental and economic accounting.

PROGRAMME AREAS

Integrating Environment and Development at the Policy, Planning and Management Levels

Basis for action

Prevailing systems for decision-making in many countries tend to separate economic, social and environmental factors at the policy, planning and management levels. This influences the actions of all groups in society, including Governments, industry and individuals, and has important implications for the efficiency and sustainability of development. An adjustment or even a fundamental reshaping of decision-making, in the light of country-specific conditions, may be necessary if environment and development is to be put at the centre of economic and political decision-making, in effect achieving a full integration of these factors. In recent years, some Governments have also begun to make significant changes in the institutional structures of government in order to enable more systematic consideration of the environment when decisions are made on economic, social, fiscal, energy, agricultural, transportation, trade and other policies, as well as the implications of policies in these areas for the environment.

New forms of dialogue are also being developed for achieving better integration among national and local government, industry, science, environmental groups and the public in the process of developing effective approaches to environment and development.

The responsibility for bringing about changes lies with Governments in partnership with the private sector and local authorities, and in collaboration with national, regional and international organizations, including in particular UNEP, UNDP and the World Bank. Exchange of experience between countries can also be significant. National plans, goals and objectives, national rules, regulations and law, and the specific situation in which different countries are placed are the overall framework in which such integration takes place. In this context, it must be borne in mind that environmental standards may pose severe economic and social costs if they are uniformly applied in developing countries.

Objectives

The overall objective is to improve or restructure the decision-making process so that consideration of socio-economic and environmental issues is fully integrated and a broader range of public participation assured. Recognizing that countries will develop their own priorities in accordance with their prevailing conditions, needs, national plans, policies and programmes, the following objectives are proposed:

(a) To conduct a national review of economic, sectoral and environmental policies, strategies and plans to ensure the progressive integration of environmental and developmental issues;

(b) To strengthen institutional structures to allow the full integration of environmental and developmental issues, at all levels of decision-making;

(c) To develop or improve mechanisms to facilitate the involvement of concerned individuals, groups and organizations in decision-making at all levels;

(d) To establish domestically determined procedures to integrate environment and development issues in decision-making.

ACTIVITIES

Improving Decision-making Processes

The primary need is to integrate environmental and developmental decision-making processes. To do this, Governments should conduct a national review and, where appropriate, improve the processes of decision-making so as to achieve the progressive integration of economic, social and environmental issues in the pursuit of development that is economically efficient, socially equitable and responsible and environmentally sound. Countries will develop their own priorities in accordance with their national plans, policies and programmes for the following activities:

(a) Ensuring the integration of economic, social and environmental considerations in decision-making at all levels and in all ministries;

(b) Adopting a domestically formulated policy framework that reflects a long-term perspective and cross-sectoral approach as the basis for decisions, taking account of the linkages between and within the various political, economic, social and environmental issues involved in the development process;

(c) Establishing domestically determined ways and means to ensure the coherence of sectoral, economic, social and environmental policies, plans and policy instruments, including fiscal measures and the budget; these mechanisms should apply at various levels and bring together those interested in the development process;

(d) Monitoring and evaluating the development process systematically, conducting regular reviews of the state of human resources development, economic and social conditions and trends, the state of the environment and natural resources; this could be complemented by annual environment and development reviews, with a view to assessing sustainable development achievements by the various sectors and departments of government;

(e) Ensuring transparency of, and accountability for, the environmental implications of economic and sectoral policies;

(f) Ensuring access by the public to relevant information, facilitating the reception of public views and allowing for effective participation.

Improving Planning and Management Systems

To support a more integrated approach to decision-making, the data systems and analytical methods used to support such decision-making processes may need to be improved. Governments, in collaboration, where appropriate, with national and international organizations, should review the status of the planning and management system and, where necessary, modify and strengthen procedures so as to facilitate the integrated consideration of social, economic and environmental issues. Countries will develop their own priorities in accordance with their national plans, policies and programmes for the following activities:

(a) Improving the use of data and information at all stages of planning and management, making systematic and simultaneous use of social, economic, developmental, ecological and environmental data; analysis should stress interactions and synergisms; a broad range of analytical methods should be encouraged so as to provide various points of view;

(b) Adopting comprehensive analytical procedures for prior and simultaneous assessment of the impacts of decisions, including the impacts within and among the economic, social and environmental spheres; these procedures should extend beyond the project level to policies and programmes; analysis should also include assessment of costs, benefits and risks;

(c) Adopting flexible and integrative planning approaches that allow the consideration of multiple goals and enable adjustment of changing needs; integrative area approaches at the ecosystem or watershed level can assist in this approach;

(d) Adopting integrated management systems, particularly for the management of natural resources; traditional or indigenous methods should be studied and considered wherever they have proved effective; women's traditional roles should not be marginalized as a result of the introduction of new management systems;

(e) Adopting integrated approaches to sustainable development at the regional level, including transboundary areas, subject to the requirements of particular circumstances and needs;

(f) Using policy instruments (legal/regulatory and economic) as a tool for planning and management, seeking incorporation of efficiency criteria in decisions; instruments should be regularly reviewed and adapted to ensure that they continue to be effective;

(g) Delegating planning and management responsibilities to the lowest level of public authority consistent with effective action; in particular the advantages of effective and equitable opportunities for participation by women should be discussed;

(h) Establishing procedures for involving local communities in contingency planning for environmental and industrial accidents, and maintaining an open exchange of information on local hazards.

Data and Information

Countries could develop systems for monitoring and evaluation of progress towards achieving sustainable development by adopting indicators that measure changes across economic, social and environmental dimensions.

Adopting a National Strategy for Sustainable Development

Governments, in cooperation, where appropriate, with international organizations, should adopt a national strategy for sustainable development based on, inter alia, the implementation of decisions taken at the Conference, particularly in respect of Agenda 21. This strategy should build upon and harmonize the various sectoral economic, social and environmental policies and plans that are operating in the country.

The experience gained through existing planning exercises such as national reports for the Conference, national conservation strategies and environment action plans should be fully used and incorporated into a country-driven sustainable development strategy. Its goals should be to ensure socially responsible economic development while protecting the resource base and the environment for the benefit of future generations. It should be developed through the widest possible participation. It should be based on a thorough assessment of the current situation and initiatives.

MEANS OF IMPLEMENTATION

Financing and Cost Evaluation

The Conference secretariat has estimated the average total annual cost (1993-2000) of implementing the activities of this programme to be about $50 million from the international community on grant or concessional terms. These are indicative and order-of-magnitude estimates only and have not been reviewed by Governments. Actual costs and financial terms, including any that are non-concessional, will depend upon, inter alia, the specific strategies and programmes Governments decide upon for implementation.

Researching Environment and Development Interactions

Governments, in collaboration with the national and international scientific community and in cooperation with international organizations, as appropriate, should intensify efforts to clarify the interactions between and within social, economic and environmental considerations. Research should be undertaken with the explicit objective of assisting policy decisions and providing recommendations on improving management practices.

Enhancing Education and Training

Countries, in cooperation, where appropriate, with national, regional or international organizations, should ensure that essential human resources exist, or be developed, to undertake the integration of environment and development at various stages of the decision-making and implementation process. To do this, they should improve education and technical training, particularly for women and girls, by including interdisciplinary approaches, as appropriate, in technical, vocational, university and other curricula. They should also undertake systematic training of government personnel, planners and managers on a regular basis, giving priority to the requisite integrative approaches and planning and management techniques that are suited to country-specific conditions.

Promoting Public Awareness

Countries, in cooperation with national institutions and groups, the media and the international community, should promote awareness in the public at large, as well as in specialized circles, of the importance of considering environment and development in an integrated manner, and should establish mechanisms for facilitating a direct exchange of information and views with the public. Priority should be given to highlighting the responsibilities and potential contributions of different social groups.

Strengthen National Institutional Capacity

Governments, in cooperation, where appropriate, with international organizations, should strengthen national institutional capability and capacity to integrate social, economic, developmental and environmental issues at all levels of development decision-making and implementation. Attention should be given to moving away from narrow sectoral approaches, progressing towards full cross-sectoral coordination and cooperation.

Providing an Effective Legal and Regulatory Framework

Basis for action

Laws and regulations suited to country-specific conditions are among the most important instruments for transforming environment and development policies into action, not only through "command and control" methods, but also as a normative framework for economic planning and market instruments. Yet, although the volume of legal texts in this field is steadily increasing, much of the law-making in many countries seems to be ad hoc and piecemeal, or has not been endowed with the necessary institutional machinery and authority for enforcement and timely adjustment. While there is continuous need for law improvement in all countries, many developing countries have been affected by shortcomings of laws and regulations. To effectively integrate environment and development in the policies and practices of each country, it is essential to develop and implement integrated, enforceable and effective laws and regulations that are based upon sound social, ecological, economic and scientific principles. It is equally critical to develop workable programmes to review and enforce compliance with the laws, regulations and standards that are adopted. Technical support may be needed for many countries to accomplish these goals. Technical cooperation requirements in this field include legal information, advisory services and specialized training and institutional capacity-building.

The enactment and enforcement of laws and regulations (at the regional, national, state/provincial or local/municipal level) are also essential for the implementation of most international agreements in the field of environment and development, as illustrated by the frequent treaty obligation to report on legislative measures. The survey of existing agreements undertaken in the context of conference preparations has indicated problems of compliance in this respect, and the need for improved national implementation and, where appropriate, related technical assistance. In developing their national priorities, countries should take account of their international obligations.

Objectives

The overall objective is to promote, in the light of country-specific conditions, the integration of environment and development policies through appropriate legal and regulatory policies, instruments and enforcement mechanisms at the national, state, provincial and local level. Recognizing that countries will develop their own priorities in accordance with their needs and national and, where appropriate, regional plans, policies and programmes, the following objectives are proposed:

(a) To disseminate information on effective legal and regulatory innovations in the field of environment and development, including appropriate instruments and compliance incentives, with a view to encouraging their wider use and adoption at the national, state, provincial and local level;

(b) To support countries that request it in their national efforts to modernize and strengthen the policy and legal framework of governance for sustainable development, having due regard for local social values and infrastructures;

(c) To encourage the development and implementation of national, state, provincial and local programmes that assess and promote compliance and respond appropriately to non-compliance.

ACTIVITIES

Making Laws and Regulations more Effective

Governments, with the support, where appropriate, of competent international organizations, should regularly assess the laws and regulations enacted and the related institutional/administrative machinery established at the national/state and local/municipal level in the field of environment and sustainable development, with a view to rendering them effective in practice. Programmes for this purpose could include the promotion of public awareness, preparation and distribution of guidance material, and specialized training, including workshops, seminars, education programmes and conferences, for public officials who design, implement, monitor and enforce laws and regulations.

Establishing Judicial and Administrative Procedures

Governments and legislators, with the support, where appropriate, of competent international organizations, should establish judicial and administrative procedures for legal redress and remedy of actions affecting environment and development that may be unlawful or infringe on rights under the law, and should provide access to individuals, groups and organizations with a recognized legal interest.

Providing Legal Reference and Support Services

Competent intergovernmental and non-governmental organizations could cooperate to provide Governments and legislators, upon request, with an integrated programme of environment and development law (sustainable development law) services, carefully adapted to the specific requirements of the recipient legal and administrative systems.

Such systems could usefully include assistance in the preparation of comprehensive inventories and reviews of national legal systems. Past experience has demonstrated the usefulness of combining specialized legal information services with legal expert advice. Within the United Nations system, closer cooperation among all agencies concerned would avoid duplication of databases and facilitate division of labour. These agencies could examine the possibility and merit of performing reviews of selected national legal systems.

Establishing a Cooperative Training Network for Sustainable Development Law

Competent international and academic institutions could, within agreed frameworks, cooperate to provide, especially for trainees from developing countries, postgraduate programmes and in-service training facilities in environment and development law.

Such training should address both the effective application and the progressive improvement of applicable laws, the related skills of negotiating, drafting and mediation, and the training of trainers. Intergovernmental and non-governmental organizations already active in this field could cooperate with related university programmes to harmonize curriculum planning and to offer an optimal range of options to interested Governments and potential sponsors.

Developing Effective National Programmes

Each country should develop integrated strategies to maximize compliance with its laws and regulations relating to sustainable development, with assistance from international organizations and other countries as appropriate. The strategies could include:

(a) Enforceable, effective laws, regulations and standards that are based on sound economic, social and environmental principles and appropriate risk assessment, incorporating sanctions designed to punish violations, obtain redress and deter future violations;

(b) Mechanisms for promoting compliance;

(c) Institutional capacity for collecting compliance data, regularly reviewing compliance, detecting violations, establishing enforcement priorities, undertaking effective enforcement, and conducting periodic evaluations of the effectiveness of compliance and enforcement programmes;

(d) Mechanisms for appropriate involvement of individuals and groups in the development and enforcement of laws and regulations on environment and development.

National Monitoring of Legal Follow-up to International Instruments

Contracting parties to international agreements, in consultation with the appropriate secretariats of relevant international conventions as appropriate, should improve practices and procedures for collecting information on legal and regulatory measures taken. Contracting parties to international agreements could undertake sample surveys of domestic follow-up action subject to agreement by the sovereign States concerned.

MEANS OF IMPLEMENTATION

Financing and Cost Evaluation

The Conference secretariat has estimated the average total annual cost (1993-2000) of implementing the activities of this programme to be about $6 million from the international community on grant or concessional terms. These are indicative and order-of-magnitude estimates only and have not been reviewed by Governments. Actual costs and financial terms, including any that are non-concessional, will depend upon, inter alia, the specific strategies and programmes Governments decide upon for implementation

Scientific and Technological Means

The programme relies essentially on a continuation of ongoing work for legal data collection, translation and assessment. Closer cooperation between existing databases may be expected to lead to better division of labour (e.g., in geographical coverage of national legislative gazettes and other reference sources) and to improved standardization and compatibility of data, as appropriate.

Human Resource Development

Participation in training is expected to benefit practitioners from developing countries and to enhance training opportunities for women. Demand for this type of postgraduate and in-service training is known to be high.

The seminars, workshops and conferences on review and enforcement that have been held to date have been very successful and well attended. The purpose of these efforts is to develop resources (both human and institutional) to design and implement effective programmes to continuously review and enforce national and local laws, regulations and standards on sustainable development.

Strengthening Legal and Institutional Capacity

A major part of the programme should be oriented towards improving the legal-institutional capacities of countries to cope with national problems of governance and effective law-making and law-applying in the field of environment and sustainable development.

Regional centres of excellence could be designated and supported to build up specialized databases and training facilities for linguistic/cultural groups of legal systems.

Making Effective use of Economic Instruments and Market and Other Incentives

Basis for action

Environmental law and regulation are important but cannot alone be expected to deal with the problems of environment and development. Prices, markets and governmental fiscal and economic policies also play a complementary role in shaping attitudes and behaviour towards the environment.

During the past several years, many Governments, primarily in industrialized countries but also in Central and Eastern Europe and in developing countries, have been making increasing use of economic approaches, including those that are market-oriented. Examples include the polluter-pays principle and the more recent natural-resource-user-pays concept.

Within a supportive international and national economic context and given the necessary legal and regulatory framework, economic and market-oriented approaches can in many cases enhance capacity to deal with the issues of environment and development. This would be achieved by providing cost-effective solutions, applying integrated pollution prevention control, promoting technological innovation and influencing environmental behaviour, as well as providing financial resources to meet sustainable development objectives.

What is needed is an appropriate effort to explore and make more effective and widespread use of economic and market-oriented approaches within a broad framework of development policies, law and regulation suited to country-specific conditions as part of a general transition to economic and environmental policies that are supportive and mutually reinforcing.

Objectives

Recognizing that countries will develop their own priorities in accordance with their needs and national plans, policies and programmes, the challenge is to achieve significant progress in the years ahead in meeting three fundamental objectives:

(a) To incorporate environmental costs in the decisions of producers and consumers, to reverse the tendency to treat the environment as a "free good" and to pass these costs on to other parts of society, other countries, or to future generations;

(b) To move more fully towards integration of social and environmental costs into economic activities, so that prices will appropriately reflect the relative scarcity and total value of resources and contribute towards the prevention of environmental degradation;

(c) To include, wherever appropriate, the use of market principles in the framing of economic instruments and policies to pursue sustainable development.

ACTIVITIES

Improving or Reorienting Governmental Policies

In the near term, Governments should consider gradually building on experience with economic instruments and market mechanisms by undertaking to reorient their policies, keeping in mind national plans, priorities and objectives, in order to:

(a) Establish effective combinations of economic, regulatory and voluntary (self-regulatory) approaches;

(b) Remove or reduce those subsidies that do not conform with sustainable development objectives;

(c) Reform or recast existing structures of economic and fiscal incentives to meet environment and development objectives;

(d) Establish a policy framework that encourages the creation of new markets in pollution control and environmentally sounder resource management;

(e) Move towards pricing consistent with sustainable development objectives.

In particular, Governments should explore, in cooperation with business and industry, as appropriate, how effective use can be made of economic instruments and market mechanisms in the following areas:

(a) Issues related to energy, transportation, agriculture and forestry, water, wastes, health, tourism and tertiary services;

(b) Global and transboundary issues;

(c) The development and introduction of environmentally sound technology and its adaptation, diffusion and transfer to developing countries in conformity with chapter 34.

Taking Account of the Particular Circumstances of Developing Countries and Countries with Economies in Transition

A special effort should be made to develop applications of the use of economic instruments and market mechanisms geared to the particular needs of developing countries and countries with economies in transition, with the assistance of regional and international economic and environmental organizations and, as appropriate, non-governmental research institutes, by:

(a) Providing technical support to those countries on issues relating to the application of economic instruments and market mechanisms;

(b) Encouraging regional seminars and, possibly, the development of regional centres of expertise.

Creating an Inventory of Effective uses of Economic Instruments and Market Mechanisms

Given the recognition that the use of economic instruments and market mechanisms is relatively recent, exchange of information about different countries' experiences with such approaches should be actively encouraged. In this regard, Governments should encourage the use of existing means of information exchange to look at effective uses of economic instruments.

Increasing Understanding of the Role of Economic Instruments and Market Mechanisms

Governments should encourage research and analysis on effective uses of economic instruments and incentives with the assistance and support of regional and international economic and environmental organizations, as well as non-governmental research institutes, with a focus on such key issues as:

(a) The role of environmental taxation suited to national conditions;
(b) The implications of economic instruments and incentives for competitiveness and international trade, and potential needs for appropriate future international cooperation and coordination;
(c) The possible social and distributive implications of using various instruments.

Establishing a Process for Focusing on Pricing

The theoretical advantages of using pricing policies, where appropriate, need to be better understood, and accompanied by greater understanding of what it means to take significant steps in this direction. Processes should therefore be initiated, in cooperation with business, industry, large enterprises, transnational corporations, as well as other social groups, as appropriate, at both the national and international levels, to examine:

(a) The practical implications of moving towards greater reliance on pricing that internalize environmental costs appropriate to help achieve sustainable development objectives;
(b) The implications for resource pricing in the case of resource-exporting countries, including the implications of such pricing policies for developing countries;
(c) The methodologies used in valuing environmental costs.

Enhancing Understanding of Sustainable Development Economics

Increased interest in economic instruments, including market mechanisms, also requires a concerted effort to improve understanding of sustainable development economics by:

(a) Encouraging institutions of higher learning to review their curricula and strengthen studies in sustainable development economics;
(b) Encouraging regional and international economic organizations and non-governmental research institutes with expertise in this area to provide training sessions and seminars for government officials;

(c) Encouraging business and industry, including large industrial enterprises and transnational corporations with expertise in environmental matters, to organize training programmes for the private sector and other groups.

MEANS OF IMPLEMENTATION

This programme involves adjustments or reorientation of policies on the part of Governments. It also involves international and regional economic and environmental organizations and agencies with expertise in this area, including transnational corporations.

Financing and Cost Evaluation

The Conference secretariat has estimated the average total annual cost (1993-2000) of implementing the activities of this programme to be about $5 million from the international community on grant or concessional terms. These are indicative and order-of-magnitude estimates only and have not been reviewed by Governments. Actual costs and financial terms, including any that are non-concessional, will depend upon, inter alia, the specific strategies and programmes Governments decide upon for implementation.

Establishing Systems for Integrated Environmental and Economic Accounting

Basis for action

A first step towards the integration of sustainability into economic management is the establishment of better measurement of the crucial role of the environment as a source of natural capital and as a sink for by-products generated during the production of man-made capital and other human activities. As sustainable development encompasses social, economic and environmental dimensions, it is also important that national accounting procedures are not restricted to measuring the production of goods and services that are conventionally remunerated. A common framework needs to be developed whereby the contributions made by all sectors and activities of society, that are not included in the conventional national accounts, are included, to the extent consistent with sound theory and practicability, in satellite accounts. A programme to develop national systems of integrated environmental and economic accounting in all countries is proposed.

Objectives

The main objective is to expand existing systems of national economic accounts in order to integrate environment and social dimensions in the accounting framework, including at least satellite systems of accounts for natural resources in all member States. The resulting systems of integrated environmental and economic accounting (IEEA) to be established in all member States at the earliest date should be seen as a complement to, rather than a substitute for, traditional national accounting practices for the foreseeable future. IEEAs would be designed to play an integral part in the national development decision-making process. National accounting agencies should work in close collaboration with national environmental statistics as well as the geographic and natural resource departments. The definition of economically active could be expanded to include people performing productive but unpaid tasks in all countries. This would enable their contribution to be adequately measured and taken into account in decision-making.

ACTIVITIES

Strengthening International Cooperation

The Statistical Office of the United Nations Secretariat should:

(a) Make available to all member States the methodologies contained in the SNA Handbook on Integrated Environmental and Economic Accounting;

(b) In collaboration with other relevant United Nations organizations, further develop, test, refine and then standardize the provisional concepts and methods such as those proposed by the SNA Handbook, keeping member States informed of the status of the work throughout this process;

(d) Coordinate, in close cooperation with other international organizations, the training of national accountants, environmental statisticians and national technical staff in small groups for the establishment, adaptation and development of national IEEAs.

The Department of Economic and Social Development of the United Nations Secretariat, in close collaboration with other relevant United Nations organizations, should:

(a) Support, in all member States, the utilization of sustainable development indicators in national economic and social planning and decision-making practices, with a view to ensuring that IEEAs are usefully integrated in economic development planning at the national level;

(b) Promote improved environmental and economic and social data collection.

Strengthening National Accounting Systems

At the national level, the programme could be adopted mainly by the agencies dealing with national accounts, in close cooperation with environmental statistics and natural resource departments, with a view to assisting national economic analysts and decision makers in charge of national economic planning. National institutions should play a crucial role not only as the depositary of the system but also in its adaptation, establishment and continuous use. Unpaid productive work such as domestic work and child care should be included, where appropriate, in satellite national accounts and economic statistics. Time-use surveys could be a first step in the process of developing these satellite accounts.

Establishing an Assessment Process

At the international level, the Statistical Commission should assemble and review experience and advise member States on technical and methodological issues related to the further development and implementation of IEEAs in member States. Governments should seek to identify and consider measures to correct price distortions arising from environmental programmes affecting land, water, energy and other natural resources. Governments should encourage corporations:

(a) To provide relevant environmental information through transparent reporting to shareholders, creditors, employees, governmental authorities, consumers and the public;

(b) To develop and implement methods and rules for accounting for sustaining development.

Strengthening Data and Information Collection

National Governments could consider implementing the necessary enhancement in data collection to set in place national IEEAs with a view to contributing pragmatically to sound economic management. Major efforts should be made to augment the capacity to collect and analyse environmental data and information and to integrate it with economic data, including gender disaggregated data. Efforts should also be made to develop physical environmental accounts. International donor agencies should consider financing the development of intersectoral data banks to help ensure that national planning for sustainable development is based on precise, reliable and effective information and is suited to national conditions.

Strengthening Technical Cooperation

The Statistical Office of the United Nations Secretariat, in close collaboration with relevant United Nations organizations, should strengthen existing mechanisms for technical cooperation among countries. This should also include exchange of experience in the establishment of IEEAs, particularly in connection with the valuation of non-marketed natural resources and standardization in data collection. The cooperation of business and industry, including large industrial enterprises and transnational corporations with experience in valuation of such resources, should also be sought.

MEANS OF IMPLEMENTATION

Financing and Cost Evaluation

The Conference secretariat has estimated the average total annual cost (1993-2000) of implementing the activities of this programme to be about $2 million from the international community on grant or concessional terms. These are indicative and order-of-magnitude estimates only and have not been reviewed by Governments. Actual costs and financial terms, including any that are non-concessional, will depend upon, inter alia, the specific strategies and programmes Governments decide upon for implementation.

Strengthening Institutions

To ensure the application of IEEAs:

(a) National institutions in developing countries could be strengthened to ensure the effective integration of environment and development at the planning and decision-making levels;

(b) The Statistical Office should provide the necessary technical support to member States, in close collaboration with the assessment process to be established by the Statistical Commission; the Statistical Office should provide appropriate support for establishing IEEAs, in collaboration with relevant United Nations agencies.

Enhancing the use of Information Technology

Guidelines and mechanisms could be developed and agreed upon for the adaptation and diffusion of information technologies to developing countries. State-of-the-art data management technologies should be adopted for the most efficient and widespread use of IEEAs.

Strengthening National Capacity

Governments, with the support of the international community, should strengthen national institutional capacity to collect, store, organize, assess and use data in decision-making. Training in all areas related to the establishment of IEEAs, and at all levels, will be required, especially in developing countries. This should include technical training of those involved in economic and environmental analysis, data collection and national accounting, as well as training decision makers to use such information in a pragmatic and appropriate way.

6

World Commission on Environment and Development

The Earth is one but the world is not. We all depend on one biosphere for sustaining our lives. Yet each community, each country, strives for survival and prosperity with little regard for its impact on others. Some consume the Earth's resources at a rate that would leave little for future generations. Others, many more in number, consume far too little and live with the prospect of hunger, squalor, disease, and early death.

Yet progress has been made. Throughout much of the world, children born today can expect to live longer and be better educated than their parents. In many parts, the newborn can also expect to attain a higher standard of living in a wider sense. Such progress provides hope as we contemplate the improvements still needed, and also as we face our failures to make this Earth a safer and sounder home for us and for those who are to come.

The failures that we need to correct arise both from poverty and from the short-sighted way in which we have often pursued prosperity. Many parts of the world are caught in a vicious downwards spiral: Poor people are forced to overuse environmental resources to survive from day to day, and their impoverishment of their environment further impoverishes them, making their survival ever more difficult and uncertain. The prosperity attained in some parts of the world is often precarious, as it has been secured through farming, forestry, and industrial practices that bring profit and progress only over the short term.

Societies have faced such pressures in the past and, as many desolate ruins remind us, sometimes succumbed to them. But generally these pressures were local. Today the scale of ow interventions in nature is increasing and the physical effects of our decisions spill across national frontiers. The growth in economic interaction between nations amplifies the wider consequences of national decisions. Economics and ecology bind us in ever-tightening networks. Today, many regions face risks of irreversible damage to the human environment that threaten the basis for human progress.

These deepening interconnections are the central justification for the establishment of this Commission. We travelled the world for nearly three years, listening. At special public hearings organized by the Commission, we heard from government leaders, scientists, and experts, from citizens' groups concerned about a wide range of environment and development issues, and from thousands of individuals farmers, shanty-town residents, young people, industrialists, and indigenous and tribal peoples.

We found everywhere deep public concern for the environment, concern that has led not just to protests but often to changed behaviour. The challenge is to ensure that these new values are more adequately reflected in the principles and operations of political and economic structures.

We also found grounds for hope: that people can cooperate to build a future that is more prosperous, more just, and more secure; that a new era of economic growth can be attained, one based on policies that sustain and expand the Earth's resource base; and that the progress that some have known over the last century can be experienced by all in the years ahead. But for this to happen, we must understand better the symptoms of stress that confront us, we must identify the causes, and we must design new approaches to managing environmental resources and to sustaining human development

SYMPTOMS AND CAUSES

Environmental stress has often been seen as the result of the growing demand on scarce resources and the pollution generated by the rising living standards of the relatively affluent. But poverty itself pollutes the environment, creating environmental stress in a different way. Those who are poor and hungry will often destroy their immediate environment in order to survive: They will cut down forests; their livestock will overgraze grasslands; they will overuse marginal land; and in growing numbers they will crowd into congested cities. The cumulative effect of these changes is so far-reaching as to make poverty itself a major global scourge.

On the other hand, where economic growth has led to improvements in living standards, it has sometimes been achieved in ways that are globally damaging in the longer term. Much of the improvement in the past has been based on the use of increasing amounts of raw materials, energy, chemicals, and synthetics and on the creation of pollution that is not adequately accounted for in figuring the costs of production processes. These trends have had unforeseen effects on the environment. Thus today's environmental challenges arise both from the lack of development and from the unintended consequences of some forms of economic growth.

Poverty

There are more hungry people in the world today than ever before in human history, and their numbers are growing. In 1980, there were 340 million people in 87 developing countries not getting enough calories to prevent stunted growth and serious health risks. This total was very slightly below the figure for 1970 in terms of share of the world population, but in terms of sheer numbers, it represented a 14 per cent increase. The World Bank predicts that these numbers are likely to go on growing.

The number of people living in slums and shanty towns is rising, not falling. A growing number lack access to clean water and sanitation and hence are prey to the diseases that arise from this lack. There is some progress, impressive in places. But, on balance, poverty persists and its victims multiply.

The pressure of poverty has to be seen in a broader context. At the international level there are large differences in per capita income, which ranged in 1984 from $190 in low income countries (other than China and India) to $11,430 in the industrial market economies.

Table : Population Size and per capita GDP by Groups of Countries

Countries	Population (millions)	Per capita GDP (1984 dollars)	Average annual growth rate of per capita GDP, 1965-1984 (per cent)
Low-income countries (excluding China, India)	611	190	0.9
China and India	1,778	390	3.2
Lower Middle-income Economies	691	740	1.0
Upper Middle-income Economies	497	1,980	3.1
High-Income Oil Exporters	19	11,350	3.2
Industrial Market Economies	732	11,430	2.4

Source: Based on data in World Bank, **World Development Report, 1985**. (New York, Oxford University rress, 1986)

Such inequalities represent great differences not merely in the quality of life today, but also in the capacity of societies to improve their quality of life in the future. Most of the world's poorest countries depend for increasing export earnings on tropical agricultural products that are vulnerable to fluctuating or declining terms of trade. Expansion can often only be achieved at the price of ecological stress. Yet diversification in ways that will alleviate both poverty and ecological stress is hampered by disadvantageous terms of technology transfer, by protectionism, and by declining financial flows to those countries that most need international finance.

Within countries, poverty has been exacerbated by the unequal distribution of land and other assets. The rapid rise in population has compromised the ability to raise living standards. These factors, combined with growing demands for the commercial use of good land, often to grow crops for exports, have pushed many subsistence farmers onto poor land and robbed them of any hope of participating in their nations' economic lives. The same forces have meant that traditional shifting cultivators, who once cut forests, grew crops, and then gave the forest time to recover, now have neither land enough nor time to let forests re-establish. So forests are being destroyed, often only to create poor farmland that cannot support those who till it. Extending cultivation onto steep slopes is increasing soil erosion in many hilly sections of both developing and developed nations. In any river valleys, areas chronically liable to floods are now farmed.

These pressures are reflected in the rising incidence of disasters. During the 1970s, six times as many people died from 'natural disasters' each year as in the 1960s, and twice as many suffered from such disasters. Droughts and floods, disasters among whose causes are widespread deforestation and overcultivation, increased most in terms of numbers affected. There were 18.5 million people affected by droughts annually in the 1960s, but 24.4 billion in the 1970s; 5.2 billion people were victims of floods yearly in the 1960s, compared with 15.4 million in the 1970s. The results are not in for the 1980s, but this disaster-prone decade seems to be carrying forward the trend, with droughts in Africa, India, and Latin America, and floods throughout Asia, parts of Africa, and the Andean region of Latin America.

Such disasters claim most of their victims among the impoverished in poor nations, where subsistence farmers must make their land more liable to droughts and floods by clearing marginal areas, and where the poor make themselves tore vulnerable to all disasters by living on steep slopes and unprotected shores - the only lands left for their shanties. Lacking food and foreign exchange reserves their economically vulnerable governments are ill-equipped to cope with such catastrophes.

The links between environmental stress and developmental disaster are most evident in sub-Saharan Africa. Per capita food production, declining since the 1960s, plummeted during the drought of the 1980s, and at the height of the food emergency some 35 million people were exposed to risk. Human overuse of land and prolonged drought threaten to turn the grasslands of Africa's Sahel region into desert. No other region more tragically suffers the vicious cycle of poverty leading to environmental degradation, which leads in turn to even greater poverty.

Growth

In some parts of the world, particularly since the mid-1950s, growth and development have vastly improved living standards and the quality of life. Many of the products and technologies that have gone into this improvement are raw material- and energy-intensive and entail a substantial amount of pollution. The consequent impact on the environment is greater than ever before in human history.

Over the past century, the use of fossil fuels has grown nearly thirtyfold, and industrial production has increased move than fiftyfold. The bulk of this increase, about three-quarters in the case of fossil fuels and a little over four-fifths in the case of industrial production, has taken place since 1950. The annual increase in industrial production today is perhaps as large as the total production in Europe around the end of the 1930s. Into every year we now squeeze the decades of industrial growth and environmental disruption that formed the basis of the pre-war European economy.

Environmental stresses also arise from more traditional forms of production. More land has been cleared for settled cultivation in the past 100 years than in all the previous centuries of human existence. Interventions in the water cycles have increased greatly. Massive dams, most of them built after 1960, impound a large proportion of the river flow. In Europe and Asia, water use has reached 10 per cent of the annual run off, a figure that is expected to rise to 20-25 per cent by the end of the century.

The impact of growth and rising income levels can be seen in the distribution of world consumption of a variety of resource intensive produce. The more affluent industrialized countries use most of the world's metals and fossil fuels. Even in the case of food products a sharp difference exists, particularly in the products that are more resource-intensive.

Table : Distribution of World Consumption, Averages for 1980-83

		Developed Countries (26% of population)		Developing Countries (74% of population)	
	Units of Per Capita Consumption	Share in World Consumption		Share in World Consumption	
Commodity		per cent	per capita	per cent	per capita
Food					
Calories	kcal/day	34	3,395	66	2,389
Protein	gms/day	38	99	62	
Fat	gms/day	53	127	47	40
Paper	kg/year	85	123	15	8
Steel	kg/year	79	459	21	41
Other Metals	kg/year	86	26	14	2
Commercial Energy	/year	80		20	0.5

Source: WCED estimates based on country-level data from FAO, UN Statistical Office, UNCTAD and American Metals Association

In recent years, industrial countries have been able to achieve economic growth using less energy and raw materials per unit of output. This, along with the efforts to reduce the emission of pollutants, will help to contain the pressure on the biosphere. But with the increase in population and the rise in incomes, per capita consumption of energy and materials will go up in the developing countries, as it has to if essential needs are to be met. Greater attention to resource efficiency can moderate the increase, but, on balance, environmental problems linked to resource use will intensify in global terms.

Survival

The scale and complexity of our requirements for natural resources have increased greatly with the rising levels of population and production. Nature is bountiful, but it is also fragile and finely balanced. There are thresholds that cannot be crossed without endangering the basic integrity of the system. Today we are close to many of these thresholds; we must be ever mindful of the risk of endangering the survival of life on Earth. Moreover, the speed with which changes in resource use are taking place gives little time in which to anticipate and prevent unexpected effects.

The 'greenhouse effect', one such threat to life support systems, springs directly from increased resource use. The burning of fossil fuels and the cutting and burning of forests release carbon dioxide (CO2). The accumulation in the atmosphere of CO2 and certain other gases traps solar radiation near the Earth's surface, causing global warming. This could cause sea level rises over the next 45 years large enough to inundate many low lying coastal cities and river deltas. It could also drastically upset national and international agricultural production and trade systems.

Another threat arises from the depletion of the atmospheric ozone layer by gases released during the production of foam and the use of refrigerants and aerosols. A substantial loss of such ozone could have catastrophic effects on human and livestock health and on some life forms at the base of the marine food chain. The 1986 discovery of a hole in the ozone layer above the Antarctic suggests the possibility of a more rapid depletion than previously suspected.

A variety of air pollutants are killing trees and lakes and damaging buildings and cultural treasures, close to and sometimes thousands of miles from points of emission. The acidification of the environment threatens large areas of Europe and North America. Central Europe is currently receiving more than one gramme of sulphur on every square metre of ground each year. The loss of forests could bring in its wake disastrous erosion, siltation, floods, and local climatic change. Air pollution damage is also becoming evident in some newly industrialized countries.

In many cases the practices used at present to dispose of toxic wastes, such as those from the chemical industries, involve unacceptable risks. Radioactive wastes from the nuclear industry remain hazardous for centuries. Many who bear these risks do not benefit in any way from the activities that produce the wastes.

Desertification - the process whereby productive arid and semi-arid land is rendered economically unproductive - and large-scale deforestation are other examples of major threats to the integrity of regional ecosystems. Desertification involves complex interactions between humans, land, and climate. The pressures of subsistence food production, commercial crops, and meat production in arid and semi-arid areas all contribute to this process.

Each year another 6 million hectares are degraded to desert-like conditions. Over three decades, this would amount to an area roughly as large as Saudi Arabia. More than 11 million hectares of tropical forests are destroyed per year and this, over 30 years, would amount to an area about the size of India. Apart from the direct and often dramatic impacts within the immediate area, nearby regions are affected by the spreading of sands or by changes in water regimes and increased risks of soil erosion and siltation.

The loss of forests and other wild lands extinguishes species of plants and animals and drastically reduces the genetic diversity of the world's ecosystems. This process robs present and future generations of genetic material with which to improve crop varieties, to make them less vulnerable to weather stress, pest attacks, and disease. The loss of species and subspecies, many as yet unstudied by science, deprives us of important potential sources of medicines and industrial chemicals. It removes forever creatures of beauty and parts of our cultural heritage; it diminishes the biosphere.

Many of the risks stemming from our productive activity and the technologies we use cross-national boundaries; many are global. Though the activities that give rise to these dangers tend to be concentrated in a few countries, the risks are shared by all, rich and poor, those who benefit from them and those who do not. Most who share in the risks have little influence on the decision processes that regulate these activities. Little time is available for corrective action. In some cases we may already be close to transgressing critical thresholds. While scientists continue to research and debate causes and effects, in many cases we already know enough to warrant action. This is true locally and regionally in the cases of such threats as desertification, deforestation, toxic wastes, and acidification; it is true globally for such threats as climate change, ozone depletion, and species loss. The risks increase faster than do our abilities to manage them.

Perhaps the greatest threat to the Earth's environment, to sustainable human progress, and indeed to survival is the possibility of nuclear war, increased daily by the continuing arms race and its spread to outer space. The search for a more viable future can only be meaningful in the context of a more vigorous effort to renounce and eliminate the development of means of annihilation.

The Economic Crisis

The environmental difficulties that confront us are not new, but only recently have we begun to understand their complexity. Previously our main concerns centred on the effects of development on the environment. Today, we need to be equally concerned about the ways in which environmental degradation can dampen or reverse economic development. In one area after another, environmental degradation is eroding the potential for development. This basic connection was brought into sharp focus by the environment and development crises of the 1980s.

The slowdown in the momentum of economic expansion and the stagnation in world trade in the 1980s challenged all nations' abilities to react and adjust. Developing countries that rely on the export of primary products have been hit particularly hard by falling commodity prices. Between 1980 and 1984, developing countries lost about $55 billion in export earnings because of the fall in commodity prices, a blow felt most keenly in Latin America and Africa.

As a consequence of this period of slow growth in the world economy - together with rising debt service obligations and a decline in the inflow of finance - many developing countries have facet) severe economic crises. Over half of all developing countries actually experienced declining per capita GDP in the years 1982-85 and per capita GDP has fallen, for developing countries as a whole, by around 10 per cent in the 1980s.

Table : Annual Rate of Increase of Gross Domestic Product in Developing Countries, 1976-85

Indicator	1976-80	1981	1982	1983	1984	1985
			(per cent)			
Gross Domestic Product	4.9	1.3	0.2	0.8	2.1	2.5
All Developing Countries						
Developing Countries Excluding Large Countries	4.5	1.0	0.6	0.1	1.5	1.4
Per Capita GDP	2.4	1.0	2.1	1.5	0.2	0.2
All developing Countries						
Developing Countries Excluding Large Countries	1.9	1.5	-3.1	-2.4	-1.0	1.1

Source: Department of International Economic and Social Affairs, **Doubling Development Finance: Meeting a Global Challenge, Views and Recommendations of the Committee on Development and Planning** (New York: UN, 1986)

The heaviest burden in international economic adjustment has been carried by the world's poorest people. The consequence has been a considerable increase in human distress and the overexploitation of land and natural resources to ensure survival in the short term.

Many international economic problems remain unresolved: Developing country indebtedness remains serious; commodity and energy markets are highly unstable; financial flows to developing countries are seriously deficient; protectionism and trade wars are a serious threat. Yet at a time when multilateral institutions, and rules, are more than ever necessary, they have been devalued. And the notion of an international responsibility for development has virtually disappeared. The trend is towards a decline in multilateralism and an assertion of national dominance.

NEW APPROACHES TO ENVIRONMENT AND DEVELOPMENT

Human progress has always depended on our technical ingenuity and a capacity for cooperative action. These qualities have often been used constructively to achieve development and environmental progress: in air and water pollution control, for example, and in increasing the efficiency of material and energy use. Many countries have increased food production and reduced population growth rates. Some technological advances, particularly in medicine, have been widely shared.

But this is not enough. Failures to manage the environment and to sustain development threaten to overwhelm all countries. Environment and development are not separate challenges; they are inexorably linked. Development cannot subsist upon a deteriorating environmental resource base; the environment cannot be protected when growth leaves out of account the costs of environmental destruction. These problems cannot be treated separately by fragmented institutions and policies. They are linked in a complex system of cause and effect.

First, environmental stresses are linked one to another. For example, deforestation, by increasing run off, accelerates soil erosion and siltation of rivers and lakes. Air pollution and acidification play their part in killing forests and lakes. Such links mean that several different problems must be tackled simultaneously. And success in one area, such as forest protection, can improve chances of success in another area, such as soil conservation.

Second, environmental stresses and patterns of economic development are linked one to another. Thus agricultural policies may lie at the root of land, water, and forest degradation. Energy policies are associated with the global greenhouse effect, with acidification, and with deforestation for fuelwood in many developing nations. These stresses all threaten economic development. Thus economics and ecology must be completely integrated in decision making and lawmaking processes not just to protect the environment, but also to protect and promote development. Economy is not just about the production of wealth, and ecology is not just about the protection of nature; they are both equally relevant for improving the lot of humankind.

Third, environmental and economic problems are linked to many social and political factors. For example, the rapid population growth that has so profound an impact on the environment and on development in many regions is driven partly by such factors as the status of women in society and other cultural values. Also, environmental stress and uneven development can increase social tensions. It could be argued that the distribution of power and influence within society lies at the heart of most environment and development challenges. Hence new approaches must involve programmes of social development, particularly to improve the position of women in society, to protect vulnerable groups, and to promote local participation in decision making.

Finally, the systemic features operate not merely within but also between nations. National boundaries have become so porous that traditional distinctions between matters of local, national, and international significance have become blurred. Ecosystems do not respect national boundaries. Water pollution moves through shared rivers, lakes, and seas. The atmosphere carries air pollution over vast distances. Major accidents - particularly those at nuclear reactors or at plants or warehouses containing toxic materials - can have widespread regional effects.

Many environment economy links also operate globally. For instance, the highly subsidized, incentive-driven agriculture of industrialized market economies generates surpluses that depress prices and erode the viability of the often neglected agriculture of developing countries. Soils and other environmental resources suffer in both systems. Each country may devise national agricultural policies to secure short-tern economic and political gains, but no nation alone can devise policies to deal effectively with the financial, economic, and ecological costs of the agricultural and trade policies of other nations.

In the past, responsibility for environmental matters has been placed in environmental ministries and institutions that often have had little or no control over destruction caused by agricultural, industrial, urban development, forestry, and transportation policies and practices. Society has failed to give the responsibility for preventing environmental damage to the 'sectoral' ministries and agencies whose policies cause it. Thus our environmental management practices have focused largely upon after-the-fact repair of damage: reforestation, reclaiming desert lands, rebuilding urban environments, restoring natural habitats, and rehabilitating wild lands. The ability to anticipate and prevent environmental damage will require that the ecological dimensions of policy be considered at the same time as the economic, trade, energy, agricultural, and other dimensions.

In most countries, environmental policies are directed at the symptoms of harmful growth; these policies have brought progress and rewards and must be continued and strengthened. But that will not be enough. What is required is a new approach in which all nations aim at a type of development that integrates production with resource conservation and enhancement, and that links both to the provision for all of an adequate livelihood base and equitable access to resources.

The concept of sustainable development provides a framework for the integration of environment policies and development strategies - the term 'development' being used here in its broadest sense. The word is often taken to refer to the processes of economic and social change in the Third World. But the integration of environment and development is required in all countries, rich and poor. The pursuit of sustainable development requires changes in the domestic and international policies of every nation.

Sustainable development seeks to meet the needs and aspirations of the present without compromising the ability to meet those of the future. Far from requiring the cessation of economic growth, it recognizes that the problems of poverty and underdevelopment cannot be solved unless we have a new era of growth in which developing countries play a large role and reap large benefits. Economic growth always brings risk of environmental damage, as it puts increased pressure on environmental resources. But policy makers guided by the concept of sustainable development will necessarily work to assure that growing economies remain firmly attached to their ecological roots and that these roots are protected and nurtured so that they may support growth over the long term. Environmental protection is thus inherent in the concept of sustainable development, as is a focus on the sources of environmental problems rather than the symptoms.

No single blueprint of sustainability will be found, as economic and social systems and ecological conditions differ widely among countries. Each nation will have to work out its own concrete policy implications. Yet irrespective of these differences, sustainable development should be seen as a global objective. No country can develop in isolation from others. Hence the pursuit of sustainable development requires a new orientation in international relations. Long term sustainable growth will requite far-reaching changes to produce trade, capital, and technology flows that are more equitable and better synchronized to environmental imperatives.

The mechanics of increased international cooperation required to assure sustainable development will vary from sector to sector and in relation to particular institutions. But it is fundamental that the transition to sustainable development be managed jointly by all nations. The unity of human needs requires a functioning multilateral system that respects the democratic principle of consent and accepts that not only the Earth but also the world is one. In the chapters that follow we examine these issues in greater detail and make a number of specific proposals for responding to the crises of a threatened future. Overall, our report carries a message of hope. But it is hope conditioned upon the establishment of a new era of international cooperation based on the premise that every human being - those here and those who are to come - has the right to life, and to a decent life. We confidently believe that the international community can rise, as it must, to the challenge of securing sustainable human progress.

7

Population and Human Resources

In 1985. some 80 million people were added to a world population of 4.8 billion. Each year the number of human beings increases, but the amount of natural resources with which to sustain this population, to improve the quality of human lives. and to eliminate mass poverty remains finite. On the other hand, expanding knowledge increases the productivity of resources.

Present rates of population growth cannot continue. They already compromise many governments' abilities to provide education, health care, and food security for people, much less their abilities to raise living standards. This gap between numbers and resources is all the more compelling because so much of the population growth is concentrated in low-income countries, ecologically disadvantaged regions, and poor households.

Yet the population issue is not solely about numbers. And poverty and resource degradation can exist on thinly populated lands, such as the drylands and the tropical forests. People are the ultimate resource. Improvements in education, health, and nutrition allow them to better use the resources they command, to stretch them further. In addition, threats to the sustainable use of resources come as much from inequalities in people's access to resources and from the ways in which they use them as from the sheer numbers of people. Thus concern over the 'population problem' also calls forth concern for human progress and human equality. Nor are population growth rates the challenge solely of those nations with high rates of increase.

An additional person in an industrial country consumer far more and places far greater pressure on natural resources than an additional person in the Third World. Consumption patterns and preferences are as important as numbers of consumers in the conservation of resources.

Thus many governments must work on several fronts to limit population growth; to control the impact of such growth on resources and, with increasing knowledge, enlarge their range and improve their productivity; to realize human potential so that people can better husband and use resources; and to provide people with forms of social security other than large numbers of children. The means of accomplishing these goals will vary from country to country, but all should keep in mind that sustainable economic growth and equitable access to resources are two of the more certain routes towards lower fertility rates.

Giving people the means to choose the size of their families is not just a method of keeping population in balance with resources; it is a way of assuring - especially for women the basic human right of self-determination. The extent to which facilities for exercising such choices are made available is itself a measure of a nation's development. In the same way. enhancing human potential not only promotes development but helps to ensure the right of all to a full and dignified life.

THE LINKS WITH ENVIRONMENT AND DEVELOPMENT

Population growth and development are linked in complex ways. Economic development generates resources that can be used to improve education and health. These improvements, along with associated social changes, reduce both fertility and mortality rates. On the other hand, high rates of population growth that eat into surpluses available for economic and social development can hinder improvements in education and health.

In the past, the intensification of agriculture and the production of higher yields helped nations cope with the increasing population pressures on available land. Migration and international trade in food and fuels eased the pressure on local resources. They permitted and helped sustain the high population densities of some industrialized countries. The situation is different in most of the developing world. There, improvements in medicine and public health have led to a sharp drop in mortality rates and have accelerated population growth rates to unprecedented levels. But fertility rates remain high; much human potential remains unrealized, and economic development is stalled. Agricultural intensification can go some way towards restoring a balance between food production and population, but there are limits beyond which intensification cannot go.

The very possibility of development can be compromised by high population growth rates. Moreover, most developing countries do not have the resources to wait for a few generations before population stabilizes. The option of migration to new lands is virtually closed. And low levels of economic and social development combined with changing trade production relationships limit possibilities of using international trade to augment access to resources. Hence, in the absence of deliberate measures, the imbalance between population growth and resource development will worsen.

Population pressure is already forcing traditional farmers to work harder, often on shrinking fame on marginal land, just to maintain household income. In Africa and Asia, rural population nearly doubled between 1950 and 1985, with a corresponding decline in land availability. Rapid population growth also creates urban economic and social problems that threaten to make cities wholly unmanageable.

Larger investments will be needed just to maintain the current inadequate levels of access to education, health care, and other services. In many cases, the resources required are just not available. Health, housing conditions, and the quality of education and public services all deteriorate; unemployment, urban drift, and social unrest increase.

Box : The Food/Population Balance

- The potential population-supporting capacity of land in developing countries has been assessed in a joint study by FAO and the International Institute for Applied

Systems Analysis. Data on soil and land characteristics were combined with climatic data to calculate the potential yields of major crops, to select the optimum crops, and to derive the overall potential for calorie production. Three levels of crop production were calculated: the first at a low level of technology with no fertilizer or chemicals, traditional crop varieties, and no soil conservation; the second at an intermediate level, where the most productive crop mix is used on half the land along with fertilizers, improved varieties, and some soil conservation; and the third at a high level of technology with an ideal crop mix and technology on all lands. The population-supporting capacity was determined by dividing the total calorie production by a minimum per capita intake level. This figure was then compared with the medium-variant UN population projections.

- The 117 developing countries covered in the study, taken together, can produce enough food to feed one-and-a-half times their projected population in the year 2000. even at a low level of technology. But the picture is less hopeful in the cases of individual countries. At the low level of technology, 64 countries with a population of around 1.1 billion lack the resources to feed themselves. With the most advanced agricultural methods, the number of countries where food production potential would fall short of requirements drops to 19, with a total population of 100 million. Most are high-income West Asian countries and some small island states. Many of these countries have the capacity to earn enough foreign exchange to import their food requirements. In the others, the real issue is the modernization of agriculture on a sustainable basis.
- Some researchers have assessed the 'theoretical' potential for global food production. One study assumes that the area under food production can be around 1.5 billion hectares (close to the current level) and that average yields could go up to 5 tons of grain equivalent

per hectare (as against the present average of 2 tons of grain equivalent}. Allowing for production from rangelands and marine sources, the total 'potential' is placed at 8 billion tons of grain equivalent.

- IIow many people can this sustain? The present global average consumption of plant energy for food, seed, and animal feed amounts to about 6,000 calories daily, with a range among countries of 3,000-15,000 calories, depending on the level of meat consumption. On this basis, the potential production could sustain a little more than 11 billion people. But if the average consumption rises substantially - say, to 9,000 calories - the population carrying capacity of the Earth comes down to 7.5 billion. These figures could be substantially higher if the area under food production and the productivity of 3 billion hectares of permanent pastures ran be increased on a sustainable basis. Nevertheless, the data do suggest, that meeting the food needs of an ultimate world population of around 10 billion would require tone changes in food habits, as well as greatly improving the efficiency of traditional agriculture.

Industrial countries seriously concerned with high population growth rates in other parts of the world have obligations beyond simply supplying aid packages of family planning hardware. Economic development, through its indirect impact on social and cultural factors, lowers fertility rates. International policies that interfere with economic development thus interfere with a developing nation's ability to manage its population growth. A concern for population growth must therefore be a part of a broader concern for a more rapid rate of economic and social development in the developing countries.

In the final analysis, and in both the developed and developing worlds, the population issue is about humane and not about numbers. It is misleading and an injustice to the human condition to see people merely fit; consumers. Their well being and security old age security, declining child mortality, health care, and so on are the goal o(development Almost any activity that increases well-being and security lessens peoples' desires to have more children than they and national ecosystems can support.

THE POPULATION PERSPECTIVE

Growth in Numbers

Population growth accelerated in the middle of the 18th century with the advent of the Industrial Revolution and associated improvements in agriculture, not just in the regions that are more developed but elsewhere as well. The recent phase of deceleration started around 1950 with the sharp reduction in mortality rates in the developing countries.

Between 1950 and 1985. world population grew at an annual rate of 1.9 per cent, compared with 0.8 per cent in the half-century preceding 1950. population growth is now concentrated in the developing regions of Asia, Africa, and Latin America, which accounted for 85 per cent of the increase of global population since 1950. The processes of population growth are changing in most developing countries as birth and death rates fall. In the early 1950s, practically all developing countries had birth rates over 40 and death rates over 20, the major exception being the low death rates in Latin America. (These rates refer to the annual number of births and deaths per 1,000 population.) Today the situation is quite different:

- Thirty-two per cent of the people in the Third World live in countries - such as China and the Republic of Korea - with birth rates below 25 and death rates below 10.
- Forty-one per cent are in countries where birth rates have fallen, but not as much as death rates, and their populations are growing at around 2 per cent - doubling, in other words, every 34 years. Such countries include Brazil, India, Indonesia, and Mexico.
- The remaining 27 per cent live in countries, such as Algeria, Bangladesh. Iran, and Nigeria, where death rates have fallen slightly but birth rates remain high. Overall population growth is in the range of 2.5 to 3 per cent (doubling every 28 to 23 years), with even higher growth rates in some countries, such as Kenya.

In the industrial world, fertility rates have declined and the population is not growing rapidly. In fact, it has stabilized in many countries. Still, the population in North America, Europe, the USSR, and Oceania is expected to increase by 230 million by the year 2025. which is as many people as live in the United States today.

Table : World Population 1950-85: Key Facts

Size and Rates	1950	1960	1970	1980	1985
Total Population			(billions)		
World	2.5	3.0	3.7	4.4	4.8
More developed regions	0.83	0.94	1.05	1.14	1.17
Less developed regions	1.68	2.07	2.65	3.31	3.66
Annual Growth *			(per cent)		
World		1.8	2.0	1.9	1.7
More developed regions		1.3	1.0	0.8	0.6
Less developed regions		2.1	2.5	2.3	2.0
Urban Population			(per cent)		
World	29	34	37	40	41
More developed regions	54	67	67	70	72
Less developed regions	17	22	25	29	31

* Data are for growth over previous decade or, for last column, over previous five years.

Source: Department of International Economic and Social Affairs, **World Population Prospects: Estimates and Projections as Assessed in 1984** (New York: UN, 1986)

The acceleration of population growth in the Third World and the decline in fertility levels in industrial countries are (changing age distribution patterns radically. In developing countries, the young predominate. In 1900, 39 per cent of developing country populations were younger than 15; the figure for industrialized countries was only 23 per cent. Yet in these countries, the proportion of the elderly is growing. Those 65 or older accounted for 11 per cent of the population in 1980; in developing countries, they represented only 4 per cent. Thus in the industrial world, relatively fewer people of working age will bear the burden of supporting relatively larger numbers of older people. A changing age structure helps to set patterns of future population growth. The large number of young people in developing countries means large numbers of future parents, so that even if each person produces fewer children. The total number of births will continue to increase. Population growth can continue to grow for some decades after fertility rates decline to the 'replacement level' of slightly over two children on average per couple. Thus in many nations, high population growth over the next few generations are assured.

Population projections indicate an increase in global population from 4.8 billion in 1985 to 6.1 billion by 2000, and to 8.2 billion by 2025 More than 90 pet cent of this increase is expected in developing regions. Large differences exist among countries in these areas, and the momentum of population growth is higher in Africa than in Latin America or Asia. In some developing countries, such as China, population growth rates are already well below 2 per cent and are expected to fall below 1 per cent by the beginning of the next century. Reflecting the 'momentum' of population growth, long term UN projections show that at the global level:

- if replacement-level fertility is reached in 2010, global population will stabilize at 7.7 billion by 2060;
- if this rate is reached in 2025, population will stabilize at 10.2 billion by 2095;
- if. however, the rate is reached only in 2065, global population in 2100 would be 14.2 billion.

These projections show that the world has real choices. Policies to bring down fertility rates could make a difference of billions to the global population next century. The greater part of the differences between the three variants is accounted for by South Asia. Africa, and Latin America. Hence much depends on the effectiveness of population policies in these regions.

Changes in Mobility

The number of people in Europe, Japan. North America. and the Soviet Union quintupled between 1750 and 1950. and these regions' share in world population increased sharply over thin period. By the latter part of the 19th century, there was growing concern about population pressures in Europe. Migration to North America, Australia, and New Zealand helped to some extent. At its peak between 1881 and 1910, permanent emigration absorbed nearly 20 per rent of the increase in population in Europe. Today, however, migration in not a major factor in determining population distribution among countries. Between 1970 and 1980 permanent emigration as a percentage of population increase fell to 4 per cent in Europe and was only 2.5 per cent in Latin America. The corresponding percentages in Asia and Africa were very much lower. Thus the option of emigration to new lands has not been and will not be a significant element in relieving demographic pressures in developing countries In effect, this reduces the time available to bring population into balance with resources. Within countries, populations are more mobile. Improved communications have enabled large movements of people. Sometimes as a natural response to the growth of economic opportunities in different places. Some governments have actively encouraged migration from densely to sparsely settled areas. A more recent phenomenon is the flight of 'ecological refugees' from areas of environmental degradation.

Table : Current and Projected Population Size and Growth Rates*

	Population			Annual Growth Rate		
	1985	2000	2025	1950 to 1985	1985 to 2000	2000 to 2025
Region	(billion)			(per cent)		
World	4.8	6.1	8.2	1.9	1.6	1.2
Africa	0.66	0.87	1.62	2.6	3.1	2.5
Latin America	0.41	0.55	0.78	2.6	2.0	1.4
Asia	2.82	3.55	4.54	2.1	1.6	1.0
North America	0.26	0.30	0.35	1.3	0.8	0.6
Europe	0.49	0.51	0.52	0.7	0.3	0.1
USSR	0.28	0.31	0.37	1.7	0.8	0.6
Oceania	0.02	0.03	0.04	1.9	1.4	0.9

* Medium-variant projections.

Source: Department of International Economic and Social Affairs, **World Population Prospects; Estimates and Projections as Assessed in 1984** (New York: UN, 1986).

Much of the movement is from countryside to city. (See Chapter 9.) In 1985. some 40 per cent of the world's population lived in cities; the magnitude of the urban drift can be seen in the fact that since 1950, the increase in urban population has been larger than the increase in rural population both in percentage and in absolute terms. This shift is most striking in developing countries, where the number of city-dwellers quadrupled during this period.

Improved Health and Education

Improvements in the health and education of all, but especially of women and in conjunction with other social changes that raise the status of women, can have a profound effect in bringing down population growth rates. In an initial period, however, better health care means that more babies live to reproduce and that women reproduce over longer time spans.

Table : Health Indicators

	Life Expectancy at Birth		Infant Mortality Rates	
Region	1950-55 (years)	1980-85	1960-65 (deaths per 1,000 live births)	1980-85
World	49.9	64.6	117	81
Africa	37.5	49.7	157	114
Asia	41.2	57.9	133	87
South America	52.3	64.0	101	64
North America	64.4	71.1	43	27
Europe	65.3	73.2	37	16
USSR	61.7	70.9	32	25
Oceania	61.0	67.6	55	39

Source: WCED, based on data in World Resources Institute / International Institute for Environment and Development, **World Resources 1986** (New York: Basic Books, 1986).

The 'health status' of a society is a complex concept that cannot be measured easily. Two widely available indicators that reflect at least some aspects of a given society's health are life expectancy and infant mortality rates. These statistics suggest that health has improved virtually everywhere; and, at least with regard to these two indicators, the gap between industrial and developing regions has narrowed. Many factors can increase life expectancy and reduce mortality rates: two are worth emphasizing. First, although generally speaking national wealth buys national health, some relatively poor nations and areas, such as China, Sri Lanka, and the Indian state of Kerala, have achieved remarkable success in lowering infant mortality and improving health through increases in education, especially of women; the establishment of primary health clinics; and other health care programmes. Second, the principal reductions in mortality rates in the industrial world came about before the advent of modern drugs; they were due to improved nutrition, housing, and hygiene. The recent gains in developing countries have also been largely due to public health programmes, particularly for the control of communicable diseases.

Education is another key dimension of 'population quality'. The past few decades have seen a great expansion of educational facilities in virtually all countries. In terms of school enrolment, literacy rates, the growth in technical education, and the development of scientific skills, much progress has been achieved.

A POLICY FRAMEWORK

Excessive population growth diffuses the fruits of development over increasing numbers instead of improving living standards in many developing countries: a reduction of current growth rates is an imperative for sustainable development. The critical issues are the balance between population size and available resources and the rate of population growth in relation to the capacity of the economy to provide for the basic needs of the population, not just today but for generations. Such a long-term view is necessary because attitudes to fertility rarely change rapidly and because, even after fertility starts declining, past increases in population impart a momentum of growth as people reach child-bearing age. However a nation proceeds towards the goals of sustainable development and lower fertility levels, the two are intimately linked and mutually reinforcing.

Measures to influence population size cannot be effective in isolation from other environment/development issues. The number, density, movement, and growth rate of a population cannot be influenced in the short run if these efforts are being overwhelmed by adverse patterns of development in other areas. Population policies must have a broader focus than controlling numbers: Measures to improve the quality of human resources in terms of health, education, and social development are as important.

A first step may be for governments to abandon the false division between 'productive' or 'economic' expenditures and 'social' expenditures. Policymakers must realize that spending on population activities and on other efforts to raise human potential is crucial to a nation's economic and productive activities and to achieving sustainable human progress - the end for which a government exists.

Managing Population Growth

Progress in population policies is uneven. Some countries with serious population problems have comprehensive policies. Some go no further than the promotion of family planning. Some do not do even that.

A population policy should set out and pursue broad national demographic goals in relation to other socio-economic objectives. Social and cultural factors dominate all others in affecting fertility. The most important of these is the roles women play in the family, the economy, and the society at large Fertility rates fall as women's employment opportunities outside the home and farm, their access to education, and their age at marriage all rise. Hence policies meant to lower fertility rates not only must include economic incentives and disincentives, but must aim to improve the position of women in society. Such policies should essentially promote women's rights.

Poverty breeds high rates of population growth: Families poor in income, employment, and social security need children first to work and later to sustain elderly parents. Measures to provide an adequate livelihood for poor households, to establish and enforce minimum-age child labour laws, and to provide publicly financed social security will all lower fertility rates. Improved public health and child nutrition programmes that bring down infant mortality rates - so parents do not need 'extra' children as insurance against child death - can also help to reduce fertility levels.

Table : Male and Female Enrolment Ratios, by Region, 1960 and 1982

	Male		Female	
Region	1960	1982	1960	1982
World				
First Level	92.2	101.3	7.1	87.3
Second Level	31.3	53.3	23.1	42.5
Africa				
First Level	56.2	89.2	32.0	72.1
Second Level	7.3	29.6	2.9	19.5
Latin America and Caribbean				
First Level	75.0	106.2	71.2	103.3
Second Level	14.9	46.6	13.6	48.5
North America				
First Level	117.4	119.7	116.4	119.9
Second Level	69.4	85.4	71.4	86.6
Asia				
First Level	94.9	100.1	63.1	79.9
Second Level	29.3	49.3	16.6	32.9
Europe and USSR				
First Level	103.4	105.4	102.7	104.5
Second Level	46.5	76.2	44.6	81.3
Oceania				
First Level	102.2	102.9	100.7	98.9
Second Level	53.8	71.1	58.8	72.0

Note; The figures are percentages of appropriate groups receiving a given level of education. As many older children are in primary school percentages can be over 100.

Source: WCED, based on data in UNESCO, 'A Summary Statistical Review of Education in the World, 1960-1982, Paris, July 1984.

All these programmes are effective in bringing down birth rates only when their benefits are shared by the majority. Societies that attempt to spread the benefits of economic growth to a wider segment of the population may do better at lowering birth rates than societies with both faster and higher levels of economic growth but a less even sharing of the benefits of that growth. Thus developing-country population strategies must deal not only with the population variable as such but also with the underlying social and economic conditions of underdevelopment. They must be multifaceted campaigns: to strengthen social, cultural, and economic motivations for couples to have small families and. through family planning programmes, to provide to all who want them the education, technological means, and services required to control family size.

Family planning services in many developing countries suffer by being isolated from other programmes that reduce fertility and even from those that increase motivation to use such services. They remain separate both in design and implementation from such fertility-related programmes as nutrition, public health, mother and child care, and preschool education that take place in the same area and that are often funded by the same agency.

Such services must therefore be integrated with other efforts to improve access to health care and education. The clinical support needed for most modern contraceptive methods makes family planning services heavily dependent on the health system. Some governments have successfully combined population programme: with health, education, and rural development projects, and implemented them as part of major socio-economic programmes in villages or regions. This integration increases motivation, improves access, and raises the effectiveness of investments in family planning.

Only about 1.5 per cent of official development aid now goes for population assistance. Regrettably, some donor countries have cut back on their assistance for multilateral population programmes and so weakened them; this must be reversed.

Zimbabwe is one nation that has successfully integrated its family planning efforts not only with its rural health services but also with efforts to improve women's abilities to organize group activities and earn money through their own labour. The government's initial efforts were aimed less at limiting population growth than at assisting women to space births in the interests of mother and child health and at helping infertile women to bear children. But gradually families have begun to use the contraceptives made available for child spacing as a way to limit fertility. Zimbabwe now leads sub-Saharan Africa in the use of modern contraceptive methods.

Managing Distribution and Mobility

Population distribution across a country's different regions is influenced by the geographical spread of economic activity and opportunity. Most countries are committed in theory to balancing regional development, but are rarely able to do this in practice. Governments able to spread employment opportunities throughout their nations and especially through their countrysides will thus limit the rapid and often uncontrolled growth of one or two cities. China's effort to support village-level industries in the countryside is perhaps the most ambitious of this sort of national programme.

Migration from countryside to city is not in itself a bad thing; it is part of the process of economic development and diversification. The issue is not so much the overall rural urban shift but the distribution of urban growth between large metropolitan cities and smaller urban settlements.

A commitment to rural development implies more attention to realizing the development potential of all regions, particularly those that are ecologically disadvantaged. This would help reduce migration from these areas due to lack of opportunities. But governments should avoid going too far in the opposite direction, encouraging people to cove into sparsely populated areas such as tropical moist forests, where the land may not be able to provide sustainable livelihoods.

Demographic phenomena constitute the heart of the African Development problematique. They are the data that lead most analysts to project a continuing and deepening crisis in Africa. There is no doubt of the imperative and urgent need for a far reaching population policy to be adopted and vigorously implemented by African governments.

One issue of relevance that requires further research is the use of the tax system as a means for controlling population growth and discouraging rural-urban migration. To slow down population growth, should families without children be given a tax incentive or tax break? Should a tax penalty be imposed for each child after a fixed number of children, considering that the tax system has not solved the population migration problem?

From Liability to Asset

When a population exceeds the carrying capacity of the available resources, it can become a liability in efforts to improve people's welfare. But talking of population just as numbers glosses over an important point: People are also a creative resource, and this creativity is an asset societies must tap. To nurture and enhance that asset, people's physical well-being must be improved through better nutrition, health care, and so on. And education must be provided to help them become more capable and creative, skilful, productive, and better able to deal with day-to-day problems. All this has to be achieved through access to and participation in the processes of sustainable development.

Improving Health

We in Asia, I feel, want to have an equilibrium between the spiritual and material life. I noticed that you have tried to separate religion from the technological side of life. Is that not exactly, the mistake in the West in developing technology, without ethics, without religion? If that is the case, and we have the chance to develop a new direction, should we not advise the group on technology to pursue a different kind of technology which has as its base not only the rationality, but also the spiritual aspect? Is this a dream or is this something we cannot avoid?

Good health is the foundation of human welfare and productivity. Hence a broad-based health policy is essential for sustainable development. In the developing world, the critical problems of ill health are closely related to environmental conditions and development problems.

Malaria is the most important parasitic disease in the tropics, and its prevalence is closely related to wastewater disposal and drainage. Large dams and irrigation systems have led to sharp increases in the incidence of schistosomiasis (snail fever) in many areas. Inadequacies in water supply and sanitation are direct causes of other widespread and debilitating diseases such as diarrhoeas and various worm infestations.

Though much has been achieved in recent years, 1.7 billion people lack access to clean water, and 1.2 billion to adequate sanitation. Many diseases can be controlled not just through therapeutic interventions but also through improvements in rural water supply, sanitation, and health education. In this sense, they really require a developmental solution. In the developing world, the number of water taps nearby is a better indication of the health of a community than is the number of hospital beds.

Other examples of links between development, environmental conditions, and health include air pollution and the respiratory illnesses it brings, the impact of housing conditions on the spread of tuberculosis, the effects of carcinogens and toxic substances, and the exposure to hazards in the workplace and elsewhere.

Many health problems arise from the nutritional deficiencies that occur in virtually all developing countries, but most acutely in low-income areas. Most malnutrition is related to a shortage of calories or protein or both, but some diets also lack specific elements and compounds, such as iron and iodine. Health will be greatly improved in low-income areas by policies that lead to the production of more of the cheap foods the poor traditionally eat - coarse grains and root crops.

These health, nutrition, environment, and development links imply that health policy cannot be conceived of purely in terms of curative or preventive medicine, or even in terms of greater attention to public health. Integrated approaches are needed that reflect key health objectives in areas such as food production; water supply and sanitation: industrial policy, particularly with regard to safety and pollution; and the planning of human settlements. Beyond this, it is necessary to identify vulnerable groups and their health risks and to ensure that the socio-economic factors that underlie these risks are taken into account in other areas of development policy.

Hence. WHO's 'Health for All' strategy should be broadened far beyond the provision of medical workers and clinics, to cover health-related interventions in all development activities. Moreover, this broader approach must be reflected in institutional arrangements to coordinate all such activities effectively. Within the narrower area of health care, providing primary health care facilities and making sure that everyone has the opportunity to use them are appropriate starting points. Maternal and child health care are also particularly important. The critical elements here are relatively inexpensive and can have a profound impact on health and well-being. An organized system of trained birth attendants, protection against tetanus and other childbirth infections, and supplemental feeding can dramatically reduce maternal mortality. Similarly, low-cost programmes to assure immunization, teach and supply oral dehydration therapy against diarrhoeas, and encourage breast-feeding (which in turn can reduce fertility) can increase child survival rates dramatically.

Health care must be supplemented by effective health education. Some parts of the Third World may soon face growing numbers of the illnesses associated with life-styles in industrial nations - cancer and heart disease especially. Few developing nations can afford the expensive treatment required for the latter diseases, and should begin efforts now to educate their citizens on the dangers of smoking and of high-fat diets.

A rapid spread of acquired immune deficiency syndrome (AIDS) in both developed and developing nations could drastically alter all countries' health priorities. AIDS is threatening to kill millions of people and disrupt the economies of many countries. Governments should overcome any lingering shyness and rapidly educate their people about this syndrome and about the ways in which it is spread. International cooperation on research and the handling of the disease is essential.

Another major health problem with international ramifications is the increase in drug addiction. It is a problem closely linked to organized crime in the production of drugs, in large-scale international traffic in these drugs, and in the networks for distribution. It distorts the economy in many poor producing areas and destroys people the world over.

International cooperation is essential in tackling this scourge. Some countries have to deploy considerable financial resources to halt the production and traffic in narcotics and to promote crop diversification and rehabilitation schemes in the producing areas, which are generally impoverished. To sustain their efforts, greater international assistance is essential

Most medical research focuses on pharmaceuticals, vaccines. and other technological interventions for disease management. Much of this research is directed at the diseases of industrialized countries, as their treatment accounts for a substantial part of the sales of pharmaceutical companies. More research is urgently needed on the environmentally related tropical diseases that are the major health problem in the Third World, This research should focus not merely on new medicines, but also on public health measures to control these diseases. Existing arrangements for international collaboration on tropical disease research should be greatly strengthened.

Education and communication are vitally important in order to impress each individual of his or her responsibility regarding the healthy future of the earth. The best way for students to recognize that their action can make a difference is to have projects organized by the school or community on which the students can work. Once convinced that they can help, people tend to change both their attitude and their behaviour. New attitudes towards the environment will be reflected in decisions at home and in corporate boardrooms around the world.

Broadening Education

Human resource development demands knowledge and skills to help people improve their economic performance. Sustainable development requires changes in values and attitudes towards environment and development - indeed, towards society and work at home, on farms, and in factories. The world's religions could help provide direction and motivation in forming new values that would stress individual and joint responsibility towards the environment and towards nurturing harmony between humanity and environment. Education should also be geared towards making people more capable of dealing with problems of overcrowding and excessive population densities, and better able to improve what could be called 'social carrying capacities'. This is essential to prevent ruptures in the social fabric, and schooling should enhance the levels of tolerance and empathy required for living in a crowded world. Improved health, lower fertility, and better nutrition will depend on greater literacy and social and civic responsibility. Education can induce all these, and can enhance a society's ability to overcome poverty, increase incomes, improve health and nutrition, and reduce family size.

The investment in education and the growth in school enrolment during the past few decades are signs of progress. Access to education is increasing and will continue to do so. Today almost all the world's boys are getting some form of primary education. In Asia and Africa, however, enrolment rates for girls are much lower than for boys at all levels. A large gap also exists between developed and developing countries in enrolment rates beyond primary schools.

UN projections of enrolment rates for the year 2000 suggest a continuation of these trends. Thus despite the growth in primary education, illiteracy will continue to rise in terms of sheer numbers: there will be more than 900 million people unable to read and write at the end of the century. By then, girls' enrolment rates are still expected to be below the current rates for boys in Asia. As for secondary education, developing countries are not expected to attain even the 1960 industrial country levels by the year 2000.

Sustainable development requires that these trends be corrected. The main task of education policy must be to make literacy universal and to close the gaps between male and female enrolment rates. Realizing these goals would improve individual productivity and earnings, as well as personal attitudes to health, nutrition, and child-bearing. It can also instill a greater awareness of everyday environmental factors. Facilities for education beyond primary school must be expanded to improve skills necessary for pursuing sustainable development. A major problem confronting many countries is the widespread unemployment and the unrest that it leads to. Education has often been unable to provide the skills needed for appropriate employment. This is evident in the large numbers of unemployed people who have been trained for white-collar employment in swelling urban populations. Education and training should also be directed towards the acquisition of practical and vocational skills, and particularly towards making people more self-reliant. All this should be supported by efforts to nurture the informal sector and the participation of community organizations.

Providing facilities is only the beginning. Education must be improved in quality and in relevance to local conditions. In many areas, it should be integrated with children's participation in farm work, a process requiring flexibility in the school system. It should impart knowledge relevant for the proper management of local resources. Rural schools must teach about local soils, water, and the conservation of both, about deforestation and how the community and the individual can reverse it. Teachers must be trained and the curriculum developed so that students learn about the agricultural balance sheet of an area.

Most people base their understanding of environmental processes and development on traditional beliefs or on information provided by a conventional education. Many thus remain ignorant about ways in which they could improve traditional production practices and better protect the natural resource base. Education should therefore provide comprehensive knowledge, encompassing and cutting across the social and natural sciences and the humanities, thus providing insights on the interaction between natural and human resources, between development and environment.

Environmental education should be included in and should run throughout the other disciplines of the formal education curriculum at all levels - to foster a sense of responsibility for the state of the environment and to teach students how to monitor, protect, and improve it. These objectives cannot be achieved without the involvement of students in the movement for a better environment, through such things as nature clubs and special interest groups. Adult education, on-the-job training, television, and other less formal methods must be used to reach out to as wide a group of individuals as possible, as environmental issues and knowledge systems now change radically in the space of a lifetime. A critical point of intervention is during teacher training. The attitudes of teachers will be key in increasing understanding of the environment and its. links with development. To enhance the awareness and capabilities of teachers in this area, multilateral and bilateral agencies must provide support for the relevant curriculum development in teacher training institutions, for the preparation of teaching aids, and for other similar activities. Global awareness could be fostered by encouraging contacts among teachers from different countries, for instance in specialized centres set up for this purpose.

When the government took our land in the valley of Rio Doce, they wanted to give us another place somewhere else. But the State, the government will never understand that we do not have another place to go.

The only possible place for the Krenak people to live and to re-establish our existence, to speak to our Gods, to speak to our nature, to weave our lives is where our God created us. It is useless for the government to put us in a very beautiful place, in a very good place with a lot of hunting and a lot of fish. The Krenak people, we continue dying and we die insisting that there is only one place for us to live.

My heart does not become happy to see humanity's incapacity. I have no pleasure at all to come here and make these statements. We can no longer see the planet that we live upon as if it were a chess-board where people just move things around. We cannot consider the planet as something isolated from the cosmic.

We are not idiots to believe that there is possibility of life for us outside of where the origin of our life is. Respect our place of living, do not degrade our living condition, respect this life. We have no arms to cause pressure, the only thing we have is the right to cry for our dignity and the need to live in our land.

Empowering Vulnerable Groups

The processes of development generally lead to the gradual integration of local communities into a larger social and economic framework. But some communities - so-called indigenous or tribal peoples - remain isolated because of such factors as physical barriers to communication or marked differences in social and cultural practices. Such groups are found in North America, in Australia, in the Amazon Basin, in Central America, in the forests and hills of Asia, in the deserts of North Africa, and elsewhere.

The isolation of many such people has meant the preservation of a traditional way of life in close harmony with the natural environment. Their very survival has depended on their ecological awareness and adaptation. But their isolation has also meant that few of them have shared in national economic and social development; this may be reflected in their poor health, nutrition, and education.

With the gradual advance of organized development into remote regions, these groups are becoming less isolated. Many live in areas rich in valuable natural resources that planners and 'developers' want to exploit, and this exploitation disrupts the local environment so as to endanger traditional ways of life. The legal and institutional changes that accompany organized development add to such pressures.

Growing interaction with the larger world is increasing the vulnerability of these groups, since they are often left out of the processes of economic development. Social discrimination, cultural barriers, and the exclusion of these people from national political processes makes these groups vulnerable and subject to exploitation. Many groups become dispossessed and marginalized, and their traditional practices disappear. They become the victims of what could be described as cultural extinction.

These communities are the repositories of vast accumulations of traditional knowledge and experience that links humanity with its ancient origins. Their disappearance is a loss for the larger society, which could learn a great deal from their traditional skills in sustainably managing very complex ecological systems. It is a terrible irony that as formal development reaches more deeply into rain forests, deserts, and other isolated environments, it tends to destroy the only cultures that have proved able to thrive in these environments.

The starting point for a just and humane policy for such groups is the recognition and protection of their traditional rights to land and the other resources that sustain their way of life - rights they may define in terms that do not fit into standard legal systems. These groups' own institutions to regulate rights and obligations are crucial for maintaining the harmony with nature and the environmental awareness characteristic of the traditional way of life. Hence the recognition of traditional rights must go hand in hand with measures to protect the local institutions that enforce responsibility in resource use. And this recognition must also give local communities a decisive voice in the decisions about resource use in their area.

Protection of traditional rights should be accompanied by positive measures to enhance the well-being of the community in ways appropriate to the group's life-style. For example, earnings from traditional activities can be increased through the introduction of marketing arrangements that ensure a fair price for produce, but also through steps to conserve and enhance the resource base and increase resource productivity.

Those promoting policies that have an impact on the lives of an isolated, traditional people must tread a fine line between keeping them in artificial, perhaps unwanted isolation and wantonly destroying their life-styles. Hence broader measures of human resource development are essential. Health facilities must be provided to supplement and improve traditional practices; nutritional deficiencies have to be corrected, and educational institutions established. These steps should precede new projects that open up an area to economic development. Special efforts should also be made to ensure that the local community can derive the full benefit of such projects, particularly through jobs.

In terms of sheer numbers, these isolated, vulnerable groups are small. But their marginalization is a symptom of a style of development that tends to neglect both human and environmental considerations. Hence a more careful and sensitive consideration of their interests is a touchstone of a sustainable development policy.

8

Towards Sustainable Development

Sustainable development is development that meets the needs of the present without compromising the ability of future generations to meet their own needs. It contains within it two key concepts:

- the concept of 'needs', in particular the essential needs of the world's poor, to which overriding priority should be given; and
- the idea of limitations imposed by the state of technology and social organization on the environment's ability to meet present and future needs.

Thus the goals of economic and social development must be defined in terms of sustainability in all countries - developed or developing, market-oriented or centrally planned. Interpretations will vary, but must share certain general features and must flow from a consensus on the basic concept of sustainable development and on a broad strategic framework for achieving it.

Development involves a progressive transformation of economy and society. A development path that is sustainable in a physical sense could theoretically be pursued even in a rigid social and political setting. But physical sustainability cannot be secured unless development policies pay attention to such considerations as changes in access to resources and in the distribution of costs and benefits. Even the narrow notion of physical sustainability implies a concern for social equity between generations, a concern that must logically be extended to equity within each generation.

THE CONCEPT OF SUSTAINABLE DEVELOPMENT

The satisfaction of human needs and aspirations in the major objective of development. The essential needs of vast numbers of people in developing countries for food, clothing, shelter, jobs - are not being met, and beyond their basic needs these people have legitimate aspirations for an improved quality of life. A world in which poverty and inequity are endemic will always be prone to ecological and other crises. Sustainable development requires meeting the basic needs of all and extending to all the opportunity to satisfy their aspirations for a better life.

Living standards that go beyond the basic minimum are sustainable only if consumption standards everywhere have regard for long-term sustainability. Yet many of us live beyond the world's ecological means, for instance in our patterns of energy use. Perceived needs are socially and culturally determined, and sustainable development requires the promotion of values that encourage consumption standards that are within the bounds of the ecological possible and to which all can reasonably aspire.

Meeting essential needs depends in part on achieving full growth potential, and sustainable development clearly requires economic growth in places where such needs are not being met. Elsewhere, it can be consistent with economic growth, provided the content of growth reflects the broad principles of sustainability and non-exploitation of others. But growth by itself is not enough. High levels of productive activity and widespread poverty can coexist, and can endanger the environment. Hence sustainable development requires that societies meet human needs both by increasing productive potential and by ensuring equitable opportunities for all.

An expansion in numbers can increase the pressure on resources and slow the rise in living standards in areas where deprivation is widespread. Though the issue is not merely one of population size but of the distribution of resources, sustainable development can only be pursued if demographic developments are in harmony with the changing productive potential of the ecosystem.

A society may in many ways compromise its ability to meet the essential needs of its people in the future - by overexploiting resources, for example. The direction of technological developments may solve some immediate problems but lead to even greater ones. Large sections of the population may be marginalized by ill-considered development.

Settled agriculture, the diversion of watercourses, the extraction of minerals, the emission of heat and noxious gases into the atmosphere, commercial forests, and genetic manipulation are all examples or human intervention in natural systems during the course of development. Until recently, such interventions were small in scale and their impact limited. Today's interventions are more drastic in scale and impact, and more threatening to life-support systems both locally and globally. This need not happen. At a minimum, sustainable development must not endanger the natural systems that support life on Earth: the atmosphere, the waters, the soils, and the living beings.

Growth has no set limits in terms of population or resource use beyond which lies ecological disaster. Different limits hold for the use of energy, materials, water, and land. Many of these will manifest themselves in the form of rising costs and diminishing returns, rather than in the form of any sudden loss of a resource base. The accumulation of knowledge and the development of technology can enhance the carrying capacity of the resource base. But ultimate limits there are, and sustainability requires that long before these are reached, the world must ensure equitable access to the constrained resource and reorient technological efforts to relieve the presume.

A communications gap has kept environmental, population, and development assistance groups apart for too long, preventing us from being aware of our common interest and realizing our combined power. Fortunately, the gap is closing. We now know that what unites us is vastly more important than what divides us.

We recognize that poverty, environmental degradation, and population growth are inextricably related and that none of these fundamental problems can be successfully addressed in isolation. We will succeed or fail together. Arriving at a commonly accepted definition of 'sustainable development' remains a challenge for all the actors in the development process.

MAKING COMMON CAUSE

Economic growth and development obviously involve changes in the physical ecosystem. Every ecosystem everywhere cannot be preserved intact. A forest may be depleted in one part of a watershed and extended elsewhere, which is not a bad thing if the exploitation has been planned and the effects on soil erosion rates, water regimes, and genetic losses have been taken into account. In general, renewable resources like forests and fish stocks need not be depleted provided the rate of use is within the limits of regeneration and natural growth. But most renewable resources are part of a complex and interlinked ecosystem, and maximum sustainable yield must be defined after taking into account system-wide effects of exploitation.

As for non-renewable resources, like fossil fuels and minerals, their use reduces the stock available for future generations. But this does not mean that such resources should not be used. In general the rate of depletion should take into account the criticality of that resource, the availability of technologies tor minimizing depletion, and the likelihood of substitutes being available. Thus land should not be degraded beyond reasonable recovery. With minerals and fossil fuels, the rate of depletion and the emphasis on recycling and economy of use should be calibrated to ensure that the resource does not run out before acceptable substitutes are available. Sustainable development requires that the rate of depletion of non renewable resources should foreclose as few future options as possible.

Development tends to simplify ecosystems and to reduce their diversity of species. And species, once extinct, are not renewable. The loss of plant and animal species can greatly limit the options of future generations; so sustainable development requires the conservation of plant and animal species.

So-called free goods like air and water are also resources. The raw materials and energy of production processes are only partly converted to useful products. The rest comes out as wastes. Sustainable development requires that the adverse impacts on the quality of air, water, and other natural elements are minimized so as to sustain the ecosystem's overall integrity.

In essence, sustainable development is a process of change in which the exploitation of resources, the direction of investments, the orientation of technological development; and institutional change are all in harmony and enhance both current and future potential to meet human needs and aspirations.

EQUITY AND THE COMMON INTEREST

Sustainable development has been described here in general terms. How are individuals in the real world to be persuaded or made to act in the common interest? The answer lies partly in education, institutional development, and law enforcement. But many problems of resource depletion and environmental stress arise from disparities in economic and political power. An industry may get away with unacceptable levels or air and water pollution because the people who bear the brunt of it are poor and unable to complain effectively. A forest may be destroyed by excessive felling because the people living there have no alternatives or because timber contractors generally have more influence then forest dwellers.

Ecological interactions do not respect the boundaries of individual ownership and political jurisdiction. Thus:

- In a watershed, the ways in which a farmer up the slope uses land directly affect run-off on farms downstream.
- the irrigation practices, pesticides, and fertilizers used on one farm affect the productivity of neighbouring ones, especially among small farms.
- The efficiency of a factory boiler determines its rate of emission of soot and noxious chemicals and affects all who live and work around it.
- The hot water discharged by a thermal power plant into a river or a local sea affects the catch of all who fish locally.

Traditional social systems recognized some aspects of this interdependence and enforced community control over agricultural practices and traditional rights relating to water, forests, and land. This enforcement of the 'common interest' did not necessarily impede growth and expansion though it may have limited the acceptance and diffusion of technical innovations.

Local interdependence has, if anything, increased because of the technology used in modern agriculture and manufacturing. Yet with this surge of technical progress, the growing 'enclosure' of common lands, the erosion of common rights in forests and other resources, and the spread of commerce and production for the market, the responsibilities for decision making are being taken away from both groups and individuals. This shift is still under way in many developing countries.

If the desert is growing, forest disappearing, malnutrition increasing, and people in urban areas living in very bad conditions, it is not because we are lacking resources but the kind of policy implemented by our rulers, by the elite group. Denying people rights and peoples' interests is pushing us to a situation where it is only the poverty that has a very prosperous future in Africa. And it is our hope that your Commission, the World Commission, will not overlook these problems of human rights in Africa and will put emphasis on it. Because it is only free people, people who have rights, who are mature and responsible citizens, who then participate in the development and in the protection of the environment.

It is not that there is one set of villains and another of victims. All would be better off if each person took into account the effect oœ" his or her acts upon others. But each is unwilling to assume that others will behave in this socially desirable fashion, and hence all continue to pursue narrow self-interest. Communities or governments can compensate for this isolation through laws, education, taxes, subsidies, and other methods. Well-enforced laws and strict liability legislation can control harmful side effects. Most important, effective participation in decision-making processes by local communities can help them articulate and effectively enforce their common interest.

Interdependence is not simply a local phenomenon. Rapid growth in production has extended it to the international plane, with both physical and economic manifestations. There are growing global and regional pollution effects, such as in the more than 200 international river basins and the large number of shared seas.

The enforcement of common interest often suffers because areas of political jurisdiction and areas of impact do not coincide. Energy policies in one jurisdiction cause acid precipitation in another. The fishing policies of one state affect the fish catch of another. No supranational authority exists to resolve such issues, and the common interest can only be articulated through international cooperation.

In the same way, the ability of a government to control its national economy is reduced by growing international economic interactions. For example, foreign trade in commodities makes issues of carrying capacities and resource scarcities an international concern. If economic power and the benefits of trade were more equally distributed, common interests would be generally recognized. But the gains from trade are unequally distributed, and patterns of trade in, say, sugar affect not merely a local sugar-producing sector, but the economies and ecologies of the many developing countries that depend heavily on this product.

The search for common interest would be less difficult if all development and environment problems had solutions that would leave everyone better off. This is seldom the case, and there are usually winners and losers. Many problems arise from inequalities in access to resources. An inequitable landowner ship structure can lead to overexploitation of resources in the smallest holdings, with harmful effects on both environment and development. Internationally, monopolistic control over resources can drive those who do not share in them to excessive exploitation of marginal resources. The differing capacities of exploiters to commandeer 'free' goods - locally, nationally, and internationally - is another manifestation of unequal access to resources. 'Losers' in environment/ development conflicts include those who suffer more than their fair share of the health, property, and ecosystem damage costs of pollution. As a system approaches ecological limits, inequalities sharpen. Thus when a watershed deteriorates, poor farmers suffer more because they cannot afford the same anti-erosion measures as richer farmers. When urban air quality deteriorates, the poor, in their more vulnerable areas, suffer more health damage than the rich, who usually live in more pristine neighbourhoods. When mineral resources become depleted, late-comers to the industrialization process lose the benefits of low-cost supplies. Globally, wealthier nations are better placed financially and technologically to cope with the effects of possible climatic change.

Hence, our inability to promote the common interest in sustainable development is often a product of the relative neglect of economic and social justice within and amongst nations.

STRATEGIC IMPERATIVES

The world must quickly design strategies that will allow nations to move from their present, often destructive, processes of growth and development onto sustainable development paths. This will require policy changes in all countries, with respect both to their own development and to their impacts on other nations' development possibilities. Critical objectives for environment and development policies that follow from the concept of sustainable development include:

- reviving growth;
- changing the quality of growth;
- meeting essential needs for jobs, food, energy, water, and sanitation;
- ensuring a sustainable level of population;
- conserving and enhancing the resource base:
- reorienting technology and managing risk; and
- merging environment and economics in decision making.

Reviving Growth

As indicated earlier, development that is sustainable has to address the problem of the large number of people who live in absolute poverty - that is, who are unable to satisfy even the most basic of their needs. Poverty reduces people's capacity to use resources in a sustainable manner; it intensifies pressure on the environment. Most such absolute poverty is in developing countries; in many, it has been aggravated by the economic stagnation of the 1980s. A necessary but not a sufficient condition for the elimination of absolute poverty is a relatively rapid rise in per capita incomes in the Third World. It is therefore essential that the stagnant or declining growth trends of this decade be reversed.

While attainable growth rates will vary, a certain minimum is needed to have any impact on absolute poverty. It seems unlikely that, taking developing countries as a whole, these objectives can be accomplished with per capita income growth of under 3 per cent. Given current population growth rates, this would require overall national income growth of around 5 per cent a year in the developing economies of Asia, 5.5 per cent in Latin America, and 6 per cent in Africa and West Asia.

Are these orders of magnitude attainable? The record in South and East Asia over the past quarter-century and especially over the last five years suggests that 5 per cent annual growth can be attained in most countries, including the two largest, India and China. In Latin America, average growth rates on the order of 5 per cent were achieved during the 1960s and 1970s, but fell well below that in the first half of this decade, mainly because of the debt crisis. A revival of Latin American growth depends on the resolution of this crisis. In Africa, growth rates during the 1960s and 1970s were around 4-4.5 per cent, which at current rates of population growth would mean per capita income growth of only a little over 1 per cent. Moreover, during the 1980s, growth nearly halted and in two-thirds of the countries per capita income declined. Attaining a minimum level of growth in Africa requires the correction of short-term imbalances, and also the removal of deep-rooted constraints on the growth process.

Growth must be revived in developing countries because that is where the links between economic growth, the alleviation of poverty, and environmental conditions operate most directly.

Yet developing countries are part of an interdependent world economy; their prospects also depend on the levels and patterns of growth in industrialized nations. The medium-term prospects for industrial countries are for growth of 3-4 per cent, the minimum that international financial institutions consider necessary if these countries are going to play a part in expanding the world economy. Such growth rates could be environmentally sustainable if industrialized nations can continue the recent shifts in the content of their growth towards less material- and energy-intensive activities and the improvement of their efficiency in using materials and energy.

GROWTH, REDISTRIBUTION, AND POVERTY

The poverty line is that level of income below which an individual or household cannot afford on a regular basis the necessities of life. The percentage of the population below that line will depend on per capita national income and the manner in which it is distributed. How quickly can a developing country expect to eliminate absolute poverty? The answer will vary from country to country, but much can be learned from a typical case.

Consider a nation in which half the population lives below the poverty line and where the distribution of household incomes is as follows: the top one-fifth of households have 50 per cent of total income, the next fifth have 20 per cent, the next fifth have 14 per cent, the next fifth have 9 per cent, and the bottom fifth have just 7 per cent. This is a fair representation of the situation in many low-income developing countries.

In this case, if the income distribution remains unchanged, per capita national income would have to double before the poverty ratio drops from 50 to 10 per cent. If income is redistributed in favour of the poor, this reduction can occur sooner. Consider the case in which 25 per cent of the incremental income of the richest one-fifth of the population is redistributed equally to the others. The assumptions here about redistribution reflect three judgements. First, in most situations redistributive policies can only operate on increases in income. Second, in low-income developing countries the surplus that can be skimmed off for redistribution is available only from the wealthier groups. Third, redistributive policies cannot be so precisely targeted that they deliver benefits only to those who are below the poverty line, so some of the benefits will accrue to those who are just a littlc above it.

The number of years required to bring the poverty ratio down from 50 to 10 per cent ranges from:

- o 18-24 years if per capita income grows at 3 per cent,
- o 26-36 years if it grown at 2 per cent, and
- o 51-70 years if it grows only at 1 per cent.

In each case, the shorter time is associated with the redistribution of 25 per cent of the incremental income of the richest fifth of the population and the longer period with no redistribution.

So with per capita national income growing only at 1 pcr cent a year, the time required to eliminate absolute poverty would stretch well into the next century. If, however, the aim is to ensure that the world is well on its way towards sustainable development by the beginning of the next century, it is necessary to aim at a minimum of 3 per cent per capita national income growth and to pursue vigorous redistributive policies.

As industrialized nations use less materials and energy, however, they will provide smaller markets for commodities and minerals from the developing nations. Yet if developing nations focus their efforts upon eliminating poverty and satisfying essential human needs, then domestic demand will increase for both agricultural products and manufactured goods and some services. Hence the very logic of sustainable development implies an internal stimulus to Third World growth.

Nonetheless, in large numbers of developing countries markets are very small; and for all developing countries high export growth, especially of non-traditional items, will also be necessary to finance imports, demand for which will be generated by rapid development. Thus a reorientation of international economic relations will be necessary for sustainable development.

Changing the quality of Growth

Sustainable development involves more than growth. It requires a change in the content of growth, to make it less Material- and energy-intensive and more equitable in its impact. These changes are required in all countries as part of a package of measures to maintain the stock of ecological capital, to improve the distribution of income, and to reduce the degree of vulnerability to economic crises.

The process of economic development must be more soundly based upon the realities of the stock of capital that sustains it. This is rarely done in either developed or developing countries. For example, income from forestry operations is conventionally measured in terms of the value of timber and other products extracted, minus the costs of extraction. The costs of regenerating the forest are not taken into account, unless money is actually spent on such work. Thus figuring profits from logging rarely takes full account of the losses in future revenue incurred through degradation of the forest. Similar incomplete accounting occurs in the exploitation of other natural resources, especially in the case of resources that are not capitalized in enterprise or national accounts: air, water, and soil. In all countries, rich or poor, economic development must take full account in its measurements of growth of the improvement or deterioration in the stock of natural resources.

Income distribution is one aspect of the quality of growth, as described in the preceding section, and rapid growth combined with deteriorating income distribution may be worse than slower growth combined with redistribution in favour of the poor. For instance, in many developing countries the introduction of large-scale commercial agriculture may produce revenue rapidly, but may also dispossess a large number of small farmers and make income distribution more inequitable. In the long run, such a path may not be sustainable; it impoverishes many people and can increase pressures on the natural resource base through overcommercialized agriculture and through the marginalization of subsistence farmers. Relying more on smallholder cultivation may be slower at first, but more easily sustained over the long term.

People have acquired, often for the first time in history, both an idea of their relative poverty and a desire to emerge from it and improve the quality of their lives. As people advance materially, and eat and live better, what, were once luxuries tend to be regarded as necessities. The net result is that the demand for food, raw materials, and power increases to an even greater degree than the population. As demand increases, a greater and greater strain is put on the finite area of the world's land to produce the products needed.

Economic development is unsustainable if it increases vulnerability to crises. A drought may force farmers to slaughter animals needed for sustaining production in future years. A drop in prices may cause farmers or other producers to overexploit natural resources to maintain incomes. But vulnerability can be reduced by using technologies that lower production risks, by choosing institutional options that reduce market fluctuations, and by building up reserves, especially of food and foreign exchange. A development path that combines growth with reduced vulnerability is more sustainable than one that does not.

Yet it is not enough to broaden the range of economic variables taken into account. Sustainability requires views of human needs and well-being that incorporate such non-economic variables as education and health enjoyed for their own sake, clean air and water, and the protection of natural beauty. It must also work to remove disabilities from disadvantaged groups, many of whom live in ecologically vulnerable areas, such as many tribal groups in forests, desert nomads, groups in remote hill areas, and indigenous peoples of the Americas and Australasia.

Changing the quality of growth requires changing our approach to development efforts to take account of all of their effects. For instance, a hydropower project should not be seen merely as a way of producing more electricity; its effects upon the local environment and the livelihood of the local community must be included in any balance sheets. Thus the abandonment of a hydro project because it will disturb a rare ecological system could be a measure of progress, not a setback to development. Nevertheless, in some cases, sustainability considerations will involve a rejection of activities that are financially attractive in the short run.

Economic and social development can and should be mutually reinforcing. Money spent on education and health can raise human productivity. Economic developments can accelerate social development by providing opportunities for underprivileged groups or by spreading education more rapidly.

Meeting Essential Human Needs

The satisfaction of human needs and aspirations is so obviously an objective of productive activity that it may appear redundant to assert its central role in the concept of sustainable development. All too often poverty is such that people cannot satisfy their needs for survival and well-being even if goods and services are available. At the same time, the demands of those not in poverty may have major environmental consequences.

The principal development challenge is to meet the needs and aspirations of an expanding developing world population. The most basic of all needs is for a livelihood: that is, employment. Between 1985 and 2000 the labour force in developing countries will increase by nearly 800 million, and new livelihood opportunities will have to be generated for 60 million persons every year. The pace and pattern of economic development have to generate sustainable work opportunities on this scale and at a level of productivity that would enable poor households to meet minimum consumption standards.

More food is required not merely to feed more people but to attack undernourishment. For the developing world to eat, person for person, as well as the industrial world by the year 2000, annual increases of 5.0 per cent in calories and 5.8 per cent in proteins are needed in Africa; of 3.4 and 4.0 per cent, respectively, in Latin America; and of 3.5 and 4.5 per cent in Asia. Foodgrains and starchy roots are the primary sources of calories, while proteins are obtained primarily from products like milk, meat, fish, pulses, and oil-seeds.

Though the focus at present is necessarily on staple foods, the projections given above also highlight the need for a high rate of growth of protein availability. In Africa, the task is particularly challenging given the recent declining per capita food production and the current constraints on growth. In Asia and Latin America, the required growth rates in calorie and protein consumption seem to be more readily attainable. But increased food production should not be based on ecologically unsound production policies and compromise long-term prospects for food security.

Energy is another essential human need, one that cannot be universally met unless energy consumption patterns change. The most urgent problem is the requirements of poor Third World households, which depend mainly on fuelwood. By the turn of the century, 3 billion people may live in areas where wood is cut faster than it grows or where fuelwood is extremely scarce. Corrective action would both reduce the drudgery of collecting wood over long distances and preserve the ecological base. The minimum requirements for cooking fuel in most developing countries appear to be on the order of 250 kilogrammes of coal equivalent per capita per year. This is a fraction of the household energy consumption in industrial countries. In the developing world, mostly in the Third World, we realize that the main problem we have is that we do not have employment opportunities, and most of these people who are unemployed move from rural areas and they migrate into the cities and those who remain behind always indulge in processes - for example charcoal burning - and all this leads to deforestation. So maybe the environmental organizations should step in and look for ways to prevent this kind of destruction. The linked basic needs of housing, water supply, sanitation, and health care are also environmentally important. Deficiencies in these areas are often visible manifestations of environmental stress. In the Third World, the failure to meet these key needs is one of the major causes of many communicable diseases such as malaria, gastro-intestinal infestations, cholera, and typhoid. Population growth and the drift into cities threaten to make these problems worse. Planners must find ways of relying more on supporting community initiatives and self-help efforts and on effectively using low-cost technologies.

Ensuring a Sustainable Level of Population

The sustainability of development is intimately linked to the dynamics of population growth. The issue, however, is not simply one of global population size. A child born in a country where levels of material and energy use are high places a greater burden on the Earth's resources than a child born in a poorer country. A similar argument applies within countries. Nonetheless, sustainable development can be pursued more easily when population size is stabilized at a level consistent with the productive capacity of the ecosystem.

In industrial countries, the overall rate of population growth is under 1 per cent, and several countries have reached or are approaching zero population growth. The total population of the industrialized world could increase from its current 1.2 billion to about 1.4 billion in the year 2025.

The greater part of global population increase will take place in developing countries, where the 1985 population of 3.7 billion may increase to 6.8 billion by 2025. The Third World does not have the option of migration to 'new' lands, and the time available for adjustment is much less than industrial countries had. Hence the challenge now is to quickly lower population growth rates, especially in regions such as Africa, where these rates are increasing.

Birth rates declined in industrial countries largely because of economic and social development. Rising levels of income and urbanization and the changing role of women all played important roles. Similar processes are now at work in developing countries. These should be recognized and encouraged. Population policies should be integrated with other economic and social development programmes female education, health care, and the expansion of the livelihood base of the poor. But time is short, and developing countries will also have to promote direct measures to reduce fertility, to avoid going radically beyond the productive potential to support their populations. In fact, increased access to family planning services is itself a form of social development that allows couples, and women in particular, the right to self-determination.

Population growth in developing countries will remain unevenly distributed between rural and urban areas. UK projections suggest that by the first decade of the next century, the absolute size of rural populations in most developing countries will start declining. Nearly 90 per cent of the increase in the developing world will take place in urban areas, the population of which in expected to rise from 1.15 billion in 1985 to 3.25 million in 2025. The increase will be particularly marked in Africa and, to a lesser extent, in Asia.

Developing-country cities are growing much faster than the capacity of authorities to cope. Shortages of housing, water, sanitation, and mass transit are widespread. A growing proportion of city-dwellers live in slums and shanty towns, many of them exposed to air and water pollution and to industrial and natural hazards. Further deterioration is likely, given that most urban growth will take place in the largest cities. Thus more manageable cities may be the principal gain from slower rates of population growth.

Urbanization is itself part of the development process. The challenge is to manage the process so as to avoid a severe deterioration in the quality of life. Thus the development of smaller urban centres needs to be encouraged to reduce pressures in large cities. Solving the impending urban crisis will require the promotion of self-help housing and urban services by and for the poor, and a more positive approach to the role of the informal sector, supported by sufficient funds for water supply, sanitation, and other services.

Conserving and Enhancing the Resource Base

If needs are to be met on a sustainable basis the Earth's natural resource base must be conserved and enhanced. Major changes in policies will be needed to cope with the industrial world's current high levels of consumption, the increases in consumption needed to meet minimum standards in developing countries, and expected population growth. However, the case for the conservation of nature should not rest only with development goals. It is part of our moral obligation to other living beings and future generations.

Pressure on resources increases when people lack alternatives. Development policies must widen people's options for earning a sustainable livelihood, particularly for resource-poor households and in areas under ecological stress. In a hilly area, for instance, economic self-interest and ecology can be combined by helping farmers shift from grain to tree crops by providing them with advice, equipment, and marketing assistance. Programmes to protect the incomes of farmers, fishermen, and foresters against short-term price declines may decrease their need to overexploit resources.

The conservation of agricultural resources is an urgent task because in many parts of the world cultivation has already been extended to marginal lands, and fishery and forestry resources have been overexploited. These resources must be conserved and enhanced to meet the needs of growing populations. Land use in agriculture and forestry must be based on a scientific assessment of land capacity, and the annual depletion of topsoil, fish stock, or forest resources must not exceed the rate of regeneration.

The pressures on agricultural land from crop and livestock production can be partly relieved by increasing productivity. But short-sighted, short-term improvements in productivity can create different forms of ecological stress, such as the loss of genetic diversity in standing crops, salinization and alkalization of irrigated lands, nitrate pollution of ground-water, and pesticide residues in food. Ecologically more benign alternatives are available. Future increases in productivity, in both developed and developing countries, should be based on the better controlled application of water and agrochemicals, as well as on more extensive use of organic manures and non-chemical means of pest control. These alternatives can be promoted only by an agricultural policy based on ecological realities. In the case of fisheries and tropical forestry, we rely largely on the exploitation of the naturally available stocks. The sustainable yield from these stocks may well fall short of demand. Hence it will be necessary to turn to methods that produce more fish, fuelwood, and forest products under controlled conditions. Substitutes for fuelwood can be promoted.

The ultimate limits to global development are perhaps determined by the availability of energy resources and by the biosphere's capacity to absorb the by-products of energy use. These energy limits may be approached far sooner than the limits imposed by other material resources. First, there are the supply problems: the depletion of oil reserves, the high cost and environmental impact of coal mining, and the hazards of nuclear technology. Second, there are emission problems, most notably acid pollution and carbon dioxide build up leading to global warming.

We live from this forest they want to destroy. And we want to take this opportunity of having so many people here gathered with the same objective in mind to defend our habitat, the conservation of forest, of tropical forest.

In my area, we have about 14-16 native products that we extract from the forest, besides all the other activities we have. So I think this must be preserved. Because it is not only with cattle, not only with pasture lands, and not only with highways that we will be able to develop the Amazon.

When they think of falling trees, they always think of building roads and the roads bring destruction under a mask called progress. Let us put this progress where the lands have already been deforested, where it is idle of labour and where we have to find people work, and where we have to make the city grow. But let us leave those who want to live in the forest, who want to keep it as it is.

Some of these problems can be met by increased use of renewable energy sources. But the exploitation of renewable sources such as fuelwood and hydropower also entails ecological problems. Hence sustainability requires a clear focus on conserving and efficiently using energy.

Industrialized countries must recognize that their energy consumption is polluting the biosphere and eating into scarce fossil fuel supplies. Recent improvements in energy efficiency and a shift towards less energy-intensive sectors have helped limit consumption. But the process must be accelerated to reduce per capita consumption and encourage a shift to non polluting sources and technologies. The simple duplication in the developing world of industrial countries' energy use patterns is neither feasible nor desirable. Changing these patterns for the better will call for new policies in urban development, industry location, housing design, transportation systems, and the choice of agricultural and industrial technologies.

Non-fuel mineral resources appear to pose fewer supply problems. Studies done before 1960 that assumed an exponentially growing demand did not envisage a problem until well into the next century since then, world consumption of most metals has remained nearly constant, which suggests that the exhaustion of non-fuel minerals is even more distant. The history of technological developments also suggests that industry can adjust to scarcity through greater efficiency in use, recycling, and substitution. More immediate needs include modifying the pattern of world trade in minerals to allow exporters a higher share in the value added from mineral use, and improving the access of developing countries to mineral supplies, as their demands increase.

Indigenous peoples are the base of what I guess could be called the environmental security system. We are the gate-keepers of success or failure to husband our resources. For many of us, however, the last few centuries have meant a major loss of control over our lands and waters. We are still the first to know about changes in the environment, but we are now the last to be asked or consulted.

We are the first to detect when the forests are being threatened, as they are under the slash and grab economics of this country. And we are the last to be asked about the future of our forests. We are the first to feel the pollution of our waters, as the Ojibway peoples of my own homelands in northern Ontario will attest. And, of course, we are the last to be consulted about how, when, and where developments should take place in order to assure continuing harmony for the seventh generation.

The most we have learned to expect is to be compensated, always too late and too little. We are seldom asked to help avoid the need for compensation by lending our expertise and our consent to development.

The prevention and reduction of air and water pollution will remain a critical task of resource conservation. Air and water quality come under pressure from such activities as fertilizer and pesticide use, urban sewage, fossil fuel burning, the use of certain chemicals, and various other industrial activities. Each of these is expected to increase the pollution load on the biosphere substantially, particularly in developing countries. Cleaning up after the event is an expensive solution. Hence all countries need to anticipate and prevent these pollution problems, by, for instance, enforcing emission standards that reflect likely long-term effects, promoting low-waste technologies, and anticipating the impact of new products, technologies, and wastes.

Reorienting Technology and Managing Risk

The fulfilment of all these tasks will require the reorientation of technology the key link between humans and nature. First, the capacity for technological innovation needs to be greatly enhanced in developing countries so that they can respond more effectively to the challenges of sustainable development. Second, the orientation of technology development must be changed to pay greater attention to environmental factors.

The technologies of industrial countries are not always suited or easily adaptable to the socio-economic and environmental conditions of developing countries. To compound the problem, the bulk of world research and development addresses few of the pressing issues facing these countries, such as arid-land agriculture or the control of tropical diseases. Not enough is being done to adapt recent innovations in materials technology, energy conservation, information technology, and biotechnology to the needs of developing countries. These gaps must be covered by enhancing research, design, development, and extension capabilities in the Third World.

In all countries, the processes of generating alternative technologies, upgrading traditional ones, and selecting and adapting imported technologies should be informed by environmental resource concerns. Most technological research by commercial organizations is devoted to product and process innovations that have market value. Technologies are needed that produce 'social goods', such as improved air quality or increased product life, or that resolve problems normally outside the cost calculus of individual enterprises, such as the external costs of pollution or waste disposal.

The role of public policy is to ensure, through incentives and disincentives, that commercial organizations find it worthwhile to take fuller account of environmental factors in the technologies they develop. Publicly funded research institutions also need such direction, and the objectives of sustainable development and environmental protection must be built into the mandates of the institutions that work in environmentally sensitive areas.

The development of environmentally appropriate technologies is closely related to questions of risk management. Such systems as nuclear reactors, electric and other utility distribution networks, communication systems, and mass transportation are vulnerable if stressed beyond a certain point. The fact that they are connected through networks tends to make them immune to small disturbances but more vulnerable to unexpected disruptions that exceed a finite threshold. Applying sophisticated analyses of vulnerabilities and past failures to technology design, manufacturing standards, and contingency plans in operations can make the consequences of a failure or accident much less catastrophic.

The best vulnerability and risk analysis has not been applied consistently across technologies or systems. A major purpose of large system design should be to make the consequences of failure or sabotage less serious. There is thus a need for new techniques and technologies - as well as legal and institutional mechanisms - for safety design and control, accident prevention, contingency planning, damage mitigation, and provision of relief.

Environmental risks arising from technological and developmental decisions impinge on individuals and areas that have little or no influence on those decisions. Their interests must be taken into account. National and international institutional mechanisms are needed to assess potential impacts of new technologies before they are widely used, in order to ensure that their production, use, and disposal do not overstress environmental resources. Similar arrangements are required for major interventions in natural systems, such as river diversion or forest clearance. In addition, liability for damages from unintended consequences must be strengthened and enforced.

Merging Environment and Economics in Decision Making

The common theme throughout this strategy for sustainable development is the need to integrate economic and ecological considerations in decision making. They are, after all, integrated in the workings of the real world. This will require a change in attitudes and objectives and in institutional arrangements at every level.

Economic and ecological concerns are not necessarily in opposition. For example, policies that conserve the quality of agricultural land and protect forests improve the long-term prospects for agricultural development. An increase in the efficiency of energy and material use serves ecological purposes but can also reduce costs. But the compatibility of environmental and economic objectives is often lost in the pursuit of individual or group gains, with little regard for the impacts on others, with a blind faith in science's ability to find solutions, and in ignorance of the distant consequences of today's decisions. Institutional rigidities add to this myopia.

One important rigidity is the tendency to deal with one industry or sector in isolation, failing to recognize the importance of intersectoral linkages. Modern agriculture uses substantial amounts of commercially produced energy and large quantities of industrial products. At the same time, the more traditional connection - in which agriculture is a source of raw materials for industry - is being diluted by the widening use of synthetics. The energy-industry connection is also changing, with a strong tendency towards a decline in the energy intensity of industrial production in industrial countries. In the Third World, however, the gradual shift of the industrial base towards the basic material producing sectors is leading to an increase in the energy intensity of industrial production.

These inter sectoral connections create patterns of economic and ecological interdependence rarely reflected in the ways in which policy is made. Sectoral organizations tend to pursue sectoral objectives and to treat their impacts on other sectors as side effects, taken into account only if compelled to do so. Hence impacts on forests rarely worry those involved in guiding public policy or business activities in the fields of energy, industrial development, crop husbandry, or foreign trade. Many of the environment and development problems that confront us have their roots in this sectoral fragmentation of responsibility. Sustainable development requires that such fragmentation be overcome.

The issues that have been brought forward here, I think, are wide-ranging and maybe you know, maybe you don't know, the answers to all those issues. But at least by hearing all those questions, stories, all these expressions that have been put forward, at least you could have some idea.

You don't know the answers nor the solutions, but you could suggest the way to solve many problems and this is by suggesting either to governments, or the UN, or international agencies, to solve any problem the best way: that is to include those with direct interests in it. The beneficiaries, as well as the victims of any development issue should be included, should be heard.

Sustainability requires the enforcement of wider responsibilities for the impacts of decisions. This requires changes in the legal and institutional frameworks that will enforce the common interest. Some necessary changes in the legal framework start from the proposition that an environment adequate for health and well-being is essential for all human beings including future generations. Such a view places the right to use public and private resources in its proper social context and provides a goal for more specific measures.

The law alone cannot enforce the common interest. It principally needs community knowledge and support, which entails greater public participation in the decisions that affect the environment. This is best secured by decentralizing the management of resources upon which local communities defend, and giving these communities an effective say over the use f these resources. It will also require promoting citizens' initiatives, empowering people's organizations, and strengthening local democracy.

Some large-scale projects, however, require participation on a different basis. Public inquiries and hearings on the development and environment impacts can help greatly in drawing attention to different points of view. Free access to relevant information and the availability of alternative sources of technical expertise can provide an informed basis for public discussion. When the environmental impact of a proposed project is particularly high, public scrutiny of the case should be mandatory and, wherever feasible, the decision should be subject to prior public approval, perhaps by referendum.

It has not been too difficult to push the environment lobby of the North and the development lobby of the South together. And there is now in fact a blurring of the distinction between the two, so they are coming to have a common consensus around the theme of sustainable development.

The building blocks are there. Environmental concern is common to both sides. Humanitarian concern is common to both sides. The difference lies in the methods of each and the degree to which each side tries to achieve its own economic interest through the development assistance process.

The time is right for bridging this gap for some very pragmatic political reasons. First of all, the people of the North do not want to see their taxes wasted. Secondly, they do not want to see growing poverty, and they obviously care for the environment, be it the environment of the North, where they live, or of the South. And the majority of people in the South do not want short-term overpass solutions.

In effect, there is a political community of interest, North and South, in the concept of sustainable development that you can build upon.

Changes are also required in the attitudes and procedures of both public and private-sector enterprises. Moreover, environmental regulation must move beyond the usual menu of safety regulations, zoning laws, and pollution control enactments; environmental objectives must be built into taxation, prior approval procedures for investment and technology choice, foreign trade incentives, and all components of development policy.

The integration of economic and ecological factors into the law and into decision making systems within countries has to be matched at the international level. The growth in fuel and material use dictates that direct physical linkages between ecosystems of different countries will increase. Economic interactions through trade, finance, investment, and travel will also grow and heighten economic and ecological interdependence. Hence in the future, even more so than now, sustainable development requires the unification of economics and ecology in international relations, as discussed in the next chapter.

CONCLUSION

In its broadest sense, the strategy for sustainable development aims to promote harmony among human brings and between humanity and nature. In the specific context of the development and environment crises of the 1980s, which current national and international political and economic institutions have not and perhaps cannot overcome, the pursuit of sustainable development requires:

- a political system that secures effective citizen participation in decision making.
- an economic system that is able to generate surpluses and technical knowledge on a self-reliant and sustained basis
- a social system that provides for solutions for the tensions arising from disharmonious development.
- a production system that respects the obligation to preserve the ecological base for development,

- a technological system that can search continuously for new solutions,
- an international system that fosters sustainable patterns of trade and finance, and
- an administrative system that is flexible and has the capacity for self-correction.

These requirements are more in the nature of goals that should underlie national and international action on development. What matters is the sincerity with which these goals are pursued and the effectiveness with which departures from them are corrected

9

Food Security: Sustaining the Potential

The world produces more food per head of population today than ever before in human history. In 1985, it produced nearly 500 kilogrammes per head of cereals and root crops, the primary sources of food. Yet amid this abundance, more than 730 million people did not eat enough to lead fully productive working lives. There are places where too little is grown; there are places where large numbers cannot afford to buy food. And there are broad areas of the Earth, in both industrial and developing nations, where increases in food production are undermining the base for future production. The agricultural resources and the technology needed to feed growing populations are available. Much has been achieved over the past few decades. Agriculture does not lack resources; it lacks policies to ensure that the food is produced where it is needed and in a manner that sustains the livelihoods of the rural poor. He can meet this challenge by building on our achievements and devising new strategies for sustaining food and livelihood security.

ACHIEVEMENTS

Between 1950 and 1985, cereal production outstripped population growth, increasing from around 700 million tons to over 1,800 million tons, an annual growth rate of around 2.7 per cent. This increase helped to meet escalating demands for cereals caused by population growth and rising incomes in developing countries and by growing needs for animal feed in developed countries. Yet regional differences in performance have been large. As production has increased sharply in some regions and demand in others, the pattern of world trade in foods, especially cereals, has changed radically. North America exported barely 5 million tons of foodgrains yearly before the Second World War; it exported nearly 120 million tons during the 1980s. Europe's grain deficit is very much lower now. and the bulk of North American exports are to the USSR. Asia, and Africa. Three countries - China, Japan, and the USSR - took half the world exports in the early 1980s; much of the rest went to relatively wealthy developing countries, such as Middle Eastern oil exporters. Several poor agricultural countries, especially in sub-Saharan Africa, have become net importers of foodgrains. Still, although one-fourth of sub-Saharan Africa's population relied on imported grains in 1984, that region's imports have accounted for less than 10 per cent of world grain trade thus far in the 1980s.

Table : Two Decades of Agricultural Development

	Per Capita Food Production (Index 1961-64 = 100)		Per Capita Gross Cropped Area (Hectares)		Per Hectare Fertilizer use (kg.)	
	1961-64	1981-84	1964	1984	1964	1984
World	100	112	0.44	0.31	29.3	85.3
North America	100	121	1.05	0.90	47.3	93.2
Western Europe	100	131	0.11	0.25	114.4	124.1
Eastern Europe and USSR	100	128	0.84	0.71	30.4	122.1
Africa	100	88	0.74	0.35	1.8	9.7
Near East*	100	107	0.53	0.35	6.9	53.6
Far East**	100	116	0.10	0.20	4.4	45.4
Latin America	100	108	0.49	0.45	11.6	11.4
CPE's of Asia***	100	135	0.17	0.10	15.5	170.3

* An FAO grouping that includes West Asia plus Egypt, Libya and Sudan

** An FAO grouping that covers South and South-East Asia excluding the centrally planned economies of Asia.

*** An FAO grouping of Centrally Planned Economies of Asia which covers China, Kampuchea, North Korea. Mongolia and Vietnam.

Other foods besides grains are changing the patterns of world food demand and production. Demand for milk and meat is growing as incomes rise in societies that prefer animal protein. and much agricultural development in the industrialized nations has been devoted to meeting these demands. In Europe, meat production more than tripled between 1950 and 1984, and milk production nearly doubled. Meat production for exports increased sharply, particularly in the rangelands of Latin America and Africa. World meat exports have risen from around 2 million tons in 1950-52 to over 11 million tons in 1984.

To produce this milk and meat required in 1984 about 1.4 billion cattle and buffaloes, 1.6 billion sheep and goats, 800 million pigs, and a great deal of poultry - all of which weigh more than the people on the planet. Most of these animals graze or browse or are fed local plants collected for them. However, rising demands for livestock feedgrains led to sharp increases in the production of cereals such as corn, which accounted for nearly two-thirds of the total increase in grain production in North America and Europe between 1950 and 1985.

This unprecedented growth in food production has been achieved partly by an extension of the production base: larger cropped areas, more livestock, more fishing vessels, and so on. But most of it is due to a phenomenal rise in productivity. Population increases have meant a decline in the area of cropped land in most of the world in per capita terms. And as the availability of arable land has declined, planners and farmers have focused on increasing productivity. In the past 35 years this has been achieved by:

- using new seed varieties designed to maximize yields, facilitate multiple cropping, and resist disease;
- applying more chemical fertilizers, the consumption of which rose more than ninefold;
- using more pesticides and similar chemicals, the use of which increased thirty-two-fold; and
- increasing irrigated area, which more than doubled.

Global statistics mask substantial regional differences. The impacts of new technology have been uneven, and in some respects the agricultural technology gap has widened. For instance, average African foodgrain productivity declined in relation to European productivity from roughly one-half to about one-fifth over the past 35 years. Even in Asia, where new technology has spread rapidly, productivity in relation to European levels dropped. Similar 'technology gaps' have emerged between regions within countries.

The past few decades have seen the emergence of three broad types of food production systems, 'Industrial agriculture', capital- and input-intensive and usually large-scale, is dominant in North America, Western and Eastern Europe, Australia and New Zealand, and in some small areas in developing countries. 'Green Revolution agriculture' is found in uniform, resource-rich, often flat and irrigated areas in the agricultural heartlands of some developing countries. It is more widespread in Asia but is also found in parts of Latin America and North Africa. Though initially the new technologies may have favoured large farmers, they are today accessible to a growing number of small producers. 'Resource-poor agriculture' relies on uncertain rain rather than irrigation and is usually found in developing regions difficult to farm - drylands, highlands, and forests - with fragile soils. This includes most of sub-Saharan Africa and the remoter areas of Asia and Latin America. Here, per capita production has been declining and hunger is a critical problem. But today, all three systems of food production display signs of crises that endanger their growth.

SIGNS OF CRISIS

Agricultural policies in practically all countries have focused on output growth. Despite this, it has proved far more difficult to raise world agricultural output by a consistent 3 per cent a year in the mid-1980s than it was in the mid-1950s. Moreover, production records have been offset by the appearance

Box : Regional Perspectives on Agricultural Development

Africa

- a drop in per capita food output of about 1 per cent a year since the beginning of the 1970s

- a focus on cash crops and a growing dependence on imported food, fostered by pricing policies and foreign exchange compulsions
- major gaps in infrastructure for research, extension, input supply, and marketing
- degradation of the agricultural resource base due to desertification, droughts, and other processes
- large untapped potential of arable land, irrigation, and fertilizer use

West Asia and North Africa

- improvements in productivity due to better irrigation, the cultivation of high-yielding varieties, and higher fertilizer use
- limited arable land and considerable amounts of desert, making food self-sufficiency a challenge
- a need for controlled irrigation to cope with dry conditions South and East Asia
- increased production and productivity, with some countries registering grain surpluses
- rapid growth in fertilizer use in some countries and extensive development of irrigation
- government commitments to be self-reliant in food, leading to national research centres, development of high-yielding seeds, and the fostering of location-specific technologies
- little unused land, and extensive, unabated deforestation
- growing numbers of rural landless

Latin America

- declining food imports since 1980, as food production kept pace with population growth over the last decade
- government support in the form of research centres to develop high-yielding seeds and other technologies
- inequitable distribution of land
- deforestation and degradation of the agricultural resource base, fueled partly by foreign trade and debt crisis

- a huge land resource and high productivity potential, though most of the potentially arable land is in the remote, lightly populated Amazon Basin, where perhaps only 20 per cent of the land is suitable for sustainable agriculture

North America and Western Europe

- North America—the world's leading source of surplus foodgrain, though the rate of increase in output per hectare and in total productivity slowed in the 1970s
- subsidies for production that are ecologically and economically expensive
- depressing effect of surpluses on world markets and consequent impact on developing countries
- a resource base increasingly degraded through erosion, acidification, and water contamination
- in North America, some scope for future agricultural expansion in frontier areas that can be intensively farmed only at high cost

Eastern Europe and the Soviet Union

- food deficits met through imports, with the Soviet Union being the world's largest grain importer
- increased government investment in agriculture accompanied by eased farm distribution and organization to meet desires for food self-reliance, leading to production increases in meat and root crops
- pressures on agricultural resources through soil erosion. acidification, salinization, alkalization, and water contamination of linked economic and ecological crises: Industrialized countries are finding it increasingly difficult to manage their surplus food production, the livelihood base of millions of poor producers in developing countries is deteriorating, and the resource base for agriculture is under pressure virtually everywhere.

Impact of Subsidies

The food surpluses in North America and Europe result mainly from subsidies and other incentives that stimulate production even in the absence of demand. Direct or indirect subsidies, which now cover virtually the entire food cycle, have become extremely expensive. In the United States, the cost of farm support has grown from $2.7 billion in 1980 to $25.8 billion in 1986. In the EEC, such costs have risen from $6.2 billion in 1976 to $21.5 billion in 1986.

It has become politically more attractive, and usually cheaper, to export surpluses - often as food aid - rather than to store them. These heavily subsidized surpluses depress the international market prices of commodities such as sugar and have created severe problems for several developing countries whose economies are based on agriculture. Non-emergency food aid and low-priced imports also keep down prices received by Third World farmers and reduce the incentive to improve domestic food production.

The environmental consequences of a heavily subsidized production system are becoming evident within industrialized nations;

- lower productivity as soil quality declines due to intensive soil cultivation and overuse of chemical fertilizers and pesticides;
- the destruction of the countryside, through clearing of hedgerows, park: belts, and other protective cover and the levelling, occupation, and cultivation of marginal land and watershed protection areas; and
- nitrate pollution of ground-water aquifers due to the often subsidized overuse of nitrate fertilizers,

The financial, economic, and environmental effects of the current incentive systems are beginning to be questioned by many governments and groups, including farm organizations. A particular area of concern is the impact of these policies on developing countries. They depress international prices of products, such as rice and sugar, that are important exports for many developing countries and so reduce exchange earnings of developing countries. They increase the instability of world prices. And they discourage the processing of agricultural commodities in the producing countries.

It is in the interests of all, including the farmers, that the policies be changed. Indeed, in recent years some conservation-oriented changes have taken place and some subsidy systems have increasingly stressed the need to retire land from production. The financial and economic burden of subsidies must be reduced. The harm that these policies do to the agriculture of developing countries by disrupting world markets must be eliminated.

Neglect of the Small Producer

The new technology behind increases in agricultural productivity requires scientific and technological skills, a system for technology extension and other services for farmers, and commercial orientation in farm management. In many' parts of Asia, in particular, small farmers have shown a remarkable capacity to use new technology once they are given incentives and adequate financial and infrastructural support. Small cash-crop farmers in Africa have demonstrated the potential of the smallholder on that continent, and in the last few years successes have been recorded in food crops also. But ecologically disadvantaged areas and land-poor rural masses have not benefited from advances in technology and will not until governments are willing and able to redistribute land and resources, and give them the necessary support and incentives.

Agricultural support systems seldom take into account the special circumstances of subsistence farmers and herders. subsistence farmers cannot afford the high cash outlay of modern inputs. Many are shifting cultivators who do not have a clear title to the land they use. They may plant a variety of crops on one plot to meet their own needs, and are thus unable to use methods developed for large stands of a single crop.

Many herders are nomadic and difficult to reach with education, advice, and equipment. They, like subsistence farmers, depend on certain traditional rights, which are threatened by commercial developments. They herd traditional breeds, which are hardy but rarely highly productive.

Women farmers, though they play a critical role in food produotion, are often ignored by programmes meant to improve production. In Latin America, the Caribbean, and Asia they form a large agricultural labour force, while most of sub-Saharan Africa's food is grown by women. Yet almost all agricultural programmes tend to neglect the special needs of women farmers.

Degradation of the Resource Base

Short-sighted policies are leading to degradation of the agricultural resource base on almost every continent: soil erosion in North America: soil acidification in Europe; deforestation and desertification in Asia. Africa, and Latin America; and waste and pollution of water almost everywhere. Within 40-70 years, global warming may cause the flooding of important coastal production areas. Some of these effects arise from trends in energy use and industrial production. Some arise from the pressure of population on limited resources. But agricultural policies emphasizing increased production at the expense of environmental considerations have also contributed greatly to this deterioration.

Loss of Soil Resources

Increases in cropped areas in recent decades have often extended cultivation in marginal lands prone to erosion. By the late 1970s, soil erosion exceeded soil formation on about a third of U.S. cropland, much of it in the midwestern agricultural heartland. In Canada, soil degradation has been costing farmers $1 billion a year. In the USSR, the extension of cultivation to the so-called Virgin Lands was a major plank of agricultural policy, but now it is believed that much of this land is marginal. In India, soil erosion affects 25-30 per cent of the total land under cultivation. Without conservation measures, the total area of rainfed cropland in developing countries in Asia, Africa, and Latin America would shrink by 544 million hectares over the long term because of soil erosion and degradation, according to an FAO study.

Erosion makes soil less able to retain water, depletes it of nutrients, and reduces the depth available for the roots to take hold. Land productivity declines. Eroded topsoil is carried to rivers. lakes, and reservoirs, silts up ports and waterways, reduces reservoir storage capacity, and increases the incidence and severity of floods. Poorly designed and implemented irrigation systems have caused waterlogging, salinization, and alkalization of soils. FAO and UNESCO estimate that as much as half the world's irrigation schemes suffer in some degree from these problems. These estimates indicate that some 10 million hectares of irrigated land are being abandoned each year.

Soil degradation erodes the overall resource base for agriculture. The loss of croplands encourages farmers to overuse the remaining land and to move into forests and onto rangelands. Sustainable agriculture cannot be based on methods that mine and deplete the soil,

Impact of Chemicals

Chemical fertilizers and pesticides have played a large role in production increases since the Second World War, but clear warnings have been raised against over-reliance on them. The run-off of nitrogen and phosphates from excess use of fertilizers damages water resources, and such damage is spreading.

Using chemicals to control insects, pests, weeds, and fungi enhances productivity, but overuse threatens the health of humans and the lives of other species. Continuing, long-term exposure to pesticide and chemical residues in food, water, and even in the air is hazardous, particularly to children. A 1983 study estimated that approximately 10.000 people died each year in developing countries from pesticide poisoning and about 400,000 suffered acutely. The effects are not limited to the area where pesticides are used but travel through the food chain.

Commercial fisheries have been depleted, bird species endangered, and insects that prey on pests wiped out. The number of pesticide-resistant insect pest species worldwide has increased and many resist even the newest chemicals. The variety and severity of pest infestations multiply, threatening the productivity of agriculture in the areas concerned.

The use of agricultural chemicals is not in itself harmful. In fact, the level of use is still quite low in many regions. In these areas, response rates are high and the environmental consequences of residues are not yet a problem. Hence these regions would benefit by using more agrochemicals. However, the growth in the use of chemicals tends to be concentrated precisely where they may be doing more overall harm than good.

Pressure on Forests

Forests are crucial for maintaining and improving the productivity of agricultural land. Yet agricultural expansion, a growing world timber trade, and woodfuel demand have destroyed much forest cover. Although this destruction has occurred worldwide, today the greatest challenge is in developing countries, particularly in tropical forests.

Growing populations and the decreasing availability of arable land lead poor farmers in these countries to seek new land in forests to grow more food. Some government policies encourage the conversion of forests to pastures and others encourage large resettlement schemes in forests. There is nothing inherently wrong with clearing forests for farming, provided that the land is the best there is for new farming, can support the numbers encouraged to settle upon it, and is not already serving a more useful function, such as watershed protection. But often forests are cleared without forethought or planning.

Deforestation most severely disrupts mountainous areas and upland watersheds and the ecosystems that depend on them. The uplands influence precipitation, and the state of their soil and vegetation systems influence how this precipitation is released into the streams and rivers and onto the croplands of the plains below. The growing numbers and growing severity of both floods and droughts in many parts of the world have been linked to the deforestation of upland watersheds.

Advancing Deserts

Some 29 per cent of the earth's land area suffers slight, moderate, or severe desertification; an additional 6 per cent is classified as extremely severely desertified. In 1984, the world's drylands supported some 850 million people, of whom 230 million were on lands affected by severe desertification.

The process of desertification affects almost every region of the globe, but it is most destructive in the drylands of South America, Asia, and Africa; for these three areas combined. 18.5 per cent (870 million hectares) of productive lands are severely desertified. Of the drylands in developing countries. Africa's Sudano-Sahelian zones and, to a lesser extent, some countries south of this zone suffer the most. In their arid and semi-arid lands are to be found 80 per cent of the moderately affected and 85 per cent of the severely affected people.

Land permanently degraded to desert-like conditions continues to grow at an annual rate of 6 million hectares. Each year. 21 million additional hectares provide no economic return because of the spread of desertification. These trends are expected to continue despite some local improvements.

Desertification is caused by a complex mix of climatic and human effects. The human effects, over which we have more control, include the rapid growth of both human and animal populations, detrimental land use practices (especially deforestation), adverse terms of trade, and civil strife. The cultivation of cash crops on unsuitable rangelands has forced herders and their cattle onto marginal lands. The unfavourable international terms of trade for primary products and the policies of aid donors have reinforced pressures to encourage increasing cash-crop production at any cost.

A Plan of Action conceived by UNEP and drawn up at the 1977 UN Conference on Desertification has led to some slight, mainly local gains. Progress on the plan has been hampered by lack of financial support from the international community, by inadequacies of the regional organizations established to respond to the regional nature of the problem, and by the lack of involvement of grass-roots communities.

THE CHALLENGE

Food demand will increase as populations increase and their consumption patterns change. In the remaining years of this century, about 1.3 billion people will be added to the human family; rising incomes, however, may account for 30 to 40 per cent of the increased demand for food in developing countries and about 10 per cent in industrial nations. Thus over the next few decades, the global food system must be managed to increase food production by 3 to 4 per cent yearly.

Global food security depends not only on raising global production, but on reducing distortions in the structure of the world food market and on shifting the focus of food production to food-deficit countries, regions, and households. Many of the countries not growing enough food to feed themselves possess the largest remaining reservoirs of untapped agricultural resources. Latin America and sub-Saharan Africa have much unused land. although its quality and quantity vary greatly from nation to nation and much of it is ecologically vulnerable. The Soviet Union and parts of North America have significant amounts of frontier land suitable for agriculture; only Asia and Europe are truly land-starved.

Global food security also depends on ensuring that all people, even the poorest of the poor, can get food. While on the world scale this challenge requires a reappraisal of global food distribution, the task weighs more immediately and heavily on national governments. Inequitable distribution of production assets, unemployment, and underemployment are at the heart of the problem of hunger in many countries.

Rapid, sound agricultural development will mean not only more food but more opportunities for people to earn money to purchase food. Thus when countries with untapped agricultural resources provide food by importing more, they are effectively importing unemployment. By the same token, countries that are subsidizing food exports are increasing unemployment in food-importing countries. This marginalizes people, and marginalized people are forced to destroy the resource base to survive. Shifting production to food-deficit countries and to the resource-poor farmers within those countries is a way of securing sustainable livelihoods.

Conserving the agricultural resource base and livelihood security of the poor can be mutually supportive in three ways. First, secure resources and adequate livelihoods lead to good husbandry and sustainable management. Second, they ease rural-to-urban migration, stimulate agricultural production from resources that otherwise would be underused, and reduce the need for food to be produced elsewhere. Third, by combating poverty, they help to slow population growth.

Shifting the focus of production to food-deficit countries will also reduce pressures on agricultural resources in the industrialized market economies, enabling them to move towards more sustainable agricultural practices. Incentive structures can be changed so that instead of encouraging overproduction, they encourage farm practices that improve soil and water quality. Government budgets will be relieved of the burdens of storing and exporting surplus products.

This shift in agricultural production will be sustainable only if the resource base is secure. As indicated, this is far from the case today. Thus to achieve global food security, the resource base for food production must be sustained, enhanced, and, where it has been diminished or destroyed, restored.

STRATEGIES FOR SUSTAINABLE FOOD SECURITY

Food security requires more than good conservation programmes, which can be - and usually are - overridden and undermined by inappropriate agricultural, economic, and trade policies. Nor is it just a matter of adding an environmental component to programmes. Food strategies must take into account all the policies that bear upon the threefold challenge of shifting production to where it is most needed, of securing the livelihoods of the rural poor, and of conserving resources.

Government Intervention

Government intervention in agriculture is the rule in both industrial and developing countries, and it is here to stay. Public investment in agricultural research and extension services, assisted farm credit and marketing services, and a range of other support systems have all played parts in the successes of the last half-century. In fact, the real problem in many developing countries is the weakness of these systems.

Intervention has taken other forms as well. Many governments regulate virtually the entire food cycle - inputs and outputs, domestic sales, exports, public procurement, storage and distribution, price controls and subsidies - as well as imposing various land use regulations: acreage, crop variety, and so on.

In general, patterns of government intervention suffer three basic defects. First, the criteria that underlie the planning of these interventions lack an ecological orientation and are often dominated by short-term considerations. These criteria should discourage environmentally unsound farm practices and encourage farmers to maintain and improve their soils, forests, and waters.

The second defect is that agricultural policy tends to operate within a national framework with uniform prices and subsidies, standardized criteria for the provision of support services, indiscriminate financing of infrastructure investments, and so forth. Policies that vary from region to region are needed to reflect different regional needs, encouraging farmers to adopt practices that are ecologically sustainable in their own areas.

The importance of regional policy differentiation can be easily illustrated:

- Hill areas may require incentive prices for fruits and subsidized supplies of foodgrains to induce farmers to shift towards horticulture, which may be ecologically more sustainable.
- In areas prone to wind and water erosion, public intervention through subsidies and other measures should encourage farmers to conserve soil and water.
- Farmers on land over recharge areas for underground aquifers subject to nitrate pollution might be given incentives to maintain soil fertility and increase productivity by means other than nitrate fertilizers.

The third defect in government intervention lies in incentive structures. In industrialized countries, overprotection of farmers and overproduction represent the accumulated result of tax reliefs, direct subsidies, and price controls. Such policies are now studded with contradictions that encourage the degradation of the agricultural resource base and. in the long run, do more harm than good to the agricultural industry. Some governments now recognize this and are making efforts to change the focus of the subsidies from production growth to conservation.

On the other hand, in most developing countries the incentive structure is weak. Market interventions are often ineffective for lack of an organizational structure for procurement and distribution. Farmers are exposed to a high degree of uncertainty, and price support systems have often favoured the urban dweller or are limited to a few commercial crops, leading to distortions of cropping patterns that add to destructive pressures on the resource base. In some cases, price controls reduce the incentive to produce. What is required, in many cases, is nothing less than a radical attempt to turn the 'terms of trade' in favour of farmers through pricing policy and government expenditure reallocation.

Strengthening food security from a global point of view requires reducing incentives that force overproduction and non-competitive production in the developed market economies and enhancing those that encourage food production in developing countries. At the same time, these incentive structures must be redesigned to promote farming practices that conserve and enhance the agricultural resource base.

A Global Perspective

Trade in agricultural products tripled between 1950 and 1970; it has doubled since then. Yet, when it comes to farming, countries are at their most conservative, continuing to think mainly in local or national terms and concerned, above all, to protect their own farmers at the expense of competitors.

Shifting food production towards food-deficit countries will require a major shift in trading patterns. Countries must recognize that all parties lose through protectionist barriers, which reduce trade in food products in which some nations may have genuine advantage. They must begin by redesigning their trade, tax, and incentive systems using criteria that include ecological and economic sustainability and international comparative advantage.

The incentive-driven surpluses in developed market economies increase pressures to export these surpluses at subsidized prices or as non-emergency food aid. Donor and receiving countries should be responsible for the impacts of aid and use it for long-term objectives. It can be beneficially used in projects to restore degraded lands, build up rural infrastructure, and raise the nutrition level of vulnerable groups.

The Resource Base

Agricultural production can only be sustained on a long-term basis if the land, water, and forests on which it is based are not degraded. As suggested, a reorientation of public intervention will provide a framework for this. But more specific policies that protect the resource base are needed to maintain and even enhance agricultural productivity and the livelihoods of all rural dwellers.

Land Use

The initial task in enhancing the resource base will be to delineate broad land categories:

- enhancement areas, which are capable of sustaining intensive cropping and higher population and consumption levels;
- prevention areas, which by common consent should not be developed for intensive agriculture or. where developed, should be converted to other uses; and
- restoration areas, where land stripped of vegetative cover has either totally lost its productivity or had it drastically reduced.

Identifying land according to 'best use' criteria requires information that is not always available. Most industrial nations possess inventories and descriptions of their lands, forests, and waters that are detailed enough to provide a basis for delineating land categories. Few developing countries have such inventories, but they can and should develop them quickly using satellite monitoring and other rapidly changing techniques.

Selection of land for each category could be made the responsibility of a board or commission representing the interests involved, especially the poor and more marginalized segments of the population. The process must be public in character, with publicly agreed criteria that combine the best use approach with the level of development required to sustain livelihood. Classifying land according to best use will determine variations in infrastructure provision, support services, promotional measures, regulatory restrictions, fiscal subsidies, and other incentives and disincentives.

Lands identified as prevention areas should be denied supports and subsidies that would encourage their development for intensive agriculture. But such areas might well support certain ecologically and economically sustainable uses such as grazing. fuelwood plantations, fruit farming, and forestry. Those redesigning support systems and incentives should focus on a broader range of crops, including those that enhance grazing, soil and water conservation, and so on.

In vast areas today natural factors and land use practices have reduced productivity to a point too low to sustain even subsistence farming. Treatment of these areas must vary from site to site. Governments should give priority to establishing a national policy and multidisciplinary programmes and to creating or strengthening institutions to restore such areas. Where these already exist, thev should be better coordinated and designed. The UN Plan of Action to Combat Desertification, which is already in place, requires more support, particularly financial.

Restoration may require limits on human activities so as to permit the regeneration of vegetation. This can be difficult where there are large herds of animals or large numbers of people. for the agreement and participation of the local people are of the highest importance. The state, with the cooperation of those living locally, could protect these areas by declaring them national reserves. Where these areas are privately held, the state might wish either to purchase the land from the owners or to provide incentives for its restoration.

Water Management

Improvements in water management are essential to raise agricultural productivity and to reduce land degradation and water pollution. Critical issues concern the design of irrigation projects and the efficiency of water use. Where water is scarce, an irrigation project should maximize productivity per unit of water; where water is plentiful, it must maximize productivity per unit of land. But local conditions will dictate how much water can be used without damaging the soil. Salinization. alkalization, and waterlogging can be avoided by a more careful approach to drainage, maintenance, cropping patterns. the regulation of water quantities, and more rational water charges. Many of these objectives will be easier to realize in small-scale irrigation projects. But whether small or large, the projects must be designed with the abilities and aims of the participating farmers in mind, and then involve them in the management.

In some areas excessive use of ground-water is rapidly lowering the water table - usually a case where private benefits are being realized at society's expense. Where ground-water use exceeds the recharge capacity of local aquifers, regulatory or fiscal controls become essential. The combined use of ground and surface water can improve the timing of water availability and stretch limited supplies.

Alternatives to Chemicals

Many countries can and should increase yields by greater use of chemical fertilizers and pesticides, particularly in the developing world. But countries can also improve yields by helping farmers to use organic nutrients more efficiently. Hence governments must encourage the use of more organic plant nutrients to complement chemicals. Pest control must also be based increasingly on the use of natural methods. These strategies require changes in public policies, which now encourage the increased use of chemical pesticides and fertilizers. The legislative, policy, and research capacity for advancing non-chemical and less-chemical strategies must be established and sustained.

Chemical fertilisers and pesticides are heavily subsidized in many countries. These subsidies promote chemical use precisely in the more commercially oriented agricultural areas where their environmental damage may already outweigh any increases in productivity they bring. Hence different regions will require different policies to regulate and promote chemical use. Legislative and institutional frameworks for controlling agrochemicals must be greatly strengthened everywhere.

Industrialized countries must tighten controls on pesticide exports. Developing countries must possess the basic legislative and institutional instruments to manage the use of agricultural chemicals within their countries. And they will need technical and financial assistance to do so.

Forestry and Agriculture

Undisturbed forests protect watersheds, reduce erosion. offer habitats for wild species, and play key roles in climatic systems. They are also an economic resource providing timber, fuelwood, and other products. The crucial task is to balance the need to exploit forests against the need to preserve them.

Sound forest policies can be based only on an analysis of the capacity of the forests and the land under them to perform various functions. Such an analysis might lead to some forests being cleared for intensive cultivation, others for livestock; some forestland might be managed for increased timber production or agroforestry use and some left intact for watershed protection, recreation, or species conservation. The extension of agriculture into forest areas must be based on scientific classification of land capacities.

Programmes to preserve forest resources must start with the local people who are both victims and agents of destruction, and who will bear the burden of any new management scheme. They should be at the centre of integrated forest management, which is the basis of sustainable agriculture.

Such an approach would entail changes in the way governments set development priorities, as well as the evolution of greater responsibility to local governments and communities. Contracts covering forest use will have to be negotiated, or overall environmental sustainability of forest exploitation and overall environmental and ecosystem conservation. Prices for forest products need to reflect the true resource value of the goods.

Box : Natural Systems of Nutrient Supply and Peat Control

- Crop residues and farmyard manure are potential sources of soil nutrients.
- Organic wastes reduce run-off, increase the take-up of other nutrients, and improve soil's water-holding and erosion-resistance capacity.
- Using farmyard manure, especially in conjunction with intercropping and crop rotation, can greatly lower production costs.
- Overall systems efficiency is enhanced if manure or vegetable biomass is anaerobically digested in biogas plants, yielding energy for cooking and to run pumps, motors, or electric generators.
- Natural systems of biological nitrogen fixation through the use of certain annual plants, trees, and micro-organisms have a high potential.
- Integrated pest management (IPM) reduces the need for agrochemicals. improves a country's balance of payments. releases foreign exchange for other development projects, and creates jobs where they are most needed.
- IPM requires detailed information about pests and their natural enemies, seed varieties tailored to resist pests, integrated cropping patterns, and farmers who support the approach and are willing to modify farm practices to adopt it.

Portions of forests may be designated as prevention areas. These are predominantly national parks, which could be set aside from agricultural exploitation to conserve soil, water, and wildlife. They may also include marginal lands whose exploitation accelerates land degradation through erosion or desertification. In this connection, the reforestation of degraded forest areas is of utmost importance. Conservation areas or national parks can also conserve genetic resources in their natural habitats.

Forestry can also be extended into agriculture. Farmers can use agroforestry systems to produce food and fuel. In such systems, one or more tree crops are combined with one or more food crops or animal farming on the same land, though sometimes at different times. Well-chosen crops reinforce each other and yield more food and fuel than when grown separately. The technology is particularly suitable for small farmers and for poor-quality lands. Agroforestry has been practised by traditional farmers everywhere. The challenge today is to revive the old methods, improve them, adapt them to the new conditions. and develop new ones.

International forestry research organizations should work in various tropical countries in various ecosystems along the lines now followed by the Consultative Group on International Agricultural Research. There is considerable scope for institution building and additional research on forestry's role in agricultural production, for example by developing models that better predict the effects on water and soil loss of removing specific portions of forest cover.

Aquaculture

Fisheries and aquaculture are critical to food security in that they provide both protein and employment. The greater part of world fish supply comes from marine fisheries, which yielded 76.8 million tons in 1983. Landings have increased by 1 million tons per year over the past few years; by the end of the century, a catch of around 100 million tons should be possible. This is well short of the projected demand. There are indications that much of the naturally available freshwater fish stocks are fully exploited or damaged by pollution.

Aquaculture. or 'fish-farming', which differs from conventional fishing in that fish are deliberately reared in controlled water bodies, can help meet future needs. Yields from aquaculture have doubled during the last decade and now represent about 10 per cent of world production of fishery products. A five- to tenfold increase is projected by the year 2000, given the necessary scientific, financial, and organizational support. Aquaculture can be undertaken in paddy fields, abandoned raining excavations, small ponds, and many other areas with some water, as well as on various commercial scales: individual, family, cooperative, or corporate. The expansion of aquaculture should be given high priority in developing and developed countries.

PRODUCTIVITY AND YIELDS

The conservation and enhancement of agriculture's resource base will increase production and productivity. But specific measures are required to make inputs more effective. This is best done by strengthening the technological and human resource base for agriculture in developing countries.

The Technological Base

Blends of traditional and modern technologies offer possibilities for improving nutrition and increasing rural employment on a sustainable basis. Biotechnology, including tissue culture techniques, technologies for preparing value-added products from biomass, micro-electronics, computer sciences, satellite imagery, and communication. technology are all aspects of frontier technologies that can improve agricultural productivity and resource management.

Providing sustainable livelihoods for resource-poor farmers presents a special challenge for agricultural research. The major advances in agricultural technology in recent decades are better suited to stable, uniform, resource-rich conditions with good soils and ample water supplies. New technologies are most urgently needed in sub-Saharan Africa and the remoter areas of Asia and Latin America, which typically have unreliable rainfall, uneven topography, and poorer soils, and hence are unsuited to Green Revolution technologies.

To serve agriculture in these areas, research has to be less centralized and more sensitive to farmers' conditions and priorities. Scientists will need to start talking to poor farmers and basing research priorities on growers' priorities. Researchers must learn from and develop the innovations of farmers and not just the reverse. More adaptive research should be done right on the farm, using research stations for referral and with farmers eventually evaluating the results.

Commercial enterprises can help develop and diffuse technology, but public institutions must provide the essential framework for agricultural research and extension. Pew academic and research institutions in developing regions are adequately funded. The problem is most acute in the low-income countries, where expenditure on agricultural research and extension amounts to 0.9 per cent of total agricultural income, as against 1.5 per cent in the middle-income countries. Research and extension efforts must be greatly expanded, especially in areas where climate, soils, and terrain pose special problems.

These areas particularly will need new seed varieties, but so will much developing-country agriculture. At present, 55 per cent of the world's scientifically stored plant genetic resources is controlled by institutions in industrial countries, 31 per cent by institutions in developing countries, and 14 per cent by International Agricultural Research centres. Much of this genetic material originated in developing countries. These gene banks must increase their inventories of material, improve their storage techniques, and ensure that the resources are readily accessible to research centres in developing countries.

Private companies increasingly seek proprietary rights to improved seed varieties, often without recognizing the rights of the countries from which the plant matter was obtained. This could discourage countries rich in genetic resources from making these internationally available and thus reduce the options for seed development in all countries. The genetic research capabilities of developing countries are so limited that agriculture there could become excessively dependent on private gene banks and seed companies elsewhere. Thus international cooperation and a clear understanding on the sharing of gains are vital in critical areas of agricultural technology, such as the development of new seed varieties.

Human Resources

The technological transformation of traditional agriculture will be difficult without a matching effort to develop human resources. This means educational reforms to produce researchers more attuned to the needs of rural peoples and agriculture. Illiteracy is still widespread among the rural poor.

But efforts to promote literacy should focus attention on functional literacy covering the efficient use of land, water, and forests.

Despite women's critical role in agriculture, their access to education and their representation in research, extension, and other support services is woefully inadequate. Women should be given the same educational opportunities as men. There should be more female extension workers, and women should participate in field visits. Women should be given more power to take decisions regarding agricultural and forestry programmes.

Productivity of Inputs

In traditional agriculture, local organic material provided farmers with sources of energy, nutrients, and ways of controlling pests. Today, these needs are increasingly met by electricity, petroleum products, chemical fertilizers, and pesticides. The cost of these inputs forms a growing proportion of agricultural costs, and wasteful use does economic and ecological harm.

One of the most important energy-related needs is mechanical power for irrigation. The efficiency of pumps could be greatly improved by providing appropriate incentives for equipment producers and farmers, and through effective extension work. Energy for irrigation pumps can also be provided by wind generators or by conventional internal combustion engines running on biogas produced from local biomass wastes. Solar dryers and solar coolers can save agricultural products. These non-conventional sources should be promoted, particularly in areas poor in energy resources.

Nutrients are lost when fertilizers are improperly applied. Often they leach away with the flow of water in a field and degrade local water supplies. Similar problems of waste and destructive side effects occur in the use of pesticides. Hence extension systems and chemical manufacturers will need to give priority to programmes to promote careful and economical use of these expensive, toxic materials.

Equity

The challenge of sustainable agriculture is to raise not just average productivity and incomes, but also the productivity and incomes of those poor in resources. And food security is not just a question of raising food production, but of ensuring that the rural and urban poor do not go hungry during the short term or midst a local food scarcity. All this requires the systematic promotion of equity in food production and distribution.

Land Reforms

In many countries where land is very unequally distributed land reform is a basic requirement. Without it, institutional and policy changes meant to protect the resource base can actually promote inequalities by shutting the poor off from resources and by favouring those with large farms, who are better able to obtain the limited credit and services available. By leaving hundreds of millions without options, such changes can have the opposite of their intended effect, ensuring the continued violation of ecological imperatives. Given institutional and ecological variations, a universal approach to land reform is impossible. Each country should work out its own programme of land reform to assist the land-poor and to provide a base for coordinated resource conservation. The redistribution of land is particularly important where large estates and vast numbers of the land-poor coexist. Crucial components include the reform of tenancy arrangements, security of tenure, and the clear recording of land rights. In agrarian reforms the productivity of the land and. in forest areas, the protection of forests should be a major concern.

In areas where holdings are fragmented into many non-contiguous plots, land consolidation can ease the implementation of resource conservation measures. Promoting cooperative efforts by small farmers - in pest control or water management, for instance - would also help conserve resources. In many countries women do not have direct land rights; titles go to men only. In the interests of food security, land reforms should recognize women's role in growing food. Women, especially those heading households, should be given direct land rights.

Subsistence Farmers and Pastoralists

Subsistence farmers, pastoralists, and nomads threaten the environmental resource base when processes beyond their control squeeze their numbers onto land or into areas that cannot support them. The traditional rights of subsistence farmers, particularly shifting cultivators, pastoralists. and nomads, must therefore be protected from encroachments. Land tenure rights and communal rights in particular must be respected. When their traditional practices threaten the resource base, their rights may have to be curtailed, but only when alternatives have been provided. Most of these groups will need to be helped to diversify their livelihoods by entering the market economy through employment programmes and some cash-crop production. Research should give early attention to the varied requirements of the mixed farming typical in subsistence agriculture. Extension and input supply systems must become more mobile to reach shifting cultivators and nomads and priority given to public investment to improve their cropland, grazing areas, and water sources.

Integrated Rural Development

Rural populations will continue to increase in many countries. With existing patterns of land distribution, the number of smallholders and landless households will increase by about 50 million, to nearly 220 million, by the year 2000. Together, these groups represent three-quarters of the agricultural households in developing countries. Without adequate livelihood opportunities, these resource-poor households will remain poor and be forced to overuse the resource base to survive.

Considerable effort has gone into creating strategies of integrated rural development, and the requirements and pitfalls are well known. Experience has shown that land reform is necessary but alone is not enough without support through the distribution of inputs and rural services. Smallholders, including- indeed especially - women, must be given preference when allocating scarce resources, staff, and credit. Small farmers must also be more involved in formulating agricultural policies.

Integrated rural development also requires resources to absorb the large increases in rural working populations expected in most developing countries through non-agricultural work opportunities, which should be promoted in rural areas. Successful agricultural development and the growth in incomes should open up opportunities in service activities and small-scale manufacturing if supported by public policy.

Food Availability Fluctuations

Environmental degradation can make food shortages more frequent and more severe. Hence sustainable agricultural development will reduce the season-to-season variability in food supplies. But such systems cannot eliminate it. There will be weather-induced fluctuations, and the growing dependence on only a few crop varieties over large areas may amplify the effects of weather and pest damage. Often it is the poorest households and the ecologically disadvantaged regions that suffer most from these shortages. Food stocks are crucial in dealing with shortages. At present, the world stock of cereals is on the order of 20 per cent of annual consumption: The developing world controls about one-third of the stock and the industrial world, two-thirds. More than half the developing-country stock is in two countries - China and India. Stock levels in most of the others provide only for immediate operational requirements; there is little by way of a reserve.

The food stocks of industrialized countries are essentially surpluses, and provide a basis for emergency assistance, which must be maintained. But emergency food aid is a precarious basis for food security: developing countries should build up national stocks in surplus years to provide reserves as well as encouraging development of food security at the household level. To do this, they will need an effective system of public support for measures facilitating the purchase, transportation, and distribution of food. The provision of strategically located storage facilities is critical both to reduce post-harvest losses and to provide a base for quick interventions in emergencies.

During most food shortages, poor households not only cannot produce food but also lose their usual sources of income and cannot buy the food that is available. Hence food security also requires that machinery is available promptly to put purchasing power in the hands of disaster-struck households, through emergency public works programme, and through measures to protect small farmers from crop failures.

FOOD FOR THE FUTURE

The challenge of increasing food production to keep pace with demand, while retaining the essential ecological integrity of production systems, is colossal both in its magnitude and complexity. But we have the Knowledge we need to conserve our land and water resources. New technologies provide opportunities for increasing productivity while reducing pressures on resources. A new generation of farmers combine experience with education. With these resources at our command, we can meet the needs of the human family. Standing in the way is the narrow focus of agricultural planning and policies.

The application of the concept of sustainable development to the effort to ensure food security requires systematic attention to the renewal of natural resources. It requires a holistic approach focused on ecosystems at national, regional. and global levels, with coordinated land use and careful planning of water usage and forest exploitation. The goal of ecological security should be embedded firmly in the mandates of FAO. other UN organizations that deal with agriculture, and all other appropriate international agencies. It will also require an enhancement and reorientation of international assistance.

The agricultural systems that have been built up over the past few decades have contributed greatly to the alleviation of hunger and the raising of living standards. They have served their purposes up to a point. But they were built for the purposes of a smaller, more fragmented world. New realities reveal their inherent contradictions. These realities require agricultural systems that focus as much attention on people as they do on technology, as much on resources as on production, as much on the long term as on the short term. Only such systems can meet the challenge of the future.

10

The Role of the International Economy

Through the ages, people have reached beyond their own borders to obtain essential, valued, or exotic materials. Today's surer communications and larger trade and capital movements have greatly enlarged this process, quickened its pace, and endowed it with far-reaching ecological implications. Thus the pursuit of sustainability requires major changes in international economic relations.

THE INTERNATIONAL ECONOMY, THE ENVIRONMENT, AND DEVELOPMENT

Two conditions must be satisfied before international economic exchanges can become beneficial for all involved. The sustainability of ecosystems on which the global economy depends must be guaranteed. And the economic partners must be satisfied that the basis of exchange is equitable; relationships that are unequal and based on dominance of one kind or another are not a sound and durable basis for interdependence. For many developing countries, neither condition is met.

Economic and ecological links between nations have grown rapidly. This widens the impact of the growing inequalities in the economic development and strength of nations. The asymmetry in international economic relations compounds the imbalance, as developing nations are generally influenced by - but unable to influence - international economic conditions.

International economic relationships pose a particular problem for poor countries trying to manage their environments, since the export of natural resources remains a large factor in their economies, especially those of the least developed nations. The instability and adverse price trends faced by most of these countries make it impossible for them to manage their natural resource bases for sustained production. The rising burden of debt servicing and the decline in new capital flows intensify those forces that lead to environmental deterioration and resource depletion occurring at the expense of long-term development. The trade in tropical timber, for example, is one factor underlying tropical deforestation. Needs for foreign exchange encourage many developing countries to cut timber faster than forests can be regenerated. This overcutting not only depletes the resource that underpins the world timber trade, it causes the lost of forest-based livelihoods, increases soil erosion and downstream flooding, and accelerates the loss of species and genetic resources. International trade patterns can also encourage the unsustainable development policies and practices that have steadily degraded the croplands and rangelands in the drylands of Asia and Africa; an example of that is provided by the growth of cotton production for export in the Sahel region.

Box : Cotton Produced for Export in the Sahel

In 1963-64, as drought and hunger were taking hold in the Sahel region of Africa, five Sahelian nations - Burkina Faso, Chad, Mali, Niger, and Senegal - produced record amounts of cotton. They harvested 154 million tons of cotton fibre, up from 22.7 million tons in 1961-62. The Sahel as a whole set another record in 1984: It imported a record 1.77 million tons of cereals, up from 200,000 tons yearly in the early 1960s. Over the period that Sahelian cotton harvests were steadily rising, world cotton prices were steadily falling in real terms. These figures do not suggest that Sahelian nations should plough up all cotton to plant sorghum and millet. But the fact that farmers who can grow cotton cannot grow enough food to feed themselves suggests that cash crops are getting too much attention and food crops too little.

Source: J. Giri, 'Retrospective de l'Economie Sahelienne', Club du Sahel, Paris, 1984.

Growth in many developing countries also requires external capital inflows. Without reasonable flows, the prospect for any improvements in living standards is bleak. As a result, the poor will be forced to overuse the environment to ensure their own survival. Long-term development thus becomes much harder, and in some cases impossible.

Yet trends in the movement of capital are worrying. Net resource flows to developing countries have fallen in real terms; in aggregate, there is now actually an outflow. The increase of international capital flows to developing countries expected over the rest of the 1980s is only half that thought necessary to restore growth to levels where a reduction in poverty can occur.

A mere increase in flows of capital to developing countries will not necessarily contribute to development. Domestic efforts are of paramount importance. More external funding is also required, but it must come in ways that are sensitive to the environmental impacts. The point is that the reduction of poverty itself is a precondition for environmentally sound development. And resource flows from rich to poor flows improved both qualitatively and quantitatively are a precondition for the eradication of poverty.

Table :

Net Transfer of Resources to Capital-Importing Developing Countries

	1979	1980	1981	1982	1983	1984	1985
	(billion dollars)						
Net Transfer from Loans (all IDCs)*	30.7	0.8	27.7	0.8	-8.6	-22.0	-41.0
Net Transfer from all Resource Flows (all IDCs)**	41.4	39.3	41.5	10.1	-0.3	-12.5	-31.0
Net Transfer from all Resource Flows (to Latin America)	15.6	11.9	11.4	- 16.7	- 25.9	-23.2	-30.0

* Net transfers on loans are net capital flows minus net interest paid. All loans, official and private, short and long-term, are included together with IMF credit

** Total net resource flows relate to net loan transfers, grants and net direct investment (less net direct investment income)

Source: UN, **World Economic Survey 1986** (New York: 1986).

DECLINE IN THE 1980S

The pressures of poverty and rising populations make it enormously difficult for developing countries to pursue environmentally sound policies even in the best of circumstances. But when international economic conditions are bad, the problems can become unmanageable. During the 1980s, economic growth rates declined sharply or even turned negative in much of the Third World, particularly in Africa and Latin America. Over the five years from 1981 to 1985, population growth outstripped economic growth in most developing countries.

Deteriorating terms of trade, rising debt service obligations, stagnating flows of aid, and growing protectionism in the developed market economies caused severe external payment problems. The increased cost of foreign borrowing, at a time when exports were depressed, also helped to plunge many developing countries into debt crises. Austerity programmes laid down by the IMF as a prerequisite for extending credit to meet short-term balance-of-payments needs became particularly onerous after the debt crisis. Growth was cut back and many social objectives fell by the wayside, including those having to do with employment, health, education, environment, and human settlements.

This was a radical change from the 1960s and 1970s. Then it was rapid economic growth that was seen as an ecological threat. Now it is recession, austerity, and falling living standards. The decline of the 1980s has aggravated pressures on the environment in several ways:

- Austerity measures and general recessionary conditions have brought sharp declines in per capita incomes and increased unemployment. This forces more people back into subsistence agriculture, where they draw heavily on the natural resource base and thus degrade it.
- Austerity programmes inevitably include government cutbacks in both the staff and expenditure of fledgling, weak environmental agencies, undermining even the minimal efforts being made to bring ecological considerations into development planning.

- Conservation always taken a back seat in times of economic stress. As economic conditions have worsened in developing countries and debt pressures have mounted, planners have tended to ignore environmental planning and conservation in both industrial and rural development projects.

The critical situations in sub Saharan Africa and the debt strapped countries of Latin America demonstrate, in an extreme way, the damaging impacts that unreformed international economic arrangements are having on both development and the environment.

The African Continent

Africa on the whole has been caught up in a series of downward spirals:

- poverty and hunger leading to environmental degradation, deteriorating agriculture, and hence more poverty and hunger;
- falling savings and a neglect of new investment in the wake of growing poverty;
- high infant mortality, poverty, and lack of education;
- high population growth rates; and
- a flight from rural hunger to the cities, leading to explosive levels of urban growth and squalor, compounding the problems of inadequate food supplies.

The situation is not everywhere so bleak. Some nations have coped well, and some far-reaching and courageous policy reforms begun in the last few years have begun to bear fruit. Encouragement also comes from South Asia, where a comparable crisis 20 years ago has given way to an upward spiral of rising food production, diminishing (but still vast) poverty, slowing population growth, rising savings and investment, and greater attention to the long-term questions of environmental management and appropriate technology.

Among the many causes of the African crisis, the workings of the international economy stand out. Sub-Saharan Africa's economic well-being depends even more than low-income Asia's on developments in the world economy. Within the last decade, many sub-Saharan countries have been hit by adverse trends in commodity terms of trade and external shocks such as higher oil prices, fluctuating exchange rates, and higher interest rates. Over the last 10 years, the prices of major commodities such as copper, iron ore, sugar, ground-nuts, rubber, timber, and cotton have fallen significantly. In 1985, the terms of trade of sub-Saharan countries (except oil-exporting countries) were 10 per cent below 1970 levels. In countries eligible for funds from the International Development Association (IDA), the average fall was well over 20 per cent, with even greater drops in some, including Ethiopia, Liberia, Sierra Leone, Zaire, and Zambia.

The problem has been compounded by growing difficulties in attracting development capital from the industrial world. At the same time, debt repayments and interest charges have risen Debt service rose in sub-Saharan Africa as a whole from 15 per cent of export earnings in 1980 to 31 per cent in 1985. This combination of events has led to a situation where net resource transfers to the area fell from an estimated $10 billion a year in 1982 to $1 billion in 1985. Thus nations have been able to import far less. In countries eligible for IDA loans, the import volume per person in 1984 was only 62 per cent of the volume in 1970. Imports for agriculture - machinery, fertilizers, and pesticides - and of essential supplies to meet basic needs have all been cut. The combination of diverse international and internal factors cut per capita incomes by 16 per cent in sub-Saharan Africa between 1960 and 1985.

The economic difficulties of sub-Saharan countries have had devastating social impacts. Declining per capita rood production has contributed to growing undernourishment. The recent drought placed some 35 million lives at risk in 1984/85, and as the drought receded some 19 million people continued to suffer famine. Malnutrition and hunger have weakened much of the population, reducing their productivity, and made more of them (especially children and the old) more susceptible to debilitating diseases and premature death. The crisis has reversed progress in supplying safe drinking water and sanitation.

It is now more widely recognized that it is necessary to deal with the long-term causes rather than the symptoms. The vast misery brought on by the drought in Africa is now generally acknowledged, and the world community has responded with a substantial emergency programme. But emergency food aid is only a short-term reaction, and, at best, a partial answer. The roots of the problem lie in national and international policies that have bo far prevented African economies from realizing their full potential for economic expansion and thus for easing poverty and the environmental pressures that it generates.

The resolution lies in large part with African decision makers, but the international community also has a heavy responsibility to support Africa's adjustment efforts with adequate aid and trade arrangements and to see to it that more capital flows into poorer nations than out. These two complementary aspects of the resolution of the problems have been fully recognized by the African countries themselves and generally acknowledged by the international community. The World Bank estimates that even if external economic conditions are favourable over the next five years, and even if African governments implement key policy reforms, a substantial gap will still remain between the finance or debt relief available on current donor policies and the amounts needed to prevent a further deterioration in the living standards of low-income Africa. And there is no money in this grim equation for restoring the damaged environment.

The international community must realize that Africa cannot pull itself out of the planet's most serious economic and ecological crisis without much more long-term assistance than is currently envisioned. In addition, greatly increased external financing for development must be accompanied by policy changes that recognize the need to avoid environmental degradation.

Latin American Debt

Debt is an acute problem for many countries of Africa. But, because of the magnitudes of debt involved, it has had its most visible impact in some middle-income countries - particularly in Latin America. The debt crisis remains a threat to international financial stability, but its main impact so far has been on the process of development, both in its economic and ecological aspects. Of the total world debt of around $950 billion in 1985, roughly 30 per cent was owed by four countries: Argentina, Brazil, Mexico, and Venezuela. Their debts constitute roughly two-thirds of the outstanding loans of banks to developing countries.

In the 1970s, Latin America's economic growth was facilitated by external borrowing. Commercial banks were happy to lend to growing countries rich in natural resources. Then major changes in international conditions made the debt unsustainable. A global recession restricted export markets, and tight monetary policies forced up global interest rates to levels far exceeding any in living memory. Bankers, alarmed by deteriorating creditworthiness, stopped lending. A flight of indigenous capital from developing countries compounded the problem.

The ensuing crisis forced governments into austerity policies to cut back imports. As a result, Latin American imports fell by 40 per cent in real terms over three years. The consequent economic contraction reduced per capita gross domestic product by an average of B per cent in the eight main Latin American countries. Much of the burden was carried by the poor, as real wages fell and unemployment rose. Growing poverty and deteriorating environmental conditions are clearly visible in every major Latin American country.

Further, the lack of new credit and the continuing burden of debt service forced these countries to service their debts by running trade surpluses. The net transfers from seven major Latin American countries to creditors rose to almost $39 billion in 1984, and in that year 35 per cent of export earnings went to pay interest on overseas debt. This massive drain represents 5 to 6 per cent of the region's GDP, around a third of the internal savings, and nearly 40 per cent of export earnings. It has been achieved by adjustment policies that impose severe and regressively skewed cuts in wages, social services, investment, consumption, and employment, both public and private, further aggravating social inequity and widespread poverty. Pressures on the environment and resources have increased sharply in the search for new and expanded exports and replacements for imports, together with the deterioration and overexploitation of the environment brought about by the swelling number of the urban and rural poor in desperate struggle for survival. A substantial part of Latin America's rapid growth in exports are raw materials, food, and resource-based manufactures.

So Latin American natural resources ate being used not for development or to raise living standards, but to meet the financial requirements of industrialized country creditors. This approach to the debt problem raises questions of economic, political, and environmental sustainability. To require relatively poor countries to simultaneously curb their living standards, accept growing poverty, and export growing amounts of scarce resources to maintain external creditworthiness reflects priorities few democratically elected governments are likely to be able to tolerate for long. The present situation is not consistent with sustainable development. This conflict is aggravated by the economic policies of some major industrial countries, which have depressed and destabilized the international economy. In order to bring about socially and environmentally sustainable development it is indispensable, among other elements, for industrial countries to resume internationally expansionary policies of growth, trade, and investment. The Commission noted that, in these circumstances, some debtor countries have felt forced to suspend or limit the outflow of funds.

Growing numbers of creditor banks and official agencies are realizing that many debtors simply will not be able to keep servicing their debts unless the burden is eased. Measures under discussion include additional new lending, forgiveness of part of the debt, longer-term rescheduling, and conversion to softer terms. But a necessary sense of urgency is lacking. Any such measures must incorporate the legitimate interests of creditors and debtors and represent a fairer sharing of the burden of resolving the debt crisis.

ENABLING SUSTAINABLE DEVELOPMENT

Developing countries have sought, for many years, fundamental changes in international economic arrangements so as to make them more equitable, particularly with regard to financial flows, trade, transnational investment, and technology transfer. Their arguments must now be recast to reflect the ecological dimensions, frequently overlooked in the past. In the short run, for most developing countries except the largest a new era of economic growth hinges on effective and coordinated economic management among major industrial countries - designed to facilitate expansion, to reduce real interest rates, and to halt the slide to protectionism. In the longer term, major changes are also required to make consumption and production patterns sustainable in a context of higher global growth. International cooperation to achieve the former is embryonic, and to achieve the latter, negligible. In practice, and in the absence of global management of the economy or the environment, attention must be focused on the improvement of policies in areas where the scope for cooperation is already defined: aid, trade, transnational corporations, and technology transfer.

Enhancing the Flow of Resources to Developing Countries

Two interrelated concerns lie at the heart of our recommendations on financial flows: one concerns the quantity, the other the 'quality of resource flows to developing countries. The need for more resources cannot be evaded. The idea that developing countries would do better to live within their limited means is a cruel illusion. Global poverty cannot be reduced by the governments of poor countries acting alone. At the same time, more aid and other forms of finance, while necessary, are not sufficient. Projects and programmes must be designed for sustainable development.

Increasing the Flow of Finance

As regards the quantity of resources, the stringency of external finance has already contributed to an unacceptable decline in living standards in developing countries. The patterns and the needs of the heavily indebted countries that rely mainly on commercial finance have been described, along with those of low-income countries that depend on aid. But there are other poor countries that have made impressive progress in recent years but still face immense problems, not least in countering environmental degradation. Low-income Asia has a continuing need for large amounts of aid; in general, the main recipients in this region have a good record of aid management. Without such aid it will be much more difficult, to sustain the growth that, together with poverty-focused programmes, could improve the lot of hundreds of millions of the 'absolute poor'.

To meet such needs requires that the main donors and lending institutions re-examine their policies. Official development assistance (ODA) levels have stagnated in absolute terms, and most donor countries fall well short of internationally agreed targets. Commercial lending and lending by export credit agencies has fallen sharply. As part of a concerted effort to reverse these trends it is vitally important for development that there should be a substantial increase in resources available to the World Bank and IDA. Increased commercial bank lending is also necessary for major debtors.

Lending for Sustainable Development

In the past, development assistance has not always contributed to sustainable development and in some cases detracted from it. Lending for agriculture, forestry, fishing, and energy has usually been made on narrow economic criteria that take little account of environmental effects For instance, development agencies have sometimes promoted chemical-dependent agriculture, rather than sustainable, regenerative agriculture. It is important therefore that there should be a qualitative as well as a quantitative improvement.

A larger portion of total development assistance should go to investments needed to enhance the environment and the productivity of the resource sectors. Such efforts include reforestation and fuelwood development, watershed protection, soil conservation, agroforestry, rehabilitation of irrigation projects, small scale agriculture, low-cost sanitation measures, and the conversion of crops into fuel. Experience has shown that the most effective efforts of this type are small projects with maximum grass-roots participation. The programmes most directly related to the objective of sustainable development may therefore involve higher local costs, a higher ratio of recurrent to capital costs, and a greater use of local technology and expertise.

A shift towards projects of this kind would also require donors to re-examine the content of their aid programmes, particularly with regard to commodity assistance, which has sometimes served to reduce rather than enhance the possibilities for sustainable development.

The major priority is for sustainability considerations to be diffused throughout the work of international financial institutions. The roles of the World Bank and the IMF are particularly crucial because their lending conditions are being used as benchmarks for parallel lending by other institutions - commercial banks and export credit agencies. It is important in this context that sustainability considerations be taken into account by the Bank in the appraisal of structural adjustment lending and other policy-oriented lending directed to resource-based sectors - agriculture, fishing, forestry, and energy in particular - as well as specific projects.

A similar shift of emphasis is required in respect of adjustment programmes undertaken by developing countries. To date, 'adjustment' - particularly under IMF auspices - has led more often than not to cutbacks in living standards in the interest of financial stabilization. Implicit in many suggested plans for coping with the debt crisis is the growing recognition that future adjustment should be growth-oriented. Yet it also needs to be environmentally sensitive.

The IMF also has a mandate for structural adjustment lending, as in its new Structural Adjustment Facility. There has been a strongly expressed demand from developing-country borrowers for the Fund to take into account wider and longer-term development objectives than financial stabilization: growth, social goals, and environmental impacts. Development agencies, and the World Bank in particular, should develop easily usable methodologies to augment their own appraisal techniques and to assist developing countries to improve their capacity for environmental assessment.

Linking Trade, Environment, and Development

The importance of foreign trade to national development has greatly increased for most countries in the post-war period. This is one measure of the extent to which trade has made nations, economically and ecologically, more interdependent. Patterns of world trade also have changed markedly. First, the value of trade in manufactured goods grew at a faster rate than that in primary products other than fuel, and a growing number of developing countries have emerged as major exporters of such goods. Manufactured goods now account for twice the value of developing countries' non-oil exports. Second, the industrialized market economies have come to depend more on fuel imports from developing countries, which accounted for 43 per cent of consumption in 1980-81 compared with only 16 per cent in 1959-60 and even less in pre-war years

The dependence of the developed market economies on other mineral imports from the developing countries has also grown, and the share of these imports in consumption increased from 19 per cent in 1959-60 to 30 per cent in 1980-81. Non-renewable resources like fuels and minerals, as well as manufactured goods, are now far more important than tropical products and other agricultural materials in the flow of primary products from developing to industrial countries. In fact, the flow of food grains is in the opposite direction.

The main link between trade and sustainable development is the use of non-renewable raw materials to earn foreign exchange. Developing countries face the dilemma of having to use commodities as exports, in order to break foreign exchange constraints on growth, while also having to minimize damage to the environmental resource base supporting this growth. There are other links between trade and sustainable development; if protectionism raises barriers against manufactured exports, for example, developing nations have less scope for diversifying away from traditional commodities.

And unsustainable development may arise not only from overuse of certain commodities but from manufactured goods that are potentially polluting.

International Commodity Trade

Although a growing number of developing countries have diversified into manufactured exports, primary commodities other than petroleum continue to account for more than one-third of the export earnings of the group as a whole. Dependence on such exports is particularly high in Latin America (52 per cent) and Africa (62 per cent). The countries recognized as 'least developed' for the purposes of the UN Special Programme use primary commodities for 73 per cent of their export earnings.

Non-oil commodity prices fell during the early 1980s, not only in real but also in nominal terms. By early 1985, the UNCTAD commodity price index was 30 per cent below the 1980 average. This recent weakness of commodity prices may not be only a temporary phenomenon. Commodity prices have not yet recovered from the depth of the world recession despite increased economic growth in consuming countries. The reasons may be partly technological (an acceleration in raw material substitution); partly monetary, caused by the high cost of holding stocks of commodities; and partly due to increases in supplies by countries desperate to earn foreign exchange.

Table : The Growing Importance of Trade

	1950	1982
Economic Group	(exports as a per cent of GDP or NMP)	
Developed Market Economies	7.7	15.3
Developing Market Economies	15.5	23.8
Socialist Countries of Eastern Europe	3.4*	16.6*
Socialist Countries of Asia	2.9*	9.7*

* percentages to net material product (NMP).

Source: Based on UNCTAD, Handbook of International Trade and Development Statistics, 1985 Supplement (New York: United Nations, 1985).

These countries are turning the terms of trade against themselves, earning less while exporting more. The promotion of increased volumes of commodity exports has led to cases of unsustainable overuse of the natural resource base. While individual cases may not exactly fit this generalization, it has been argued that such processes have been at work in ranching for beef, fishing in both coastal and deep sea waters, forestry, and the growing of some cash crops. Moreover, the prices of commodity exports do not fully reflect the environmental costs to the resource base. In a sense, then, poor developing countries are being caused to subsidize the wealthier importers of their products.

The experience of oil has of course been different from that of most other commodities. It does provide one example of producers combining to restrict output and raise prices in ways that greatly increased export earnings while conserving the resource base and promoting energy saving and substitution on a large scale. Recent events suggest that regulation of the market by producers is very difficult in the long term, whether or not it is desirable in the wider, global interest, and in any event the conditions have not existed for other commodity exporters to operate in a like manner. Any arrangement encompassing measures to enhance the export earnings of producers, as well as to ensure the resource basis, would require consumer as well as producer support.

In recent years, Third World commodity exporters have sought to earn more by doing the first-stage processing of raw materials themselves. This first stage often involves subsidized energy, other concessions, and substantial pollution costs. But these countries often find that they do not gain much from this capital- and energy-intensive first-stage processing, as the price spread shifts in favour of downstream products, most of which continue to be manufactured mainly in industrial countries. Tariff escalation in the industrial market economies reinforces this tendency.

The main international response to commodity problems has been the development of international commodity agreements to stabilize and raise developing countries' earnings from these exports. But real progress has been very limited and in fact there have been reversals. Moreover, environmental resource considerations have not played any part in commodity agreements, with the notable exception of the International Tropical Timber Agreement. Commodity agreements have not been easy to negotiate, and regulation of commodity trade has been notoriously controversial and difficult. Current arrangements could be improved in two crucial respects:

- Larger sums for compensatory financing to even out economic shocks - as under the IMF's Compensatory Financing Facility - would encourage producers to take a long-term view, and not to overproduce commodities where production is close to the limits of environmental sustainability during periods of market glut.
- Where producers need to diversify from traditional, single-crop production patterns, more assistance could be given for diversification programmes. The second window of the Common Fund could be used for promoting resource regeneration and conservation.

Individual governments can better use renewable resources such as forests and fisheries to ensure that exploitation rates stay within the limits of sustainable yields and that finances are available to regenerate resources and deal with all linked environmental effects. As for non-renewable resources like minerals, governments should ensure that:

- the leaseholder undertakes exploration aimed at adding to proven reserves at least the amount extracted;
- that the ratio of production to proven reserve remains below a pre-specified limit;
- that the funds generated by royalties are used in a way that compensates for the declining income when the resource deposit is exhausted; and
- that the leaseholder is responsible for land restoration and other environmental control measures in the urea affected by mining.

Relevant international organizations such as various UN agencies, the World Bank, and regional groups could develop further their work on model contracts and guidelines incorporating these principles.

Protectionism and International Trade

The increase in protectionism in industrial countries stifles export growth and prevents diversification from traditional exports. The success of some Far Eastern developing countries in increasing exports of labour-intensive manufactured goods shows the development potential of such trace. However, other countries - especially low-income Asian and Latin American nations - seeking to follow the same route have found themselves severely handicapped by growing trade barriers, particularly in textiles and clothing. If developing countries are to reconcile a need for rapid export growth with a need to conserve the resource base, it is imperative that they enjoy access to industrial country markets for non traditional exports where they enjoy a comparative advantage. In many cases, the problems of protectionism relate to manufactures; but there are cases - sugar is a good example - where industrial countries employ agricultural trade restrictions in ways that are damaging ecologically as well as economically.

'Pollution-intensive' Goods

The processing of certain raw materials - pulp and paper, oil, and alumina, for example - can have substantial environmental side effects. Industrial countries have generally been more successful than developing ones in seeing to it that export product prices reflect the costs of environmental damage and of controlling that damage. Thus in the case of exports from industrial countries, these costs are paid by consumers in importing nations, including those in the Third World. But in the case of exports from developing countries, such costs continue to be borne entirely domestically, largely in the form of damage costs to human health, property, and ecosystems.

Box : Sugar and Sustainable Development

Thirty million poor people in the Third World depend on sugar cane for their survival. Many developing countries have a genuine comparative advantage in production and could earn valuable foreign exchange by expanding output. Some small states - Fiji, Mauritius, and several Caribbean islands - depend for their economic survival on cane sugar exports.

Industrial countries have actively promoted, and protected, beet sugar production, which competes with cane and has had quite damaging effects on developing countries: High-cost, protected beet production encourages artificial sweeteners; quotas have kept out Third World imports (except for some guaranteed imports as under the EEC's Sugar Protocol); and surpluses are dumped on world markets depressing prices.

In the 1986 World Development Report, the World Bank estimated that industrial countries' sugar policies cost developing countries About $7.4 billion in lost revenues during 1963, reduced their real income by about $2.1 billion and increased price instability by about 25 per cent.

Over and above the increased developing country poverty that results from these practices, the promotion of beet production in industrial countries has had adverse ecological side effects. Modern beet growing is highly capital-intensive, it depends heavily on chemical herbicides, and the crop has poorer regenerative properties than others. The same product could be grown in developing countries, as cane, more cheaply, using more labour and fewer chemical additives.

In 1980 the industries of developing countries exporting to OECD members would have incurred direct pollution control costs of $5.5 billion if they had been required to meet the environmental standards then prevailing in the United States, according to a study conducted for this Commission. If the pollution control expenditures associated with the materials that went into the final product are also counted, the costs would have mounted to $14.2 billion. The evidence also suggests that OECD imports from developing countries involve products that entail higher average environmental and resource damage costs than do overall OECD imports. These hypothetical pollution control costs probably understate the real costs of environmental and resource damage in the exporting countries. Furthermore, these costs relate only to environmental pollution and net to the economic damage costs associated with resource depletion.

The fact that these costs remain hidden means that developing countries are able to attract more investment to export manufactured goods than they would under a more rigorous system of global environmental control. Many Third World policymakers see this as beneficial in that it gives developing countries a comparative advantage in 'pollution-intensive' goods that should be exploited. They also see that passing along more of the real costs could reduce the competitive position of their country in some markets, and thus regard any pressure in this direction as a form of disguised protectionism from established producers. Yet it is in developing countries' own long-term interests that more of the environmental and resource costs associated with production be reflected in prices. Such changes must come from the developing countries themselves.

The Mandates of Multilateral Trade Forums

Although a number of UNCTAD research projects have considered the links between trade and environment, these issues have not been taken up systematically by intergovernmental organizations. The mandates of these organizations - principally GATT and UNCTAD - should include sustainable development. Their activities should reflect concern with the impacts of trading patterns on the environment and the need for more effective instruments to integrate environment and development concerns into international trading arrangements.

International organizations dealing with trade will find it easier to reorientate their activities if each nation designates a lead agency with a broad mandate to assess the effects of international trade on sustaining the environmental and resource base of economic growth. This agency could be responsible for raising sustainability issues in the work of UNCTAD, GATT, OECD, CMEA, and other relevant organizations.

Ensuring Responsibility in Transnational Investment

Overseas investment activity by companies in market economies has grown substantially over the past 40 years. Foreign affiliates now account for 40 per cent of sales, 33 per cent of net assets, and 56 per cent of net earnings for 380 of the largest industrial corporations in the market economies, according to data compiled by the UN Centre for Transnational Corporations. A high proportion of transnational investment is within industrial market economies, another aspect of the growing integration of these economies.

Transnationals play an important role as owners, as partners in joint ventures, and as suppliers of technology in the mining and manufacturing sectors in many developing countries, especially in such environmentally sensitive areas as petroleum, chemicals, metals, paper, and automobiles. They also dominate world trade in many primary commodities.

In recent years, many developing countries have begun to take a more positive view of the role TNC investment can play in their development process. This has been somewhat influenced by these countries' needs for foreign exchange and their awareness of the role that foreign investment might play in providing it. Effective cooperation with TNCs is possible in creating equal conditions for all parties. This can be attained by a strict observance of the principle of sovereignty of the host country For their part, many corporations have recognized the need to share managerial skills and technological know-how with host country nationals and to pursue profit-seeking objectives within a framework of long-tern sustainable development.

The Role of Transnational Corporations

- *In 1983 chemicals accounted for roughly one-fourth of the stock of foreign direct investment in manufacturing in developing countries by companies from four leading countries - Japan (23 per cent), the United States (23 per cent), the United Kingdom (27 per cent), and the Federal Republic of Germany (14 per cent).*
- *Agriculture, mining, and other extractive industries accounted for 38 per cent of the stock of U.S. investment in developing countries in 1983, 29 per cent of the stock of Japanese investment in 1983, 21 per cent of the total FRG investment in 1981-83, and 9 per cent of the stock of U.K. investment in 1978.*

- *Eighty to ninety per cent of the trade in tea, coffee, cocoa, cotton, forest products, tobacco, jute, copper, iron ore, and bauxite is controlled in the case of each commodity by the three to six largest transnationals.*

Source: UN Centre on Transnational Corporations, Environmental Aspects of the Activities of Transnational Corporations: A Survey (New York: UN, 1985).

But mutual suspicions still exist, usually because of an asymmetry in bargaining power between large corporations and small, poor, developing countries. Negotiations are often made one sided by a developing country's lack of information, technical unpreparedness, and political and institutional weaknesses. Suspicions and disagreements remain, particularly concerning the introduction of new technologies, the development of natural resources, and the use of the environment. If multinationals are to play a larger role in development, these conflicts and suspicions must be reduced.

Strengthening the bargaining posture and response of developing countries vis a vis transnationals is therefore critical. Where nations lack indigenous capacity to deal with large TNCs, regional and other international institutions should assist. As indicated earlier, they could expand existing help in the form of model agreements with transnationals for different situations, such an lease agreements for the exploitation of a mineral resource. They could also field technical assistance and advisory teams when a country negotiates with a transnational.

Transnational can have a substantial impact on the environment and resources of other countries and on the global commons. Both the home and host countries of TNCs share responsibilities and should work together to strengthen policies in this sphere. For example, information on policies and standards applied to and followed by corporations when investing in their own home country, especially concerning hazardous technologies, should be provided to host countries. Moreover, the policies of some industrialized countries that major investments are subject to prior environmental assessment should be considered for application to investments made elsewhere and should be broadened to include sustainability criteria. The information and recommendations thus arrived at should be shared with the host countries, which of course would retain the final responsibility. Despite their importance, international measures regarding transnational have been generally lacking and have proved extremely difficult to negotiate. The codes of conduct for transnational corporations formulated by the OECD and under discussion in the UN should deal explicitly with environmental matters and the objective of sustainable development. More detailed and specific instruments are needed for other problems. In particular, when introducing a new technology, plant, product, or process, or when setting up a joint venture in a developing country, the parties involved must also recognize and accept certain special responsibilities.

Broadening the Technological Base

The promotion of resource productivity is largely the work of domestic economic policy. But the international economy impinges on possibilities for productivity improvement in several ways, particularly in the transfer of technology from one country to another.

The Diffusion of Environmentally Sound Technologies

The promotion of sustainable development will require an organized effort to develop and diffuse new technologies, such as for agricultural production, renewable energy systems, and pollution control. Much of this effort will be based on the international exchange of technology: through trade in improved equipment, technology-transfer agreements, provision of experts, research collaboration, and so on. Hence the procedures and policies that influence these exchanges must stimulate innovation and ensure ready and widespread access to environmentally sound technologies. The real challenge is to ensure that the new technologies reach all those who need them, overcoming such problems as the lack of information and in some cases an inability to pay for commercially developed technologies. The measures required at the national level to deal with these problems are discussed in Part II of this report. However, both these issues also arise in the international diffusion of technology. Developing countries paid about $2 billion in 1960 by way of royalties and fees, mainly to industrial countries. The gap in scientific and technological capabilities is particularly wide in areas of direct relevance to the objectives of sustainable development, including biotechnology and genetic engineering, new energy sources, new materials and substitutes, and low-waste and non-polluting technologies.

The principal policy issue as regards the impact of payments is the impact of patents and proprietary rights. In 1980, industrialized market economies accounted for 65 per cent of the world total of patents granted, and the socialist countries of Eastern Europe held 29 per cent. Developing countries held only 6 per cent, and most of these had been granted to non-residents. Proprietary rights are a key element in the commercial development of technology. But their application in certain areas may hamper the diffusion of environmentally sound technologies and may increase inequities. In the past, publicly funded research provided new technology to small producers, particularly farmers, on a full or subsidized basis. The situation is not very different now, and in areas such as new seed varieties there is some reason to believe proprietary rights could act as a major barrier to developing countries' acquisition of new technologies. International cooperation is essential to maintain the flow of genetic material and to ensure an equitable sharing of gains.

Building Up Technological Capabilities in Developing Countries

At present, most of the global research and development effort is devoted to military purposes or the commercial objectives of large corporations. Little of this is of direct relevance to conditions in developing countries. In many areas the gap in technological capabilities is narrowing, but these efforts must be supported by international assistance, especially in such key areas as biotechnology. Unless action is taken to accumulate biological knowledge, valuable information as well as vital genetic variety will be lost forever, and developing countries will be at a permanent disadvantage in adapting the new biotechnologies to their own needs. Developing countries therefore have to work, individually and together, to build up their technological capabilities. The creation and enhancement of the infrastructure for research and technology is a precondition for such cooperation. The countries concerned could share the burden by establishing cooperative research projects along the lines of the International Agricultural Research Centres. Mission-oriented cooperative research ventures could be developed in areas such as dryland agriculture, tropical forestry, pollution control in small enterprises, and low-cost housing. Specific responsibilities would be assigned to institutions and corporations in the participating countries, and the agreement could provide for the equitable sharing and widespread diffusion of the technologies developed.

A SUSTAINABLE WORLD ECONOMY

If large parts of the developing world are to avert economic, social, and environmental catastrophes, it is essential that global economic growth be revitalized. In practical terms, this means more rapid economic growth in both industrial and developing countries, freer market access for the products of developing countries, lower interest rates, greater technology transfer, and significantly larger capital flows, both concessional and commercial. But many people fear that a more rapidly growing world economy will apply environmental pressures that are no more sustainable than the pressures presented by growing poverty. The increased demand for energy and other non-renewable raw materials could significantly raise the price of these items relative to other goods. The Commission's overall assessment is that the international economy must speed up world growth while respecting the environmental constraints. Some favourable trends have been noted in the pattern of consumption and production in industrial countries, which collectively still consume most of the world's non-renewable resources. Sustaining these trends will make it easier for developing countries to grow by diversifying their own economies. But for them to emerge from dependence a general acceleration of global economic growth is not enough. This would mean a mere perpetuation of existing economic patterns, though perhaps at a higher level of incomes. It must be ensured that the economies of developing countries grow fast enough to outpace their growing internal problems and fast enough for that first leap needed to acquire momentum. A continuation of economic growth and diversification, along with the development of technological and managerial skills, will help developing countries mitigate the strains on the rural environment, raise productivity and consumption standards, and allow nations to move beyond dependence on one or two primary products for their export earnings.

Future patterns of agricultural and forestry development, energy use, industrialization, and human settlements can be made far less material-intensive, and hence both more economically and environmentally efficient. Under these conditions, a new era of growth in the world economy can widen the options available to developing countries.

Reforms at an international level are now needed to deal simultaneously with economic and ecological aspects in ways that allow the world economy to stimulate the growth of developing countries while giving greater weight to environmental concerns. Such an agenda requires deep commitment by all countries to the satisfactory working of multilateral institutions, such as the multilateral development banks; to the making and observance of international rules in fields such as trade and investment; and to constructive dialogue on the many issues where national interests do not immediately coincide but where negotiation could help to reconcile them.

The Commission therefore regrets but cannot ignore the recent decline in multilateral cooperation in general and a negative attitude to dialogue on development in particular. At first sight, the introduction of an environmental dimension further complicates the search for such cooperation and dialogue. But it also injects an additional element of mutual self-interest, since a failure to address the interaction between resource depletion and rising poverty will accelerate global ecological deterioration. New dimensions of multilateralism are essential to human progress. The Commission feels confident that the mutual interests involved in environment and development issues can help generate the needed momentum and can secure the necessary international economic changes that it will make possible.

11

Species and Ecosystems: Resources for Development

Conservation of living natural resources - plants, animals, and micro-organisms, and the non-living elements of the environment on which they depend - is crucial for development. Today, the conservation of wild living resources is on the agenda of governments; nearly 4 per cent of the Earth's land area is managed explicitly to conserve species and ecosystems, and all but a small handful of countries have national parks. The challenge facing nations today is no longer deciding whether conservation is a good idea, but rather how it can be implemented in the national interest and within the means available in each country.

THE PROBLEM: CHARACTER AND EXTENT

Species and their genetic materials promise to play an expanding role in development, and a powerful economic rationale is emerging to bolster the ethical, aesthetic, and scientific cases for preserving them. The genetic variability and germplasm material of species make contributions to agriculture, medicine, and industry worth many billions of dollars per year.

Yet scientists have intensively investigated only one in every 100 of Earth's plant species, and a far smaller proportion of animal species. If nations can ensure the survival of species, the world can look forward to new and improved foods, new drugs and medicines, and new raw materials for industry. This - the scope for species to make a fast-growing contribution to human welfare in myriad forms - is a major justification for expanded efforts to safeguard Earth's millions of species. Equally important are the vital life processes carried out by nature, including stabilization of climate, protection of watersheds and soil, preservation of nurseries and breeding grounds, and so on. Conserving these processes cannot be divorced from conserving the individual species within natural ecosystems. Managing species and ecosystems together is clearly the most rational way to approach the problem. Numerous examples of workable solutions to local problems are available.

Species and natural ecosystems make many important contributions to human welfare. Yet these very important resources are seldom being used in ways that will be able to meet the growing pressures of future high demands for both goods and services that depend upon these natural resources.

There is a growing scientific consensus that species are disappearing at rates never before witnessed on the planet. But there is also controversy over those rates and the risks they entail. The world is losing precisely those species about which it knows nothing or little; they are being lost in the remotest habitats. The growing scientific concern is relatively new and the data base to support it fragile. But it firms yearly with each new field report and satellite study.

Many ecosystems that are rich biologically and promising in material benefits are severely threatened. Vast stocks of biological diversity are in danger of disappearing just as science is learning how to exploit genetic variability through the advances of genetic engineering. Numerous studies document this crisis with examples from tropical forests, temperate forests, mangrove forests, coral reefs, savannas, grasslands, and arid zones. Although most of these studies are generalized in their documentation and few offer lists of individual species at risk or recently extinct, some present species-by-species details.

Habitat alteration and species extinction are not the only threat. The planet is also being impoverished by the loss of races and varieties within species. The variety of genetic riches inherent in one single species can be seen in the variability manifested in the many races of dogs, or the many specialized types of maize developed by breeders.

Many species are losing whole populations at a rate that quickly reduces their genetic variability and thus their ability to adapt to climatic change and other forms of environmental adversity. For example, the remaining gene pools of major crop plants such as maize and rice amount to only a fraction of the genetic diversity they harboured only a few decades ago, even though the species themselves are anything but threatened. Thus there can be an important difference between loss of species and loss of gene reservoirs.

Some genetic variability inevitably will be lost, but all species should be safeguarded to the extent that it is technically, economically, and politically feasible. The genetic landscape is constantly changing through evolutionary processes, and there is more variability than can be expected to be protected by explicit government programmes. So in terms of genetic conservation, governments must be selective, and ask which gene reservoirs most merit a public involvement in protective measures. However, as a more general proposition, governments should enact national laws and public policies that encourage individual, community, or corporate responsibility for the protection of gene reservoirs.

But before science can focus on new ways to conserve species, policy makers and the general public for whom policy is made must grasp the size and the urgency of the threat. Species that are important to human welfare are not just wild plants that are relatives of agricultural crops, or animals that are harvested. Species such as earthworms, bees, and termites may be far more important in terms of the role they play in a healthy and productive ecosystem. It would be grim irony indeed if just as new genetic engineering techniques begin to let us peer into life's diversity and use genes more effectively to better the human condition, we looked and found this treasure sadly depleted.

Box : Some Examples of Species Extinction

- *In Madagascar, until about mid-century, there were **12,000** plant species and probably around **190,000** animal species, with at least **60** per cent of them endemic to the island's eastern strip of forest (that is, found nowhere* *else on Earth). At least 93 per cent of the original primary forest has been eliminated. Using these figures, scientists estimate that at least half the original species have already disappeared, or are on the point of doing so.*

- *Lake Malawi in Central Africa holds over 500 cichlid fish species, 99 per cent of them endemic. The lake is only one-eighth the size of North America's Great Lakes, which feature just 173 species, fewer than 10 per cent of which are endemic. Yet Lake Malawi is threatened through pollution from industrial installations and the proposed introduction of alien species.*
- *Western Ecuador is reputed to have once contained between 8,000 and 10,000 plant species, some 40 and 60 per cent of them endemic. Given that there are between 10 and 30 animal species for every one plant species in similar areas, western Ecuador must have contained about 200,000 species. Since 1960, almost all the forests of western Ecuador have been destroyed to make way for banana plantations, oil wells, and human settlements. The number of species thus eliminated is difficult to judge, but the total could well number 50.000 or more - all in just 25 years.*
- *The Pantanal area of Brazil contains 110,000 square kilometres of wetlands, probably the most extensive and richest in the world. They support the largest and most diversified populations of waterfowl in South America. The area has been classified by UNESCO as 'of international importance'. Yet it suffers increasingly from agricultural expansion, dam construction, and other forms of disruptive development. Sources: W. Rauh. 'Problems of Biological Conservation in Madagascar', in D. Bramwell (ed.), Plants and Islands (London: Academic Press, 1979): D.C.N. Barel et al., 'Destruction of Fisheries in Africa's Lakes', Nature, Vol. 315, pp. 19-20, 1985; A.H. Gentry. 'Patterns of Neotropical Plant Species Diversity', Evolutionary Biology. Vol. 15, pp.1-84, 1982; D.A. Scott and M. Carbonell, 'A Directory of Neotropical Wetlands', IUCN. Gland. Switzerland. 1985.*

EXTINCTION PATTERNS AND TRENDS

Extinction has been a fact of life since life first emerged. The present few million species are the modern-day survivors of the estimated half-billion species that have ever existed. Almost all past extinctions have occurred by natural processes, but today human activities are overwhelmingly the main cause of extinctions.

The average duration of a species is some 5 million years. The best current estimates are that on average 900,000 species have become extinct every 1 million years during the last 200 million years, so the average 'background rate' of extinction has been very roughly one in every one and one-ninth years. The present human-caused rate is hundreds of times higher, and could easily be thousands of times higher. We do not know. We have no accurate figures on the current rates of extinctions, as most of the species vanishing are those least documented, such as insects in tropical forests.

Although tropical moist forests are by far the richest biological units in terms of genetic diversity and by far the most threatened through human activities, other major ecological zones are also under pressure. Arid and semi-arid lands harbour only a very small number of species compared with tropical forests. But because of the adaptations of these species to harsh living conditions, they feature many potentially valuable biochemicals, such as the liquid wax of the jojoba shrub and the natural rubber of the guayule bush. Many of these are threatened by. among other things, the expansion of livestock herding.

Coral reefs, with an estimated half-million species in their 400,000 square kilometres, are being depleted at rates that may leave little but degraded remnants by early next century. This would be a great loss, in that coral-reef organisms, by virtue of the 'biological warfare' they engage in to ensure living space in crowded habitats, have generated an unusual number and variety of toxins valuable in modern medicine.

Tropical moist forests cover only 6 per cent of the Earth's land surface but contain at least half the Earth's species (which totals 5 million at a minimum, but could be as many as 30 million). They may contain 90 per cent or even more of all species. The mature tropical forests that still exist cover only 900 million hectares, out of the 1.5-1.6 billion hectares that once stood. Between 7.6 million and 10 million hectares are eliminated outright each year, and at least a further 10 million hectares are grossly disrupted annually. But these figures come from surveys of the late 1970s, and since then deforestation rates have probably accelerated.

By the end of the century, or shortly thereafter, there could be little virgin tropical moist forest left outside of the Zaire Basin and the western half of Brazilian Amazonia, plus some areas such as the Guyana tract of forest in northern South America and parts of the island of New Guinea. The forests in these zones are unlikely to survive beyond a few further decades, as world demand for their produce continues to expand and as the number of forestland farmers increases.

If deforestation were to continue in Amazonia at present rates until the year 2000, but then halted completely (which is unlikely), about 15 per cent of plant species would be lost. Were Amazonia's forest cover to be ultimately reduced to those areas now established as parks and reserves, 66 per cent of plant species would eventually disappear, together with almost 69 per cent of bird species and similar proportions of all other major categories of species. Almost 20 per cent of the Earth's species are found in Latin American forests outside of Amazonia; another 20 per cent are found in forests of Asia and Africa outside the Zaire Basin. All these forests are threatened, and if they were to disappear, the species loss could amount to hundreds of thousands.

Unless appropriate management measures are taken over the longer term, at least one-quarter, possibly one-third, and conceivably a still larger share of species existing today could be lost. Many experts suggest that at least 20 per cent of tropical forests should be protected, but to date well under 5 per cent has been afforded protection of any sort - and many of the tropical forest parks exist only on paper.

Even the most effectively managed parks and protected areas are unlikely to provide a sufficient answer. In Amazonia, if as much as half the forest were to be safeguarded in some way or another but the other half were to be eliminated or severely disrupted, there might well not be enough moisture in the Amazonian ecosystem to keep the remaining forest moist. It could steadily dry up until it became more like an open woodland - with the loss of most of the species adapted to tropical moist forest conditions.

More widespread climatic changes are likely to emerge within the foreseeable future as the accumulation of 'greenhouse gases' in the atmosphere leads to global warming early in the next century. Such a change will produce considerable stress for all ecosystems, making it particularly important that natural diversity be maintained as a means of adaptation.

SOME CAUSES OF EXTINCTION

The tropics, which host the greatest number and diversity of species, also host most developing nations, where population growth is fastest and poverty is most widespread. If farmers in these countries are forced to continue with extensive agriculture, which is inherently unstable and leads to constant movement, then farming will tend to spread throughout remaining wildlife environments. But if they are helped and encouraged to practise more intensive agriculture, they could make productive use of relatively limited areas, with less impact on wildlands.

They will need help: training, marketing support, and fertilizers, pesticides, and tools they can afford. This will require the full support of governments, including ensuring that conservation policies are designed with the benefit of agriculture foremost in mind. It may be expedient to stress the value to farmers rather than to wildlife of this programme, but in fact the destinies of the two are intertwined. Species conservation is tied to development, and the problems of both are more political than technical.

Population growth is a major threat to conservation efforts in many developing nations. Kenya has allocated 6 per cent of its territory as parks and reserves in order to protect its wildlife and to earn foreign exchange through tourism. But Kenya's present population of 20 million people is already pressing so hard on parks that protected land is steadily being lost to invading farmers. And the country's population is projected to grow fourfold in the next 40 years.

Similar population pressures threaten parks in Ethiopia, Uganda. Zimbabwe, and other countries in which a growing but impoverished peasantry is forced to depend on a dwindling natural resource base. The prospects are bleak for parks that do not make important and recognizable contributions to national development objectives.

Brazil, Colombia, Indonesia. Cote d'lvoire, Kenya, Madagascar, Peru, the Philippines. Thailand, and other nations with an unusual abundance of species already suffer a massive flow of farmers from traditional homelands into virgin territories. These areas often include tropical forests. perceived by the migrants encouraged to farm there as 'free' lands available for unimpeded settlement. The people who are already living on such lands at low population densities and with only traditional rights to the land are often swept aside in the rush to develop lands that might better be left in extensively used forest.

Many tropical countries with large forest resources have provoked wasteful 'timber booms' by assigning harvesting rights to concessionaires for royalty, rent, and tax payments that are only a small fraction of the net commercial value of the timber harvest. They have compounded the damage caused by these incentives by offering only short-term leases, requiring concessionaires to begin harvesting at once, and adopting royalty systems that induce loggers to harvest only the best trees while doing enormous damage to the remainder. In response, logging entrepreneurs in several countries have leased virtually the entire productive forest area within a few years and have overexploited the resource with little concern for future productivity (while unwittingly opening it for clearing by slash-and-burn cultivators).

In Central and South America, many governments have encouraged the large-scale conversion of tropical forests to livestock ranches. Many of these ranches have proved ecologically and economically unsound, as the underlying soils are soon depleted of nutrients; weed species replace planted grasses, and pasture productivity declines abruptly. Yet tens of millions of hectares of tropical forest have been lost to such ranches, largely because governments have underwritten the conversions with large land grants, tax credits and tax holidays, subsidized loans, and other inducements.

The promotion of tropical timber imports into certain industrial countries, through low tariffs and favourable trade incentives, combined with weak domestic forest policies in tropical countries and with high costs and disincentives to harvesting in industrial countries, also drives deforestation. Some industrial countries typically import unprocessed logs either duty-free or at minimal tariff rates. This encourages developed country industries to use logs from tropical forests rather than their own, a pattern that is reinforced by domestic restrictions on the amounts that can be cut in domestic forests.

ECONOMIC VALUES AT STAKE

Species conservation is not only justified in economic terms. Aesthetic, ethical, cultural, and scientific considerations provide ample grounds for conservation. For those who demand an accounting, the economic values inherent in the genetic materials of species are alone enough to justify species preservation.

Today, industrialized nations record far greater financial benefits from wild species than do developing countries, though unrecorded benefits to people living in the tropical countryside can be considerable. But the industrial countries have the scientific and industrial capacity to convert the wild material for industrial and medical use. And they also trade a higher proportion of their agricultural produce than do developing nations. Northern crop breeders are increasingly dependent on genetic materials from wild relatives of maize and wheat, two crops that play leading roles in the international grain trade. The U.S. Department of Agriculture estimates that contributions from plant genetic material lead to increases in productivity that average around 1 per cent annually, with a farm-gate value of well over $1 billion (1980 dollars). The U.S. maize crop suffered a severe setback in 1970. when a leaf fungus blighted croplands, causing losses to farmers worth more than $2 billion. Then fungus-resistant genetic material was found in genetic stocks that had originated in Mexico. More recently, a primitive species of maize was discovered in a montane forest of south-central Mexico. This wild plant is the most primitive known relative of modern maize and was surviving in only three tiny patches covering a mere four hectares in an area threatened with destruction by farmers and loggers. The wild species is a perennial; all other forms of maize are annuals. Its cross-breeding with commercial varieties of maize opens up the prospect that farmers could be spared the annual expense of ploughing and sowing, since the plant would grow again yearly of its own accord. The genetic benefits of this wild plant, discovered when not more than a few thousand last stalks remained, could total several thousand million dollars a year.

Wild species likewise contribute to medicine. Half of all prescriptions dispensed have their origins in wild organisms. The commercial value of these medicines and drugs in the United States now amounts to some $14 billion a year. Worldwide, and including non-prescription materials plus pharmaceuticals, the estimated commercial value exceeds $40 billion a year. Industry also benefits from wildlife.

Wildlife-derived materials contribute gums, oils, resins, dyes, tanning, vegetable fats and waxes, insecticides, and many other compounds. Many wild plants bear oil-rich seeds that can help in the manufacture of fibres, detergents, starch, and general edibles. For instance, the Fevillea genus of rain-forest vines in western Amazonia bear seeds with such a high oil content that a hectare of such vines in an original forest could produce more oil than a hectare of commercial oil palm plantation.

A few plant species contain hydrocarbons rather than carbohydrates. Certain of these plants can flourish in areas that have been rendered useless through such activities as strip-mining. Hence land that has been degraded by extraction of hydrocarbons such as coal could be rehabilitated by growing hydrocarbons on the surface. Moreover, unlike an oil well, a 'petroleum plantation' need never run dry. The emerging field of genetic engineering, by which science devises new variations of life forms, does not render wild genes useless. In fact, this new science must be based on existing genetic material and makes such material even more valuable and useful. Extinction, according to Professor Tom Eisner of Cornell University, 'no longer means the simple loss of one volume from the library of nature. It means the loss of a loose-leaf book whose individual pages, were the species to survive, would remain available in perpetuity for selective transfer and improvement of other species. And Professor Winston Brill of the University of Wisconsin has noted: 'We are entering an age in which genetic wealth, especially in tropical areas such as rain forests, until now a relatively inaccessible trust fund, is becoming a currency with high immediate value. Genetic engineering may mean that agriculture's Green Revolution will be superseded by a 'Gene Revolution'. This technology raises hopes of eventually harvesting crops from deserts, from seawater, and from other environments that did not previously support farming. Medical researchers foresee their own Gene Revolution bringing more innovative advances during the last two decades of this century than occurred during the previous 200 years.

Many of the nations with the least capacity for managing living resources are those richest in species; the tropics, which contain at least two-thirds of all species and a still greater proportion of threatened species, roughly coincide with the area generally referred to as the Third World. Many developing nations recognize the need to safeguard threatened species but lack the scientific skills, institutional capacities, and funds necessary for conservation. Industrial nations seeking to reap some of the economic benefits of genetic resources should support the efforts of Third World nations to conserve species; they should also seek ways to help tropical nations and particularly the rural people most directly involved with these species realize some of the economic benefits of these resources.

A NEW APPROACH; ANTICIPATE AND PREVENT

The historical approach of establishing national parks that are somehow isolated from the greater society has been overtaken by a new approach to conservation of species and ecosystems that can be characterized as 'anticipate and prevent.' This involves adding a new dimension to the now-traditional and yet viable and necessary step of protected areas. Development patterns must be altered to make them more compatible with the preservation of the extremely valuable biological diversity of the planet. Altering economic and land use patterns seems to be the best long-term approach to ensuring the survival of wild species and their ecosystems.

This more strategic approach deals with the problems of species depletion at their sources in development policies. anticipates the obvious results of the more destructive policies, and prevents damage now. A useful tool in promoting this approach is the preparation of National Conservation Strategies (NCS), which bring the processes of conservation and development together. Preparing an NCS involves government agencies, non-governmental organizations, private interests, and the community at large in analysis of natural resource issues and assessment of priority actions. In this way. it is hoped that sectoral interests will better perceive their interrelationships with other sectors and new potentials for conservation and development will be revealed.

The link between conservation and development and the need to attack the problem at the source can be seen clearly in the case of tropical forests. Sometimes it is government policy, not economic necessity, that drives the overexploitation and destruction of these resources. The direct economic and fiscal costs of this overexploitation - in addition to those of species extinction - are huge. The result has been wasteful exploitation of the tropical forests, the sacrifice of most of their timber and non-timber values. enormous losses of potential revenue to the government, and the destruction of rich biological resources.

Third World governments can stem the destruction of tropical forests and other reservoirs of biological diversity while achieving economic goals. They can conserve valuable species and habitat while reducing their economic and fiscal burdens. Reforming forest revenue systems and concession terms could raise billions of dollars of additional revenues, promote more efficient, long-term forest resource use. and curtail deforestation. Governments could save themselves enormous expense and revenue loss, promote more sustainable land uses, and slow down the destruction of tropical forests by eliminating incentives for livestock ranching.

The link between conservation and development also requires some changes in trade patterns. This has been recognized in the establishment in 1986 of the International Tropical Timber Organization, based in Yokohama, Japan, which seeks to rationalize trade flows. It has been set up to implement the first commodity agreement that incorporates a specific conservation component.

Numerous other opportunities can be found to encourage both species conservation and economic productivity. Many governments maintain unrealistically low taxes on rural land, while allowing settlers to establish title to 'virgin' land by converting it to farmland. Thus wealthy landowners can keep huge, underused estates at little or no cost, while land-hungry peasants are encouraged to clear forests to establish marginal holdings. Reforms of tax and tenure systems could increase productivity on existing holdings and reduce the pressures to expand cultivation into forests and upland watersheds.

Well-designed ecosystem conservation contributes to the predominant' goals of sustainable development in a number of ways. Safeguards for critical tracts of wildlands can serve also to safeguard agricultural land, for example. This is particularly true for upland forests of the tropics, which protect valley fields from floods and erosion, and waterways and irrigation systems from siltation.

A case in point is the Duraoga-Bone Reserve in Indonesia's northern Sulawesi, covering some 3,000 square kilometres of upland forest. It protects large populations of most of Sulawesi's endemic mammals, and many of the island's 80 endemic bird species. It also protects the Dumoga Valley Irrigation Scheme, funded by a World Bank loan, set up in the flatlands below to achieve a tripling of rice production on more then 13,000 hectares of prime agricultural land. Similar examples include the

Canaima National Park in Venezuela, which protects domestic and industrial water supplies for a major hydropower facility that, in turn, provides electricity to the nation's key industrial centre and its capital city.

One conclusion from this connection is that governments could think of 'parks for development', insofar as parks serve the dual purpose of protection for species habitats and development processes at the same time. National efforts to anticipate and prevent the adverse consequences of development policies in any of these areas would surely yield much more for species conservation than all the measures of the past 10 years in support of park building, ranger patrols, anti-poaching units, and the other conventional forms of wildlife preservation. The 3rd World Congress on National Parks, held in Bali, Indonesia, in October 1982, brought this message from protected area managers to the policy makers of the world, demonstrating the many contributions that protected areas managed in the modern way are making to sustaining human society.

INTERNATIONAL ACTION FOR NATIONAL SPECIES

Species and their genetic resources - whatever their origins - plainly supply benefits to all human beings. Wild genetic resources from Mexico and Central America serve the needs of maize growers and consumers globally. The principal cocoa-growing nations are in West Africa, while the genetic resources on which modern cocoa plantations depend for their continued productivity are found in the forests of western Amazonia.

Coffee growers and drinkers depend for the health of the crop on constant supplies of new genetic material from coffee's wild relatives, principally located in Ethiopia. Brazil, which supplies wild rubber germplasm to Southeast Asia's rubber plantation, itself depends on germplasm supplies from diverse parts of the world to sustain its sugar-cane, soybean, and other leading crops. Without access to foreign sources of fresh germplasm year by year, the nations of Europe and North America would quickly find their agricultural output declining.

The Earth's endowment of species and natural ecosystems will soon be seen as assets to be conserved and managed for the benefit of all humanity. This will necessarily add the challenge of species conservation to the international political agenda.

At the heart of the issue lies the fact that there is often a conflict between the short-term economic interest of the individual nations and the long-term interest of sustainable development and potential economic gains of the world community at large. A major thrust in actions to conserve genetic diversity must therefore be directed at making it more economically attractive both in the short term and in the longer perspective to protect wild species and their ecosystems. Developing countries must be ensured an equitable share of the economic profit from the use of genes for commercial purposes.

Some Current Initiatives

A number of international measures are already being tried. But they are limited in scope, only partially successful, and reactive in nature. UNESCO operates a clearing-house for information on natural areas and genetic resources. Its World Heritage Fund supports the management of a handful of exceptional ecosystems around the world, but all these activities receive small budgets. UNESCO has sought to establish a global system of Biosphere Reserves representing the Earth's 200 'biotic provinces' and harbouring sample communities of species. But only one-third of the needed reserves have been established, even though instituting and operating the rest would cost only about $150 million a year.

UN agencies such as FAO and UNEP run programmes concerned with threatened species, genetic resources, and outstanding ecosystems. But their combined activities are tiny in the face of the large needs. Among national agencies, the U.S. Agency for International Development leads the field in recognizing the value of species conservation. Legislation passed by the U.S. Congress in 1986 will make available $2.5 million a year for this purpose. Again, this should be considered an important gesture compared with what has been done to date by bilateral agencies, but trifling compared with the needs and opportunities.

IUCN, working in close collaboration with UNEP, WWF, the World Bank, and various international technical assistance agencies, has established a 'Conservation Monitoring Centre', to provide data on species and ecosystems for any part of the world quickly and easily. This service, which is available to all, can help ensure that development projects are designed with full information available about the species and ecosystems that might be affected. Technical assistance is also available for nations, sectors, and organizations interested in establishing local data bases for their own applications.

Species problems tend to be perceived largely in scientific and conservationist terms rather than as a leading economic and resource concern. Thus the issue lacks political clout. One important initiative that attempts to put conservation more squarely on the agenda of international development concerns has been the Tropical Forestry Action Plan. This collaborative effort coordinated by FAO involves the World Bank, IUCN, the World Resources Institute, and UNDP, along with numerous other collaborating institutions. The broad-based effort proposes the formulation of national forestry reviews, national forestry plans, identification of new projects, enhanced cooperation between development aid agencies at work in the forestry sector. and increased flows of technical and financial resources into forestry and related fields such as' smallholder agriculture.

Establishing norms and procedures with respect to resource issues is at least as important as increased funding. Precedents for such norms include the Convention on Wetlands of International Importance, the Convention on Conservation of Islands for Science (both of which safeguard prime habitats and their species), and the Convention on International Trade in Endangered Species. These three precedents all help, although the first two are essentially reactive attempts to devise 'species refuges'.

Setting Priorities

A first priority is to establish the problem of disappearing species and threatened ecosystems on political agendas as a major resource issue. The World Charter for Nature, adopted by the UN in October 1982, was an important step towards this objective. Governments should investigate the prospect of agreeing to a 'Species Convention', similar in spirit and scope to the Law of the Sea Treaty and other international conventions reflecting principles of 'universal resources'. A Species Convention, such as a draft prepared by IUCN, should articulate the concept of species and genetic variability as a common heritage. Collective responsibility for the common heritage would not mean collective international rights to particular resources within nations. This approach need not interfere with concepts of national sovereignty. But it would mean that individual nations would no longer be left to rely on their own isolated efforts to protect species within their borders.

Such a Convention would need to be supported by a financial arrangement that would have the active backing of the community of nations. Any such arrangement, and there are several possibilities, must not only seek to ensure the conservation of genetic resources for all people, but assure that the nations that possess many of these resources obtain an equitable share of the benefits and earnings derived from their development. This would greatly encourage the conservation of species. One such arrangement might be a Trust Fund to which all nations could contribute, with those benefiting most from the use of these resources contributing an appropriate share. Governments of tropical forest nations could receive payments to support the conservation of given areas of forest, with such payments rising or falling depending on the degree to which the forests are maintained and protected.

The sums required for effective conservation are large. Traditional-type conservation needs in tropical forests alone require outlays of $170 million a year for at least five years. However, the network of protected areas that the world will need by the year 2050 must include much larger areas brought under some degree of protection and a sophisticated degree of flexibility in management techniques.

More funds will also be required for conservation activities outside protected areas: wildlife management, ecodevelopment areas, education campaigns, and so on. Other approaches of a less expensive sort include the conservation of wild gene reservoirs of special significance through 'genetic conservation areas' in countries well endowed with biological wealth. Much of this work can be carried out by citizens' groups and other non-governmental means.

International development agencies - the World Bank and other major lending banks. UN agencies, and bilateral agencies -should give comprehensive and systematic attention to the problems and opportunities of species conservation. Although the international trade in wildlife and wildlife products is considerable, to date the economic values inherent in genetic variability and ecological processes have been generally disregarded. Possible measures include environmental impact analyses of development projects with particular attention to species' habitats and life-support systems, identification of crucial localities featuring exceptional concentrations of species with exceptional levels of endemism that face exceptional degrees of threat, and special opportunities for linking species conservation with development aid.

SCOPE FOR NATIONAL ACTION

As indicated earlier, governments need to follow a new approach in this field - one of anticipating the impact of their policies in numerous sectors and acting to prevent undesirable consequences. They should review programmes in areas such as agriculture, forestry, and settlements that serve to degrade and destroy species' habitats. Governments should determine how many more protected areas are needed, especially in the spirit of how such areas can contribute to national development objectives, and make further provision for protection of gene reservoirs (for instance, primitive cultivated varieties) that may not normally be preserved through conventional protected areas.

In addition, governments need to reinforce and expand existing strategies. Urgent needs include better wildlife and protected-area management, more protected areas of a non-conventional type (such as the ecological stations that are proving reasonably successful in Brazil), more game cropping and ranching projects (such as the crocodile schemes in India, Papua New Guinea, Thailand, and Zimbabwe), more promotion of wildlife-based tourism, and stronger anti-poaching measures (even though relatively few species are threatened by poaching, compared with the vast numbers threatened by habitat loss). National Conservation Strategies, such as those already prepared in over 25 countries, can be important tools for coordinating conservation and development programmes.

Other measures governments could take to confront the crisis of disappearing species, recognizing that it constitutes a major resource and development challenge, include consideration of species conservation needs and opportunities in land use planning and the explicit incorporation of their genetic resource stocks into national accounting systems. This could entail establishing a natural-resource accounting system that directs particular attention to species as high-value yet little-appreciated resources. Finally, they should support and expand programmes of public education to ensure that the species question receives the attention it deserves throughout the entire population.

Every nation has only limited resources at its disposal for dealing with conservation priorities. The dilemma is how to use these resources most effectively. Cooperation with neighbouring nations sharing species and ecosystems can help streamline programmes as well as share expenses for regional initiatives. Explicit efforts to save particular species will be possible for only relatively few of the more spectacular or important ones. Agonizing as it will be to make such choices, planners need to make conservation strategies as systematically selective as possible. No one cares for the prospect of consigning threatened species to oblivion. But insofar as choices are already being made, unwittingly, they should be made with selective discretion that takes into account the impact of the extinction of a species upon the biosphere or on the integrity of a given ecosystem.

But even though public effort may be concentrated on a few species, all species are important and deserve some degree of attention; this might take the form of tax credits to farmers willing to maintain primitive cultivars. an end to incentives to clear virgin forest, the promotion of research attention from local universities, and the preparation of basic inventories of native flora and fauna by national institutions.

THE NEED FOR ACTION

There are numerous signs that the loss of species and their ecosystems is being taken seriously as a phenomenon that carries practical implications for people all around the world, now and for generations to come.

The recent rise in public concern can be seen in such developments as the growth in Kenya's Wildlife Clubs. now numbering more than 1,500 school clubs with around 100.000 members. A parallel development in conservation education has occurred in Zambia. In Indonesia, some 400 conservation groups have joined together under the banner of the Indonesian Environmental Forum and exert strong political influence. In the United States, membership of the Audubon Society reached 385,000 in 1985. In the Soviet Union, nature clubs have over 35 million members. All of these indicate that the public puts a value on nature that is beyond the normal economic imperatives.

In response to this popular concern, governments have been moving to help species threatened within their borders, primarily through the establishment of additional protected areas. Today, the worldwide network of protected areas totals more than 4 million square kilometres, roughly equivalent to the size of most of the countries of Western Europe combined, or twice the size of Indonesia. In terms of continental coverage, protected areas in Europe (outside the USSR) amounted by 1985 to 3.9 per cent of territory; in the USSR, to 2.5 per cent; in North America, to 8.1 per cent; in South America, to 6.1 per cent; in Africa, to 6.5 per cent; and in Asia (outside the USSR) and Australia, to 4.3 per cent each.

Since 1970, the networks have expanded in extent by more than 80 per cent, around two-thirds of which are in the Third World. But a great deal more remains to be done; a consensus of professional opinion suggests that the total expanse of protected areas needs to be at least tripled if it is to constitute a representative sample of Earth's ecosystems.

There is still time to save species and their ecosystems. It is an indispensable prerequisite for sustainable development. Our failure to do so will not be forgiven by future generations.

12

Energy: Choices for Environment and Development

Energy is necessary for daily survival. Future development crucially depends on its long-term availability in increasing quantities from sources that are dependable, safe, and environmentally sound. At present, no single source or mix of sources is at hand to meet this future need.

Concern about a dependable future for energy is only natural since energy provides 'essential services' for human life - heat for warmth, cooking, and manufacturing, or power for transport and mechanical work. At present, the energy to provide these services comes from fuels - oil, gas, coal, nuclear, wood, and other primary sources (solar, wind, or water power) - that are all useless until they are converted into the energy services needed, by machines or other kinds of end-use equipment, such as stoves, turbines, or motors. In many countries worldwide, a lot of primary energy is wasted because of the inefficient design or running of the equipment used to convert it into the services required; though there is an encouraging growth in awareness of energy conservation and efficiency.

Today's primary sources of energy are mainly non-renewable: natural gas, oil, coal, peat, and conventional nuclear power. There are also renewable sources, including wood, plants, dung, falling water, geothermal sources, solar, tidal, wind, and wave energy, as well as human and animal muscle-power. Nuclear reactors that produce their own fuel ('breeders') and eventually fusion reactors are also in this category. In theory, all the various energy sources can contribute to the future energy mix worldwide. But each has its own economic, health, and environmental costs, benefits, and risks - factors that interact strongly with other governmental and global priorities. Choices must be made, but in the certain knowledge that choosing an energy strategy inevitably means choosing an environmental strategy.

Patterns and changes of energy use today are already dictating patterns well into the next century. We approach this question from the standpoint of sustainability. The key elements of sustainability that have to be reconciled are:

- sufficient growth of energy supplies to meet human needs (which means accommodating a minimum of 3 per cent per capita income growth in developing countries);
- energy efficiency and conservation measures, such that waste of primary resources is minimized;
- public health, recognizing the problems of risks to safety inherent in energy sources; and
- protection of the biosphere and prevention of more localized forms of pollution.

The period ahead must be regarded as transitional from an era in which energy has been used in an unsustainable manner. A generally acceptable pathway to a safe and sustainable energy future has not yet been found. We do not believe that these dilemmas have yet been addressed by the international community with a sufficient sense of urgency and in a global perspective.

ENERGY, ECONOMY, AND ENVIRONMENT

The growth or energy demand in response to industrialization, urbanization, and societal affluence has led to an extremely uneven global distribution of primary energy consumption. The consumption of energy per person in industrial market economies, for example, is more than 80 times greater than in sub-Saharan Africa. And about a quarter of the world's population consumes three-quarters of the world's primary energy.

Table : Global Primary Energy Consumption Per Capita, 1984

	GNP Per Capita (1984 dollars)	Energy Consumption (kW per capita*)	Mid-1984 Population (million)	Total Consumption (TW)
World Bank GNP Economy Category				
Low Income	260	0.41	2,390	0.99
Sub-Saharan Africa	210	0.08	258	0.02
Lower-middle	740	0.57	691	0.39
Upper-middle	1,950	1.76	497	0.87
Sub-Saharan Africa	660	0.25	148	0.04
High-Income Oil Exporters	11,250	5.17	19	0.10
Industrial Market Economies	11,430	7.01	733	5.14
East European Non-Market Economies		6.27	389	2.44
World		2.11**	4.718	9.94

*kW per capita is kW years/year per capita.

** Population-weighted average energy consumption (kW/capita) for first three main categories is 0.654 and for industrial market and East European categories is 6.76.

Source: Based on World Bank, World Development Report 1985 (New York: Oxford University Press, 1986).

In 1980, global energy consumption stood at around 10TW. if per capita use remained at the same levels as today, by 2025 a global population of 6.2 billion would need about 14TW (over 4TW in developing and over 9TW in industrial countries) - an increase of 40 per cent over 1980. But if energy consumption per head became uniform worldwide at current industrial country levels, by 2025 that same global population would require about 55TW.

Energy Units

A variety of units are used to measure energy production and use in physical terms. This chapter user; the kilowatt (kW);

the Gigawatt (GW), which is equal to 1 million kW; and the Terawatt (TW), which is equal to 1 billion kilowatts. One kilowatt - a thousand watts of energy - if emitted continuously for a year is lkW year. Consuming 1 kW year/year is equivalent to the energy liberated by burning 1,050 kilogrammes - approximately 1 ton - of coal annually. Thus a TW year is equal to approximately 1 billion tons of coal. Throughout the chapter, TW years/year is written as TW.

Neither the 'low' nor the 'high' figure is likely to prove realistic, but they give a rough idea of the range within which energy futures could move, at least hypothetically. Many other scenarios can be generated in-between, some of which assume an improved energy base for the developing world. For instance, if the average energy consumption in the low- and middle-income economies trebled and doubled, respectively, and if consumption in the high-income oil-exporting and industrial market and non-market countries remained the same as today, then the two groups would be consuming about the same amounts of energy. The low- and middle-income categories would need 10.5TW and the three 'high' categories would use 9.3TW - totalling 20TW globally, assuming that primary energy is used at the same levels of efficiency as today.

How practical are any of these scenarios? Energy analysts have conducted many studies of global energy futures to the years 2020-2030. Such studies do not provide forecasts of future energy needs, but they explore how various technical, economic, and environmental factors may interact with supply and demand. In general, the lower scenarios (14.4TW by 2030, 11.2TW by 2020. and 5.2 by 2030) require an energy efficiency revolution. The higher scenarios (18.8TW by 2025. 24.7TW by 2020, and 35.2 by 2030) aggravate the environmental pollution problems that we have experienced since the Second World War.

Two Indicative Energy Scenarios

Case A: High Scenario

By the year 2030, a 35TW future would involve producing 1.6 tines as much oil, 3.4 times as much natural gas, and nearly

5 times as much coal as in 1960. This increase in fossil fuel use implies bringing the equivalent of a new Alaska pipeline into production every one to two years. Nuclear capacity would have to be increased 30 times over 1960 levels - equivalent to installing a new nuclear power station generating 1-gigawatt of electricity every two to four days. This 35TW scenario is still well below the 55TW future that assumes today's levels of energy consumption per capita in industrial countries are achieved in all countries.

Case B: Low Scenario

Taking the 11.2TW scenario as a highly optimistic example of a strong conservation strategy. 2020 energy demand in developing and industrial countries is quoted as 7.3TW and 3.9TW respectively, as compared with 3.3TW and 7.0TW in 1980. This would mean a saving of 3.1TW in industrial countries by 2020 and an additional requirement of 4.0TW in developing countries. Even if developing countries were able to acquire the liberated primary resource, they would still be left with a shortfall of 0.9TW in primary supply. Such a deficit is likely to be much greater (possibly two to three times), given the extreme level of efficiency required for this scenario, which is unlikely to be realized by most governments. In 1980, the following breakdown of primary supply was quoted: oil, 4.2TW; coal, 2.4; gas, 1.7; renewables, 1.7; and nuclear, 0.2. The question is - where will the shortfall in primary energy supply come from? This rough calculation serves to illustrate that the postulated average growth of around 30 per cent per capita in primary consumption in developing countries will still require considerable amounts of primary supply even under extremely efficient energy usage regimes.

Sources: The 35TW scenario was originated in Energy Systems Group of the International Institute for Applied Systems Analysis, Energy in a Finite World - A Global Systems Analysis, (Cambridge, Mass.: Ballinger, 1981); all other calculations are from J. Goldemberg et al., 'An End-Use Oriented Global Energy Strategy', Annual Review of Energy, Vol. 10, 1985.

The economic implications of a high energy future are disturbing. A recent World Bank Study indicates that for the period 1960-95, a 4.1 per cent annual growth in energy consumption, would require an average annual investment of some $130 billion (in 1982 dollars) in developing countries alone. This would involve doubling the share of energy investment in terms of aggregate gross domestic product. About half of this would have to come from foreign exchange and the rest from internal spending on energy in developing countries.

The environmental risks and uncertainties of a high energy future are also disturbing and give rise to several reservations. Four stand out:

- the serious probability of climate change generated by the 'greenhouse effect' of gases emitted to the atmosphere, the most important of which is carbon dioxide (CO_2) produced from the combustion of fossil fuels ;
- urban-industrial air pollution caused by atmospheric pollutants from the combustion of fossil fuels ;
- acidification of the environment from the same causes ; and
- the risks of nuclear reactor accidents, the problems of waste disposal and dismantling of reactors after their service life is over, and the dangers of proliferation associated with the use of nuclear energy.

Along with these, a major problem arises from the growing scarcity of fuelwood in developing countries. If trends continue, by the year 2000 around 2.4 billion people may be living in areas where wood is extremely scarce.

These reservations apply at even lower levels of energy use. A study that proposed energy consumption at only half the levels of Case A drew special attention to the risks of global warning from CO_2. The study indicated that a realistic fuel mix - a virtual quadrupling of coal and a doubling of gas use, along with 1.4 times as much oil - could cause significant global warming by the 2020s. No technology currently exists to remove CO2 emissions from fossil fuel combustion. The high coal use would also increase emissions of oxides of sulphur and nitrogen, much of which turns to acids in the atmosphere. Technologies to remove these latter emissions are now required in some countries in all new and even some old facilities, but they can increase investment costs by 15-25 per cent. If countries are not prepared to incur these expenses, this path becomes even more infeasible, a limitation that applies much more to the higher energy futures that rely to a greater extent on fossil fuels. A near doubling of global primary energy consumption will be difficult without encountering severe economic, social, and environmental constraints.

Energy is, put most simply, the fundamental unit of the physical world. As such, we cannot conceive of development without changes in the extent or the nature of energy flows. And because it is so fundamental, every one of those changes of flows has environmental implications. The implications of this are profound. It means that there is no such thing as a simple energy choice. They are all complex. And they all involve trade-offs. However, some of the choices and some of the trade-offs appear to be unequivocally better than others, in the sense that they offer more development and less environmental damage.

This raises the desirability of a lower energy future, where GDP growth is not constrained but where investment effort is switched away from building more primary supply sources and put into the development and supply of highly efficient fuel-saving end-use equipment. In this way, the energy services needed by society could be supplied at much reduced levels of primary energy production. Case B in Box 7-2 allows for a 50 per cent fall in per capita primary energy consumption in industrial countries and a 30 per cent increase in developing countries. By using the most energy-efficient technologies and processes now available in all sectors of the economy, annual global per capita GDP growth rates of around 3 per cent can be achieved. This growth is at least as great as that regarded in this report as a minimum for reasonable development. But this path would require huge structural changes to allow market penetration of efficient technologies, and it seems unlikely to be fully realizable by most governments during the next 40 years.

The crucial point about these lower, energy-efficient futures is not whether they are perfectly realisable in their proposed time frames. Fundamental political and institutional shifts are required to restructure investment potential in order to move along these lower, more energy-efficient paths.

The Commission believes that there is no other realistic option open to the world for the 21st century. The ideas behind these lower scenarios are not fanciful. Energy efficiency has already shown cost-effective results. In many industrial countries, the primary energy required to produce a unit of GDP has fallen by as much as a quarter or even a third over the last 13 years, much of it from implementing energy efficiency measures. Properly managed, efficiency measures could allow industrial nations to stabilize their primary energy consumption by the turn of the century. They would also enable developing countries to achieve higher levels of growth with much reduced levels of investment, foreign debt, and environmental damage. But by the early decades of the 21st century they will not alleviate the ultimate need for substantial new energy supplies globally.

FOSSIL FUELS: THE CONTINUING DILEMMA

Many forecasts of recoverable oil reserves and resources suggest that oil production will level off by the early decades of the next century and then gradually fall during a period of reduced supplies and higher prices. Gas supplies should last over 200 years and coal about 3.000 years at present rates of use. These estimates persuade many analysts that the world should immediately embark on a vigorous oil conservation policy. In terms of pollution risks, gas is by far the cleanest fuel, with oil next and coal a poor third. But they all pose three interrelated atmospheric pollution problems: global warming, urban industrial air pollution, and acidification of the environment. Some of the wealthier industrial countries may possess the economic capacity to cope with such threats. Most developing countries do not.

These problems are becoming more widespread particularly in tropical and subtropical regions, but their economic, social, and political repercussions are as yet not fully appreciated by society. With the exception of CO_2, air pollutants can be removed from fossil fuel combustion processes at costs usually below the costs of damage caused by pollution. However, the risks of global warming make heavy future reliance upon fossil fuels problematic.

Managing Climatic change

The burning of fossil fuels and, to a lesser extent, the loss of vegetative cover, particularly forests, through urban-industrial growth increase the accumulation of CO_2 in the atmosphere. The pre-industrial concentration was about 280 parts of carbon dioxide per million parts of air by volume. This concentration reached 340 in 1980 and is expected to double to 560 between the middle and the end of the next century. Other gases also play an important role in this 'greenhouse effect', whereby solar radiation is trapped near the ground, warming the globe and changing the climate.

After reviewing the latest evidence on the greenhouse effect in October 1985 at a meeting in Villach, Austria, organized by the WMO, UNEP, and ICSU, scientists from 29 industrialized and developing countries concluded that climate change must be considered a 'plausible and serious probability. They further concluded that: 'Many important economic and social decisions are being made today on ... major water resource management activities such as irrigation and hydropower; drought relief; agricultural land use; structural designs and coastal engineering projects; and energy planning - all based on the assumption that past climatic data, without modification, are a reliable guide to the future. This is no longer a good assumption'.

They estimated that if present trends continue, the combined concentration of CO_2 and other greenhouse gases in the atmosphere would be equivalent to a doubling of CO_2 from pre-industrial levels, possibly as early as the 2030s, and could lead to a rise in global mean temperatures 'greater than any in man's history'. Current modelling studies and 'experiments' show a rise in globally averaged surface temperatures, for an effective CO_2 doubling, of somewhere between 1.5°C and 4.5°C,

With the warming becoming more pronounced at higher latitudes during winter than at the equator.

An important concern is that a global temperature rise of 1.5-4.5°C, with perhaps a two to three times greater warming at the poles, would lead to a sea level rise of 25-140 centimetres. A rise in the upper part of this range would inundate low-lying coastal cities and agricultural areas, and many countries could expect their economic, social, and political structures to be severely disrupted. It would also alow the 'atmospheric heat-engine', which is driven by the differences between equatorial and polar temperatures, thus influencing rainfall regimes. Experts believe that crop and forest boundaries will move to higher latitudes; the effects of warmer oceans on marine ecosystems or fisheries and food chains are also virtually unknown.

There is no way to prove that any of this will happen until it actually occurs. The key question is: How much certainty should governments require before agreeing to take action? If they wait until significant climate change is demonstrated, it may be too late for any countermeasures to be effective against the inertia by then stored in this massive global system. The very long time lags involved in negotiating international agreement on complex issues involving all nations have led some experts to conclude that it is already late. Given the complexities and uncertainties surrounding the issue, it is urgent that the process start now. A four track strategy is needed, combining:

- improved monitoring and assessment of the evolving phenomena;
- increased research to improve knowledge about the origins, mechanisms, and effects of the phenomena;
- the development of internationally agreed policies for the reduction of the causative gases; and
- adoption of strategies needed to minimize damage and cope with the climate changes, and rising sea level.

No nation has either the political mandate or the economic power to combat climatic change alone. However, the Villach statement recommended such a four track strategy for climate change, to be promoted by governments and the scientific community through WMO, UNEP, and ICSU - backed by a global convention if necessary.

It is difficult to imagine an issue with more global impacts on human societies and the natural environment than the greenhouse effect. The signal is unclear but we may already be witnessing examples, if not actual greenhouse effects, in Africa.

The ultimate potential impacts of a greenhouse warming could be catastrophic. It is our considered judgement that it is already very late to start the process of policy consideration. The process of heightening public awareness, of building support for national policies, and finally for developing multilateral efforts to slow the rate of emissions growth will take time to implement.

The greenhouse issue is an opportunity as well as a challenge; not surprisingly, it provides another important reason to implement sustainable development strategies.

While these strategies are being developed, more immediate policy measures can and should be adopted. The most urgent are those required to increase and extend the recent steady gains in energy efficiency and to shift the energy mix more towards renewables. Carbon dioxide output globally could be significantly reduced by energy efficiency measures without any reduction of the tempo of GDP growth. These measures would also serve to abate other emissions and thus reduce acidification and urban-industrial air pollution. Gaseous fuels produce less carbon dioxide per unit of energy output than oil or coal and should be promoted, especially for cooking and other domestic uses.

Gases other than carbon dioxide are thought to be responsible for about one-third of present global warming, and it is estimated that they will cause about half the problem around 2030. some of these, notably chlorofluorocarbons used as aerosols, refrigeration chemicals, and in the manufacture of plastics, may be more easily controlled than CO2. These, although not strictly energy-related, will have a decisive influence on policies for managing carbon dioxide emissions. Apart from their climatic effect, chlorofluorocarbons are responsible to a large extent for damage to the earth's stratospheric ozone. The chemical industry should make every effort to find replacements, and governments should require the use of such replacements when found (as some nations have outlawed the use of these chemicals as aerosols). Governments should ratify the existing ozone convention and develop protocols for the limitation of chlorofluorocarbon emissions, and systematically monitor and report implementation.

A lot of policy development work is needed. This should proceed hand in hand with accelerated research to reduce remaining scientific uncertainties. Nations urgently need to formulate and agree upon management policies for all environmentally reactive chemicals released into the atmosphere by human activities, particularly those that can influence the radiation balance on earth. Governments should initiate discussions leading to a convention on this matter.

If a convention on chemical containment policies cannot be implemented rapidly, governments should develop contingency strategies and plans for adaptation to climatic change. In either case, WMO, UNEP, WHO, ICSU, and other relevant international and national bodies should be encouraged to coordinate and accelerate their programmes to develop a carefully integrated strategy of research, monitoring, and assessment of the likely impacts on climate, health, and environment of all environmentally reactive chemicals released into the atmosphere in significant quantities.

Reducing Urban-Industrial Air Pollution

The past three decades of generally rapid growth worldwide have seen dramatic increases in fuel consumption for heating and cooling, automobile transport, industrial activities, and electricity generation. Concern over the effects of increasing air pollution in the late 1960s resulted in the development of curative measures, including air-quality criteria, standards, and add-on control technologies that can remove pollutants cost-effectively. All these greatly reduced emissions of some of the principal pollutants and cleaned air over many cities. Despite this, air pollution has today reached serious levels in the cities of several industrial and newly industrialized countries as well as in those of most developing countries, which in some cases are by now the world's most polluted urban areas.

The fossil fuel emissions of principal concern in terms of urban pollution, whether from stationary or mobile sources, include sulphur dioxide, nitrogen oxides, carbon monoxide, various volatile organic compounds, fly ash, and other suspended particles. They can injure human health and the environment, bringing increased respiratory complaints, some potentially fatal. But these pollutants can be contained so as to protect human health and the environment and all governments should take steps to achieve acceptable levels of air quality.

Governments can establish and monitor air quality goals and objectives, allowable atmospheric loadings, and related emission criteria or standards, as some successfully do already. Regional organizations can support this effort. Multilateral and bilateral development assistance agencies and development banks should encourage governments to require that the most energy-efficient technology be used when industries and energy utilities plan to build new or extend existing facilities.

Damage from the Long-Range Transport of Air Pollution

Measures taken by many industrialized countries in the 1970s to control urban and industrial air pollution (high chimney stacks, for example) greatly improved the quality of the air in the cities concerned. However, it quite unintentionally sent increasing amounts of pollution across national boundaries in Europe and North America, contributing to the acidification of distant environments and creating new pollution problems. This was manifest in growing damage to lakes, soils, and communities of plants and animals. Failure to control automobile pollution in some regions has seriously contributed to the problem.

Thus atmospheric pollution, once perceived only as a local urban-industrial problem involving people's health, is now also seen as a much more complex issue encompassing buildings, ecosystems, and maybe even public health over vast regions. During transport in the atmosphere, emissions of sulphur and nitrogen oxides and volatile hydrocarbons are transformed into sulphuric and nitric acids, ammonium salts, and ozone. They fall to the ground, sometimes many hundreds or thousands of kilometres from their origins, as dry particles or in rain, snow, frost, fog, and dew. Few studied of their socio-economic costs are available, but these demonstrate that they are quite large and suggest that they are growing rapidly. They damage vegetation, contribute to land and water pollution, and corrode buildings, metallic structures and vehicles, causing billions of dollars in damage annually.

Damage first became evident in Scandinavia in the 1960s. Several thousand lakes in Europe, particularly in southern Scandinavia , and several hundreds in North America have registered a steady increase in acidity levels to the point where their natural fish populations have declined or died out. The same acids enter the soil and groundwater, increasing corrosion of drinking water piping in Scandinavia.

The circumstantial evidence indicating the need for action on the sources of acid precipitation is mounting with a speed that gives scientists and governments little time to assess it scientifically. Some of the greatest observed damage has been reported in Central Europe, which is currently receiving more than one gramme of sulphur on every square metre of ground each year, at least five times greater than natural background. There was little evidence of tree damage in Europe in 1970. In 1962, the Federal Republic of Germany reported visible leaf damage in its forest plot samples nationwide, amounting in 1983 to 34 per cent, and rising in 1985 to BO per cent. Sweden reported light to moderate damage in 30 per cent of its forests, and various reports from other countries in Eastern and Western Europe are extremely disquieting. So far an estimated 14 per cent of all European forestland is affected.

The evidence is not all in, but many reports show soils in parts of Europe becoming acid throughout the tree rooting layers, particularly nutrient-poor soils such as those of Southern Sweden The precise damage mechanisms are not known, but all theories include an air pollution component. Root damage and leaf damage appear to interact - affecting the ability of the trees both to take up water from the soil and to retain it in the foliage, so that they become particularly vulnerable to dry spells and other stresses. Europe may be experiencing an immense change to irreversible acidification, the remedial costs of which could be beyond economic reach. Although there are many options for reducing sulphur, nitrogen, and hydrocarbon emissions, no single pollutant control strategy is likely to be effective in dealing with forest decline. It will require a total integrated mix of strategies and technologies to improve air quality, tailored for each region.

A forest in an ecosystem that exists under certain environmental conditions, and if you change the conditions, the system is going to change. It is a very difficult task for ecologists to foresee what changes are going to be because the systems are so enormously complex.

The direct causes behind an individual tree dying can be far removed from the primary pressure that brought the whole system into equilibrium. One time it might be ozone, another time it may be SO_2, a third time it may be aluminium poisoning.

Evidence of local air pollution and acidification in Japan and also in the newly industrialized countries of Asia, Africa, and Latin America is beginning to emerge. China and the Republic of Korea seem particularly vulnerable, as do Brazil, Colombia, Ecuador, and Venezuela. So little is known about the likely environmental loading of sulphur and nitrogen in these region and about the acid-neutralizing capacity of tropical lakes and forest soils that a comprehensive programme of investigation should be formulated without delay.

Where actual or potential threats from acidification exist, governments should map sensitive areas, assess forest damage annually and soil impoverishment every five years according to regionally agreed protocols, and publish the findings. They should support transboundary monitoring of pollution being carried out by agencies in their region and, where there is no such agency, create one or give the job to any suitable regional body. Governments in many regions could gain significantly from early agreement to prevent transboundary air pollution and the enormous damage to their economic base now being experienced in Europe and North America. Even though the exact causes of the damage are hard to prove, reduction strategies are certainly within reach and economic. They could be viewed as a cheap insurance policy compared with the vast amount of potential damage these strategies avoid.

Damage and Control Costs of Air Pollution

It is very difficult to quantify damage control costs, not least because cost figures are highly dependent on the control strategy assumed. However, in the eastern United States, it has been estimated that halving the remaining sulphur dioxide emissions from existing sources would cost $5 billion a year, increasing present electricity rates by 2-3 per cent. If nitrogen oxides are figured in, the additional costs might be as high as $6 billion a year. Materials corrosion damage alone is estimated to cost $7 billion annually in 17 states in the eastern United states.

Estimates of the annual costs of securing a 55 to 65 per cent reduction in the remaining sulphur emissions in the countries of the European Economic Community between 1980 and 2000 range from $4.6 billion to $6.7 billion (1982 dollars) per year. Controls on stationary boilers to reduce nitrogen levels by only 10 per cent annually by the year 2000 range between $100,000 and $400,000 (1982 dollars). These figures translate into a one-time increase of about 6 per cent in the price of electrical power to the consumer. Studies place damage costs due to material and fish losses alone at $3 billion a year, while damage to crops, forests, and health are estimated to exceed $10 billion per year. Technologies for drastically reducing oxides of nitrogen and hydrocarbons from automobile exhaust gases are readily available and routinely used in North America and Japan, but not in Europe.

Japanese laboratory studies indicate that air pollution and acid rain can reduce some wheat and rice crop production, perhaps by as much as 30 per cent.

Sources: U.S. Congress, Office of Technology Assessment, Acid Rain and Transported Air Pollutants: Implications for

Public Policy (Washington, DC: U.S. Government Printing Office, 1985); U.S. Environmental Protection Agency, Acid Deposition Assessment (Washington, DC: 1985); I.M. Torrens, 'Acid Rain and Air Pollution: A Problem of Industrialization', prepared for WCED, 1985; P. Mandelbaum, Acid Rain - Economic Assessment (New York: Plenum Press, 1985); M. Hashimoto, 'National Air quality Management Policy of Japan', prepared for WCED, 1985; OECD, The State of the Environment (Paris: 1985).

NUCLEAR ENERGY: UNSOLVED PROBLEMS

The Peaceful Atom

In the years following the Second World War, the nuclear knowledge that under military control had led to the production of atomic weapons was redeployed for peaceful 'energy' purposes by civilian technologists. Several benefits were obvious at the time.

It was also realized that no energy source would ever be risk-free. There was the danger of nuclear war, the spread of atomic weapons, and nuclear terrorism. But intensive international cooperation and a number of negotiated agreements suggested that these dangers could be avoided. For instance, the Nonproliferation Treaty (NPT), drafted in its final form in 1969, included a promise by signatory governments possessing nuclear weapons and expertise to pursue and undertake nuclear disarmament ad also to assist the non-nuclear signatories in developing nuclear power, but strictly for peaceful purposes only. Other problems, such as radiation risks, reactor safety, and nuclear waste disposal were all acknowledged as very important but, with the right amount of effort, containable.

And now, after almost four decades of immense technological effort to support nuclear development, nuclear energy has become widely used. Some 30 governments produce from nuclear generators a total of about 15 per cent of all the electricity used globally. Yet it has not met earlier expectations that it would be the key to ensuring an unlimited supply of low-cost energy. However, during this period of practical experience with building and running nuclear reactors, the nature of the costs, risks and benefits have become much more evident and as such, the subject of sharp controversy.

The Growing Understanding of Nuclear Issues

The potential for the spread of nuclear weapons is one of the most serious threats to world peace. It is in the interest of all nations to prevent proliferation of nuclear weapons. All nations therefore should contribute to the development of a viable non-proliferation regime. The nuclear weapon states must deliver on their promise to reduce the number and ultimately eliminate nuclear weapons in their arsenals and the role those weapons play in their strategies. And the non-nuclear-weapon states must cooperate in providing credible assurances that they are not moving towards a nuclear weapon capability.

Most schemes for non-proliferation mandate an institutional separation between military and civilian uses of nuclear energy. But for countries with full access to the complete nuclear fuel cycle, no technical separation really exists. Not all states operate the necessary clear-cut administrative separation of civilian and military access. Cooperation is needed also among suppliers and buyers of civilian nuclear facilities and materials and the International Atomic Energy Agency, in order to provide credible safeguards against the diversion of civilian reactor programmes to military purposes, especially in countries that do not open all their nuclear programmes to IAEA inspection. Thus, there still remains a danger of the proliferation of nuclear weapons.

Costs

The costs of construction and the relative economics of electricity generating stations - whether powered by nuclear energy, coal, oil or gas - are conditioned by the following factors throughout the service life of a plant:

- the cost of borrowing money to finance plant construction,
- the impact of inflation;
- the duration of the period of planning, licensing, and construction;
- the cost of fuel and maintenance ;

- the costs of protective measures, to ensure safe operation; and
- waste disposal costs (land, air, and water pollution containment) and the costs of dismantling at the end of service life.

All these factors vary widely depending on differing institutional, legal, and financial arrangements in different countries. Cost generalizations and comparisons are therefore unhelpful or misleading. However, costs associated with several of these factors have increased more rapidly for nuclear stations during the last 5-10 years, so that the earlier clear cost advantage of nuclear over the service life of the plant has been reduced or lost altogether. Nations should therefore look very closely at cost comparisons to obtain the best value when choosing an energy path.

Health and Environment Risks

Very strict codes of safety practice are implemented in nuclear plants so that under officially approved operating conditions, the danger from radiation to reactor personnel and especially to the general public is negligible. However, an accident occurring in a reactor may in certain very rare canes be serious enough to cause an external release of radioactive substances. Depending upon the level of exposure, people are under a certain level of risk of becoming ill from various forms of cancer or from alteration or genetic material, which may result in hereditary defects.

Since 1928, the International Commission on Radiological Protection (ICRP) has issued recommendations on radiation dosage levels above which exposure is unacceptable. These have been developed for occupationally exposed workers and for the general public. The 'Nuclear Safety Standards (NUSS) codes of IAEA were developed in 1975 to reduce safety differences among member states. Neither system is in any way binding on governments, if an accident occurs, individual governments have the responsibility of deciding at what level of radioactive contamination pasture land, drinking water, milk, meat, eggs, vegetables, and fish, are to be banned for consumption by livestock or humans. Different countries - even different local government authorities within a country - have different criteria. Some have none at all, ICRP and NUSS notwithstanding. States with more rigorous standards may destroy large amounts of food or may ban food imports from a neighbour states with more permissive criteria. This causes great hardship to farmers who may not receive any compensation for their losses. It may also cause trade problems and political tension between states. Both of these difficulties -occurred following the Chernobyl disaster, when the need to develop at least regionally conformable contamination criteria and compensation arrangements was overwhelmingly demonstrated.

Nuclear Accidents Risks

Nuclear safety returned to the newspaper headlines following the Three Mile Island (Harrisburg, United States) and the Chernobyl (USSR) accidents. Probabilistic estimates of the risks of component failure, leading to a radioactive release in Western style light water reactors wore made in 1975 by the U.S. Nuclear Regulatory Commission. The most serious category of release through containment failure was placed at around 1 in 1,000,000 years of reactor operation. Post-accident analysis of both Harrisburg and Chernobyl - a completely different type of reactor - have shown that in both cases, human operator error was the main cause. They occurred after about 2,000 and 4,000 reactor-years respectively. The frequencies of such occurrences are well nigh impossible to estimate probabilistically. However, available analyses indicate that although the risk of a radioactive release accident is small, it is by no means negligible for reactor operations at the present time.

The regional health and environment effects of an accident are largely predictable from radioactive fall-out studies following early atomic weapons testing in the atmosphere and have been confirmed in practice following the Chernobyl accident. What could not be confidently predicted before Chernobyl were the local effects of such an accident. A much clearer picture is now emerging as a result of the experiences there when a reactor exploded, following a series of infringements of the official safety regulations, on 26 April 1986, causing the worst reactor accident ever experienced. As a result, the whole district had to be managed on something like a 'war footing' and efforts resembling a large military operation were needed to contain the damage.

Radioactive Waste Disposal

Civil nuclear energy programmes worldwide have already generated many thousands of tons of spent fuel and high-level waste. Many governments have embarked on large-scale programmes to develop ways of isolating these from the biosphere for the many hundreds of thousands of years that they will remain hazardously radioactive.

But the problem of nuclear waste disposal remains unsolved. Nuclear waste technology has reached an advanced level of sophistication. This technology has not however been fully tested or utilized and problems remain about disposal. There is particular concern about future recourse to ocean dumping and the disposal of contaminated waste in the territories of small or poor states that lack the capacity to impose strict safeguards. There should be a clear presumption that all countries that generate nuclear waste dispose of it within their own territories or under strictly monitored agreements between states.

The Current International Situation

During the last 25 years, a growing awareness of the difficulties outlined above has resulted in a wide range of reactions from technical experts, the public, and governments. Many experts still feel that so much can be learned from the problems experienced up to now. They argue that if the public climate allows then to solve the nuclear waste disposal and decommissioning issues and the cost of borrowing money remains reasonably below its 1980-82 peak, in the absence of viable new supply alternatives there is no reason why nuclear energy should not emerge as a strong runner in the 1990s. At the other extreme, many experts take the view that there are so many unsolved problems and too many risks for society to continue with a nuclear future. Public reactions also vary.

Some countries have exhibited little public reaction, in others there appears to be a high level of anxiety that expresses itself in anti-nuclear results in public opinion polls or large anti-nuclear campaigns.

And so, whilst some states still remain nuclear-free, today nuclear reactors supply about 15 per cent of all the electricity generated. Total electricity production worldwide is in turn equivalent to around 15 per cent of global primary energy supply. Roughly one-quarter of all countries worldwide have reactors. In 1986, there were 366 working and a further 140 planned, with 10 governments possessing about 90 per cent of all installed capacity (more than 5 GW (e)). Of these, there are 8 with a total capacity of more than 9 GW (e), which provided the following percentages of electric power in 1985: France, 65; Sweden, 42; Federal Republic of Germany, 31; Japan, 23; United Kingdom, 19; United States, 16; Canada, 13; and USSR, 10. According to IAEA, in 1985 there were 55 research reactors worldwide, 33 of them in developing countries.

Nevertheless, there is little doubt that the difficulties referred to above have in one way or another contributed to a scaling back of future nuclear plans - in some countries, to a de facto nuclear pause. In Western Europe and North America, which today have almost 75 per cent of current world capacity, nuclear provides about one-third of the energy that was forecast for it 10 years ago. Apart from France, Japan, the USSR, and several other East European countries that have decided to continue with their nuclear programmes, ordering, construction, and licensing prospects for new reactors in many other countries look poor. In fact, between 1972 and 1986, earlier global projections of estimated capacity for the year 2000 have been revised downwards by a factor of nearly seven. Despite this, the growth of nuclear at around 15 per cent a year over the last 20 years is still impressive.

Following Chernobyl, there were significant changes in the nuclear stance of certain governments. Several - notably China, the Federal Republic of Germany, France, Japan, Poland, United Kingdom, United States, and the USSR - have maintained or reaffirmed their pro-nuclear policy. Others with a 'no nuclear' or a 'phase-out' policy (Australia, Austria, Denmark, Luxembourg, New Zealand, Norway, Sweden - and Ireland with an unofficial anti-nuclear position) have been joined by Greece and the Philippines. Meanwhile, Finland, Italy, the Netherlands, Switzerland, and Yugoslavia are re-investigating nuclear safety and/or the anti-nuclear arguments, or have introduced legislation tying any further growth of nuclear energy and export/import of nuclear reactor technology to a satisfactory solution of the problem of disposal of radioactive wastes. Several countries have been concerned enough to conduct referenda to test public opinion regarding nuclear power.

Conclusions and Recommendations

These national reactions indicate that as they continue to review and update all the available evidence, governments tend to take up three possible positions:

- remain non-nuclear and develop other sources of energy:
- regard their present nuclear power capacity as necessary during a finite period of transition, to safer alternative energy sources; or
- adopt and develop nuclear energy with the conviction that the associated problems and risks can and must, be solved with a level of safety that is both nationally and internationally acceptable.

The discussion in the Commission also reflected these tendencies, views, and positions.

But whichever policy is adopted, it is important that the vigorous promotion of energy-efficient practices in all energy sectors and large-scale programmes of research, development, and demonstration for the safe and environmentally benign use of all promising energy sources, especially renewables, be given the highest, priority.

Because of potential transboundary effects, it is essential that governments cooperate to develop internationally agreed codes of practice covering technical, economic, social (including health and environment aspects), and political components of nuclear energy. In particular, international agreement must be reached on the following specific items:

- full governmental ratification of the conventions on 'Early Notification of a Nuclear Accident' (including the development of an appropriate surveillance and monitoring system) and on 'Assistance in the Case of a Nuclear Accident or Radiological Emergency' as recently developed by IAEA;
- emergency response training - for accident containment and for decontamination and long-term clean-up of affected sites, personnel, and ecosystems;
- the transboundary movement of all radioactive materials - including fuels, spent fuels, and other wastes by land, sea, or air;
- a code of practice on liability and compensation;
- standards for operator training and international licensing;
- codes of practice for reactor operation, including minimum safety standards;
- the reporting of routine and accidental discharges from nuclear installations;
- effective, internationally harmonized minimum radiological protection standards;
- agreed site selection criteria as well as consultation and notification prior to the siting of all major civil nuclear - related installations;
- standards for waste repositories;
- standards for the decontamination and dismantling of time-expired nuclear reactors; and
- problems posed by the development of nuclear powered shipping.

For many reasons, especially including the failure of the nuclear weapons states to agree on disarmament, the Nonproliferation Treaty has not proved to be a sufficient instrument to prevent the proliferation of nuclear weapons, which still remains a serious danger to world peace. We therefore recommend in the strongest terms the construction of an effective international regime covering all dimensions of the problem. Both nuclear weapons states and non nuclear weapons states, should undertake to accept safeguards in accordance with the statutes of IAEA.

Additionally, an international regulatory function is required, including inspection of reactors internationally. This should be quite separate from the role of IAEA in promoting nuclear energy.

The generation of nuclear power is only justifiable if there are solid solutions to the presently unsolved problems to which it gives rise. The highest priority must be accorded to research and development on environmentally sound and economically viable alternatives, as well as on means of increasing the safety of nuclear energy.

WOOD FUELS: THE VANISHING RESOURCE

Seventy per cent of the people in developing countries use wood and, depending on availability, burn anywhere between an absolute minimum of about 350 kilogrammes to 2,900 kilogrammes of dry wood annually, with the average being around 700 kilogrammes per person. Rural woodfuel supplies appear to be steadily collapsing in many developing countries, especially in Sub-Saharan Africa. At the same time, the rapid growth of agriculture, the pace of migration to cities, and the growing numbers of people entering the money economy are placing unprecedented pressures on the biomass base and increasing the demand for commercial fuels: from wood and charcoal to kerosene, liquid propane, gas, and electricity. To cope with this, many developing country governments have no option but to immediately organize their agriculture to produce large quantities of wood and other plant fuels.

Wood is being collected faster than it can regrow in many developing countries that still rely predominantly on biomass wood, charcoal, dung, and crop residues - for cooking, for heating their dwellings, and even for lighting. FAO estimates suggest that in 1900, around 1.3 billion people lived in vood-deficit areas. If this population-driven overharvesting continues at present rates, by the year 2000 some 2.4 billion people may be living in areas where wood is 'acutely scarce or has to be obtained elsewhere'. These figures reveal great human hardship.

Precise data on supplies are unavailable because much of the wood is not commercially traded but collected by the users, principally women and children, but there is no doubt that millions are hard put to find substitute fuels, and their numbers are growing. The fuelwood crisis and deforestation - although related are not the same problems. Wood fuels destined for urban and industrial consumers do tend to come from forests. But only a small proportion of that used by the rural poor comes from forests. Even in these cases, villagers rarely chop down trees; most collect dead branches or cut them from trees.

When fuelwood is in short supply, people normally economize; when it is no longer available, rural people are forced to burn such fuels as cow dung, crop stems and husks, and weeds. Often this does no harm, since waste products such as cotton stalks are used. But the burning of dung and certain crop residues may in some cases rob the soil of needed nutrients. Eventually extreme fuel shortages can reduce the number of cooked meals and shorten the cooking time, which increases malnourishment.

Many urban people rely on wood, and most of this is purchased. Recently, as the price of wood fuels has been rising, poor families have been obliged to spend increasing proportions of their income on wood. In Addis Ababa and Maputo, families may spend a third to half of their incomes this way. Much work has been done over the past 10 years to develop fuel-efficient stoves, and some of these new models use 30-50 per cent less fuel. These, as well as aluminium cooking pots and pressure cookers that also use much less fuel, should be made more widely available in urban areas.

Fuelwood and charcoal are, and will remain, the major sources of energy for the great majority of rural people in developing countries. The removal of trees in both semiarid and humid land in African countries is a result to a large extent of increasing

RENEWABLE ENERGY: THE UNTAPPED POTENTIAL

Renewable energy sources could in theory provide 10-13TW annually - equal to current global energy consumption.

Today they provide about 2TW annually, about 21 per cent of the energy consumed worldwide, of which 15 per cent is biomass and 6 per cent hydropower. However, most of the biomass is in the form of fuelwood and agricultural and animal wastes. As noted above, fuelwood can no longer be thought of as a 'renewable' resource in many areas, because consumption rater have overtaken sustainable yields.

Although worldwide reliance on all these sources has been growing by more than 10 per cent a year since the late 1970s, it will be some time before they make up a substantial portion of the world's energy budget. Renewable energy systems are still in a relatively primitive stage of development. But they offer the world potentially huge primary energy sources, sustainable in perpetuity and available in one form or another to every nation on Earth. But it, will require a substantial and sustained commitment to further research and development if their potential is to be realized.

Wood as a renewable energy source is usually thought of as naturally occurring trees and shrubs harvested for local domestic use. Wood, however, is becoming an important feedstock, specially grown for advanced energy conversion processes in developing as well as industrial countries for the product ion of process heat, electricity, and potentially for other fuels, such as combustible gases and liquids.

Hydropower, second to wood among the renewables, has been expanding at nearly 4 per cent annually. Although hundreds of thousands of megawatts of hydropower have been harnessed throughout the world, the remaining potential is huge. In neighbouring developing countries, interstate cooperation in hydropower development could revolutionize supply potential especially in Africa.

Solar energy use is small globally, but it is beginning to assume an important place in the energy consumption patterns of some countries. Solar water and household heating is widespread in many parts of Australia, Greece, and the Middle East. A number of East European and developing countries have active solar energy programmes, and the United States and Japan support solar sales of several hundred million dollars a year. With constantly improving solar thermal and solar electric technologies, it is likely that their contribution will increase substantially. The cost of photovoltaic equipment has fallen from around $500-600 per peak watt to $5 and is approaching the $1-2 level where it can compete with conventional electricity production. But even at $5 per peak watt, it still provides electricity to remote places more cheaply than building power lines.

Wind power has been used for centuries - mainly for pumping water. Recently its use has been growing rapidly in regions such as California and Scandinavia. In these cases the wind turbines are used to generate electricity for the local electricity grid. The costs of wind-generated electricity, which benefited initially from substantial tax incentives, have fallen dramatically in California in the last five years and may possibly be competitive with other power generated there within a decade. Many countries have successful but small wind programmes, but the untapped potential is still high.

The fuel alcohol programme in Brazil produced about 10 billion litres of ethanol from sugar-cane in 1984 and replaced about 60 per cent of the gasoline that would have been required. The cost has been estimated at $50-60 per barrel of gasoline replaced. When subsidies are removed, and a true exchange rate is used, this is competitive at 1981 oil prices. With present lower oil prices, the programme has become uneconomical. But it saves the nation hard currency, and it provides the additional benefits of rural development, employment generation, increased self-reliance, and reduced vulnerability to crises in the world oil markets. The use of geothermal energy, from natural underground heat sources, has been increasing at more than 15 per cent per year in both industrial and developing countries. The experience gained during the past decades could provide the basis for a major expansion of geothermal-capacity. By contrast, technologies for low-grade heat via heat pumps or from solar ponds and ocean thermal gradients are promising but still mostly at the research and development stage.

These energy sources are not without their health and environment risks. Although they range from rather trivial to very serious problems, public reactions to them are not necessarily in proportion to the damage sustained. For instance, some of the commonest difficulties with solar energy are, somewhat surprisingly, the injuries from roof falls during solar thermal maintenance and the nuisance of sun-glare off their glass surfaces. Or a modern wind turbine can be a significant noise nuisance to people living nearby. Yet, these apparently small problems often arouse very strong public reactions.

But these are still minor issues compared with the ecosystem destruction at hydropower sites or the uprooting of homesteads in the areas to be flooded, as well as the health risks from toxic gases generated by rotting submerged vegetation and soils, or from waterborne diseases such as schistosomiasis (snail fever). Hydrodams also act as an important barrier to fish migration and frequently to the movement of land animals. Perhaps the worst problem they pose is the danger of catastrophic rupture of the dam-wall and the sweeping away or flooding of human settlements downstream - about once a year somewhere in the world. This risk is small but not insignificant.

One of the most widespread chronic problems is the eye and lung irritation caused by woodsmoke in developing countries. When agricultural wastes are burned, pesticide residues inhaled from the dusts or smoke of the crop material can be a health problem. Modern biofuel liquids have their own special hazards. Apart from competing with food crops for good agricultural land, their production generates large quantities of organic waste effluent, which if not used as a fertilizer can cause serious water pollution. Such fuels, particularly methanol, may produce irritant or toxic combustion products. All these and many other problems, both large and small, will increase as renewable energy systems are developed.

Most renewable energy systems operate best at small to medium scales, ideally suited for rural and suburban applications. They are also generally labour-intensive, which should be an added benefit where there if surplus labour. They are less susceptible than fossil fuels to wild price fluctuations and foreign exchange costs. Most countries have some renewable resources, and their use can help nations move towards self-reliance.

The need for a steady transition to a broader and more sustainable mix of energy sources is beginning to become accepted. Renewable energy sources could contribute substantially to this, particularly with new and improved technologies, but their development will depend in the short run on the reduction or removal of certain economic and institutional constraints to their use. These are formidable in many countries. The high level of hidden subsidies for conventional fuels built into the legislative and energy programmes of most countries distorts choices against renewables in research and development, depletion allowances, tax write-offs, and direct support of consumer prices. Countries should undertake a full examination of all subsidies and other forms of support to various sources of energy and remove those that are not clearly justified.

Although the situation is changing rapidly in some jurisdictions, electrical utilities in most have a supply monopoly on generation that allows them to arrange pricing policies that discriminate against other, usually small, suppliers. In some countries a relaxation of this control, requiring utilities to accept power generated by industry, small systems, and individuals, has created opportunities for the development of renewables. Beyond that, requiring utilities to adopt an end-use approach in planning, financing, developing, and marketing energy can open the door to a wide range of energy-saving measures as well as renewables.

Renewable energy sources require a much higher priority in national energy programmes. Research, development, and demonstration projects should command funding necessary to ensure their rapid development and demonstration. With a potential of 10TW or so, even if 3-4TW were realized, it would make a crucial difference to future primary supply, especially in developing countries, where the background conditions exist for the success of renewables. The technological challenges of renewables are minor compared with the challenge of creating the social and institutional frameworks that will ease these sources into energy supply systems. The Commission believes that every effort should be made to develop the potential for renewable energy, which should form the foundation of the global energy structure during the 21st Century. A much more concerted effort must be mounted if this potential is to be realized. But a major programme of renewable energy development will involve large costs and high risks, particularly massive-scale solar and biomass industries. Developing countries lack the resources to finance all but a small fraction of this cost although they will be important users and possibly even exporters. Large-scale financial and technical assistance will therefore be required.

ENERGY EFFICIENCY: MAINTAINING THE MOMENTUM

Given the above analysis, the Commission believes that energy efficiency should be the cutting edge of national energy policies for sustainable development. Impressive gains in energy efficiency have been made since the first oil price shock in the 1970s. During the past 13 years, many industrial countries saw the energy content of growth fall significantly as a result of increases in energy efficiency averaging 1.7 per cent annually between 1973 and 1983. And this energy efficiency solution costs less, by savings made on the extra primary supplies required to run traditional equipment.

The ccst-effectiveness of 'efficiency' as the most environmentally benign 'source' of energy is well established. The energy consumption per unit of output from the most efficient processes and technologies is one-third to less than one-half that of typically available equipment.

This is true of appliances for cooking, lighting and refrigeration, and space cooling and heating - needs that are growing rapidly in most countries and putting severe pressures on the available supply systems. It is also true of agricultural cultivation and irrigation systems, of the automobile, and of many industrial processes and equipment.

Given the large disproportion in per capita energy consumption between developed and developing countries in general, it is clear that the scope and need for energy saving is potentially much higher in industrial than in developing countries. Nonetheless, energy efficiency is important everywhere. The cement factory, automobile, or irrigation pump in a poor country is fundamentally no different from its equivalent in the rich world. In both, there is roughly the same scope for reducing the energy consumption or peak power demand of these devices without loss of output or welfare. But poor countries will gain much more from such reductions.

The woman who cooks in an earthen pot over an open fire uses perhaps eight times more energy than an affluent neighbour with a gas stove and aluminium pans. The poor who light their homes with a wick dipped in a jar of kerosene get one-fiftieth of the illumination of a 100-watt electric bulb, but use just as much energy. These examples illustrate the tragic paradox of poverty. For the poor, the shortage of money is a greater limitation than the shortage of energy. They are forced to use 'free' fuels and inefficient equipment because they do not have the cash or savings to purchase energy-efficient fuels and end-use devices. Consequently, collectively they pay much more for a unit of delivered energy services.

In most cases, investments in improved end-use technologies save money over time through lowered energy-supply needs The costs of improving the end-use equipment is frequently much less than the cost of building more primary supply capacity. In Brazil, for example, it has been shown that for a discounted total investment of $4 billion in more efficient end-use technologies (such as more efficient refrigerators, street-lighting, or motors) it would be feasible to defer construction of 21 gigawatts of new electrical supply capacity, corresponding to a discounted capital savings for new supplies of $19 billion in the period 1986 to 2000.

There are many examples of successful energy efficiency programmes in industrial countries. The many methods used successfully to increase awareness include information campaigns in the media, technical press, and schools; demonstrations of successful practices and technologies; free energy audits; energy 'labelling' of appliances; and training in energy-saving techniques. These should be quickly and widely extended. Industrialized countries account for such a large proportion of global energy consumption that even small gains in efficiency can have a substantial impact on conserving reserves and reducing the pollution load on the biosphere. It is particularly important that consumers, especially large commercial and industrial agencies, obtain professional audits of their energy use. This kind of energy 'book-keeping' will readily identify those places in their consumption patterns where significant savings can be made.

Energy pricing policies play a critical role in stimulating efficiency. At present, they sometimes include subsidies and seldom reflect the real costs of producing or importing the energy, particularly when exchange rates are undervalued. Very rarely do they reflect the external damage costs to health, property, and the environment. Countries should evaluate all hidden and overt subsidies to see how far real energy costs can be passed on to the consumer. The true economic pricing of energy - with safeguards for the very poor - needs to be extended in all countries. Large numbers of countries both industrial and developing are already adopting such policies.

Developing countries face particular constraints in saving energy. Foreign exchange difficulties can make it hard to purchase efficient but costly energy conversion and end-use devices. Energy can often be saved cost-effectively by fine-tuning already functioning systems. But governments and aid agencies may find it less attractive to fund such measures than to invest in new large-scale energy supply hardware that is perceived as a more tangible symbol of progress.

The manufacture, import, or sale of equipment conforming to mandatory minimal energy consumption or efficiency standards is one of the most powerful and effective tools in promoting energy efficiency and producing predictable savings. International cooperation may be required when such equipment is traded from nation to nation. Countries and appropriate regional organizations should introduce and extend increasingly strict efficiency standards for equipment and mandatory labelling of appliances. Many energy efficiency measures cost nothing to implement. But where investments are needed, they are frequently a barrier to poor households and small-scale consumers, even when pay-back times are short. In these latter cases, special small loan or hire-purchase arrangements are helpful. Where investment costs are not insurmountable, there are many possible mechanisms for reducing or spreading the initial investment, such as loans with favourable repayment periods and 'invisible' measures such as loans repaid by topping up the new, reduced energy bills to the pre-conservation levels.

Transport has a particularly important place in national energy and development planning. It is a major consumer of oil, accounting for 50-60 per cent of total petroleum use in most developing countries. It is often a major source of local air pollution and regional acidification of the environment in industrial and developing countries. Vehicle markets will grow much more rapidly in developing countries, adding greatly to urban air pollution, which in many cities already exceeds international norms. Unless strong action is taken, air pollution could become a major factor limiting industrial development in many Third World cities.

In the absence of higher fuel prices, mandatory standards providing for a steady increase in fuel economy may be necessary. Either way, the potential for substantial future gains in fuel economy is enormous. If momentum can be maintained, the current average fuel consumption of approximately 10 litres per 100 kilometres in the fleet of vehicles in use in industrial countries could be cut in half by the turn of the century.

A key issue is how developing countries can rapidly improve the fuel economy of their vehicles when these are, on average, used for twice as long those as in industrial countries, cutting rates of renewal and improvement in half. Licensing and import agreements should be reviewed to ensure access to the best available fuel efficient designs and production processes. Another important fuel-saving strategy especially in the growing cities of developing countries is the organizing of carefully planned public transport systems.

Industry accounts for 40 60 pet cent of all energy consumed in industrial countries and 10-40 per cent in developing countries. There has been significant improvement in the energy efficiency of production equipment, processes, and products. In developing countries, energy savings of as much as 20-30 per cent could be achieved by such skilful management of industrial development.

Agriculture worldwide is only a modest energy consumer, accounting for about 3.5 per cent of commercial energy use in the industrial countries and 4.5 per cent in developing countries as a whole. A strategy to double food production in the Third World through increases in fertilizers, irrigation, and mechanization would add 140 million tons of oil equivalent to their agricultural energy use. This is only some 5 per cent of present world energy consumption and almost certainly a small part of the energy that could be saved in other sectors in the developing world through appropriate efficiency measures.

Buildings offer enormous scope for energy savings, and perhaps the most widely understood ways of increasing energy efficiency are in the home and workplace. Buildings in the tropics are now commonly designed to avoid as much direct solar heating as possible by having very narrow east- and west-facing walls, but with long sides facing north and south and protected from the overhead sun by recessed windows or wide sills.

An important method of heating buildings is by hot water produced during electricity production and piped around whole districts, providing both heat and hot water. This extremely efficient use of fossil fuels demands a coordination of energy supply with local physical planning, which few countries are institutionally equipped to handle. Where it has been successful, there has usually been local authority involvement in or control of regional energy-services boards, such as in Scandinavia and the USSR. Given the development of these or similar institutional arrangements, the cogeneration of heat and electricity could revolutionize the energy efficiency of buildings worldwide.

ENERGY CONSERVATION MEASURES

There is general agreement that the efficiency gains achieved by some industrialized countries over the past 13 years were driven largely by higher energy prices, triggered by higher oil prices. Prior to the recent fall in oil prices, energy efficiency was growing at a rate of 2.0 per cent annually in some countries, having increased gradually year by year.

It is doubtful whether such steady improvements can be maintained and extended if energy prices are held below the level needed to encourage the design and adoption of more energy-efficient homes, industrial processes, and transportation vehicles. The level required will vary greatly within and between countries, depending on a wide range of factors. But whatever it is, it should be maintained. In volatile energy markets, the question is how.

Nations intervene in the 'market price' of energy in a variety of ways. Domestic taxes (or subsidies) on electrical power rates, oil, gas and other fuels are most common. They vary greatly between and even within countries where different states, provinces, and sometimes even municipalities have the right to add their own tax. Although taxes on energy have seldom been levied to encourage the design and adoption of efficiency measures, they can have that result if they cause energy prices to rise beyond a certain level - a level that varies greatly among jurisdictions.

Some nations also maintain higher than market prices on energy through duties on imported electricity, fuel, and fuel products. Others have negotiated bilateral pricing arrangements with oil and gas producers in which they stabilize prices for a period of time.

In most countries, the price of oil eventually determines the price of alternative fuels. Extreme fluctuations in oil prices, such as the world has experienced recently, endanger programmes to encourage conservation. Many positive energy developments worldwide that made sense with oil above $25 per barrel, are harder to justify at lower prices. Investments in renewables, energy-efficient industrial processes, transport vehicles, and energy-services may be reduced. Most are needed to ease the transition to a safer and more sustainable energy future beyond this century. This goal requires a long, uninterrupted effort to succeed.

Given the importance of oil prices on international energy policy, the Commission recommends that new mechanisms for encouraging dialogue between consumers and producers be explored.

If the recent momentum behind annual gains in energy efficiency is to be maintained and extended, governments need to make it an explicit goal of their policies for energy pricing to consumers. Prices needed to encourage the adoption of energy-saving measures may be achieved by any of the above means or by other means. Although the Commission expresses no preference, conservation pricing requires that governments take a long-term view in weighing the costs and benefits of the various measures. They need to operate over extended periods, dampening wild fluctuations in the price of primary energy, which can impair progress towards energy conservation.

CONCLUSION

It is clear that a low energy path is the best way towards a sustainable future. But given efficient and productive uses of primary energy, this need not mean a shortage of essential energy services. Within the next 50 years, nations have the opportunity to produce the same levels of energy services with as little as half the primary supply currently consumed. This requires profound structural changes in socio-economic and institutional arrangements and is an important challenge to global society.

More importantly, it will buy the time needed to mount major programmes on sustainable forms of renewable energy, and so begin the transition to a safer, more sustainable energy era. The development of renewable sources will depend in part on a rational approach to energy pricing to secure a stable matrix for such progress. Both the routine practice of efficient energy use and the development of renewables will help take pressure off traditional fuels, which are most needed to enable developing countries to realize their growth potential worldwide.

Energy is not so much a single product as a mix of products and services, a mix upon which the welfare of individuals, the sustainable development of nations, and the life-supporting capabilities of the global ecosystem depend. In the past, this mix has been allowed to flow together haphazardly, the proportions dictated by short-term pressures on and short-term goals of governments, institutions, and companies. Energy is too important for its development to continue in such a random manner. A safe, environmentally sound, and economically viable energy pathway that will sustain human progress into the distant future is clearly imperative. It is also possible. But it will require new dimensions of political will and institutional cooperation to achieve it.

Bibliography

Angel, Bradley: Toxic Threat to Indian Lands: A Greenpeace Report, San Francisco, Greenpeace, 1991.

Bryant, Bunyan: Environmental Justice: Issues, Policies, and Solutions, Washington, DC, Island Press, 1995.

Burch, William R. Jr.: Human Ecology: An Environmental Approach, Belmont, Duxbury Press, 1994.

Dasmann, R.F.: Environmental Conservation, New York, Wiley, 1972.

Daubenmire, R. F.: Plants and Environment, New York, Wiley, 1947.

Gay, Kathlyn: Saving the Environment: Debating the Costs, New York, Franklin Watts, 1996.

Harvey L. Molotoch: Urban Fortunes: The Political Economy of Place, Berkeley, University of California Press, 1987.

Hofrichter, Richard: The Theory and Practice of Environmental Justice, Philadelphia, New Society Publishers, 1993.

Mandelker, D.R.: Environment and Equity: A Regulatory Challenge, New York, McGraw Hill, 1981.

Meyer, Art: Earth Keepers: Environmental Perspectives on Hunger, Poverty, and Injustice, Scottsdale, Herald Press, 1991.

Paul Mohai: Race and the Incidence of Environmental Hazards: A Time for Discourse, Boulder, Westview Press, 1992.

Strahler, A. H.: Introduction to Environmental Science: Santa Barbara, New York, Hamilton Publishing Company; 1974.

Vallette, J.: The International Trade in Wastes: A Greenpeace Inventory, Washington, Greenpeace, 1989.

Zupan, J.M.: The Distribution of Air Quality in the New York Region, Baltimore, Johns Hopkins University Press, 1973.

Index

□□□